S0-CFE-054

THE TRAIN

DOESN'T

STOP HERE

ANYMORE

THE TRAIN
DOESN'T
STOP HERE
ANYMORE

An Illustrated History of Railway Stations in Canada
3rd edition

Ron Brown

THE DUNDURN GROUP
TORONTO

Copyright © Ron Brown, 2008

All rights reserved. No part of this publication may be reproduced, stored in a retrieval system, or transmitted in any form or by any means, electronic, mechanical, photocopying, recording, or otherwise (except for brief passages for purposes of review) without the prior permission of Dundurn Press. Permission to photocopy should be requested from Access Copyright.

Editor: Tony Hawke
Copy-editor: Shannon Whibbs
Designer: Erin Mallory
Printer: Transcontinental

Library and Archives Canada Cataloguing in Publication

Brown, Ron, 1945-
        The train doesn't stop here anymore : an illustrated history of railway stations in
Canada / Ron Brown. -- 3rd ed.

Includes bibliographical references and index.
ISBN 978-1-55002-794-5

        1. Railroad stations--Canada--History. 2. Railroad stations--Canada--Pictorial
works. I. Title.

TF302.C3B76 2008   385.3'140971   C2007-907446-4

1 2 3 4 5   12 11 10 09 08

  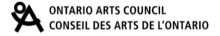

We acknowledge the support of the **Canada Council for the Arts** and the **Ontario Arts Council** for our publishing program. We also acknowledge the financial support of the **Government of Canada** through the **Book Publishing Industry Development Program** and **The Association for the Export of Canadian Books**, and the **Government of Ontario** through the **Ontario Book Publishers Tax Credit program** and the **Ontario Media Development Corporation**.

Care has been taken to trace the ownership of copyright material used in this book. The author and the publisher welcome any information enabling them to rectify any references or credits in subsequent editions.

J. Kirk Howard, President

Printed and bound in Canada
www.dundurn.com

Dundurn Press	Gazelle Book Services Limited	Dundurn Press
3 Church Street, Suite 500	White Cross Mills	2250 Military Road
Toronto, Ontario, Canada	High Town, Lancaster, England	Tonawanda, NY
M5E 1M2	LA1 4XS	U.S.A. 14150

CONTENTS

ACKNOWLEDGEMENTS

Research for this book extended over several years and many kilometres. It involved visiting railway stations from one side of Canada to the other, and ploughing through libraries, museums, and archives of all descriptions. In addition, I placed a nationwide call for former railway employees and others who had a direct connection with their stations to share their memories with me. Many replied and they are acknowledged throughout the book.

I would like especially to thank the staff of the following vital institutions and organizations for supplying photos, manuscripts, and a wide variety of railway rule books and publications. These include

National Archives of Canada, Picture Collection
Ontario Archives
Algonquin Park Museum
Glenbow Museum Archives
Saskatchewan Archives Board
The Canadian Press
Medicine Hat News
Metro Toronto Library
City of Vancouver Archives
British Columbia Archives
The Oil Museum of Canada
Lake of the Woods Museum
St. Lawrence Parks Commission
Lennox and Addington County Museum and Archives
Notman Photographic Archives, McCord Museum
Gravenhurst Archives Committee

Heritage Scarborough

Yukon Tourism, Heritage Branch

County of Bruce Museum

Provincial Archives of Alberta

Provincial Archives of Manitoba

CN Rail, especially Loren C. Perry, Doug MacKenzie, and Connie Romani

CPR Corporate Archives, especially Paul Thurston, B.C. Scott, and Nancy Battet

City of Ottawa Archives

Victoria City Archives

Provincial Archives of Newfoundland and Labrador

City of Toronto Archives

Thunder Bay Museum

Muskoka Pioneer Museum

London Public Library

Hamilton Public Library

Todmorden Mills Historic Park Archives

Sudbury Public Library

Archives Nationales du Quebec

Provincial Archives of New Brunswick

Provincial Archives of Prince Edward Island

McMichael Canadian Collection

Ontario Northland Railway Archives, especially Lorne Fleece

Queen's University Archives

Ontario Media Development Corporation, especially Donna Zucklinski

MuchMusic, especially James Woods

Parks Canada, especially Lawrence Friend and Janet Martin

Canadian Transport Commission

VIA Rail Canada

Ontario Ministry of Culture and Communications, especially Margo Teasdale and Richard Moorehouse.

All heritage enthusiasts should be inspired by the tenacity of the late Jacques Dalibard, who led the fight to save stations, and who, as head of the Heritage Canada Foundation, raised awareness among Canadians across the country of their vanishing heritage landmarks. The work of those like him is also acknowledged here. And, finally, I want to thank my family: my wife June and daughters Jeri and Ria, for enduring more "station hunts" than they care to remember. And to my late father, Arnold Robert Henry Brown, who never refused our persistent requests, as kids, to take us to the Leaside station or the Bathurst Street railway yards to indulge our fascination with our railways. It is to his memory that this book is dedicated.

Ron Brown, Toronto, November 2007

1st PASSENGER TRAIN
REACHED CALGARY
AUG, 1883.

C.P. RAILWAY STATION
CALGARY. 1884

ERNEST BROWN 813A
COPYRIGHT,

WOOD BURNING
ENGINE, NO: 144,

Calgary's first permanent passenger station was typical of a CPR divisional station. Photo, 1884. Photo courtesy of Alberta Archives, B3152.

WHAT IS A STATION? 1

Confusion often exists between the terms "station" and "depot." As defined in railway timetables, a "station" is a "stopping place" and need not be a structure. In fact, it may be nothing more than a siding, a platform, or a mail hook. "Depot," an American term, refers to the building itself. Nevertheless, in Canada the word "station" popularly refers to that wonderful old building, with its semaphore, its bay window, its platform, and its waiting room full of memories.

No matter what it was called, the station was vital for train operations and for customers. On the operational side, it housed offices for administrators, provided sidings and yards for rolling stock, maintenance and fuel for the locomotives, equipment for the orderly movement of trains, and shelter and food for the train crews. The station was a place to work, to live and to play; it was the architectural pride of the community, and was the building that, more than any other, determined the layout of the community. But its fundamental role was to serve the railway and to serve the customer, and everything about the layout, the location, and the equipment of the station, supported these two functions.

For its customers, the station was where they shipped parcels, bought money orders or sent telegrams; it was where they picked up their mail or loaded their farm produce; it was where they hurried down a meal during crew changes; it was where they bought their tickets for a trip around the world or just to the next town, and it was where they awaited the train that would take them there.

Clearly, a station could be many things, and the number of functions it had determined what kind of station it was. A station could range from something as simple as shelter for passengers with a platform for freight and a mail crane, to a large urban palace with everything from executive suites to shoeshine stands. In between were the divisional stations, and the most common of all, the way stations.

The Country Stations

Also known as way stations, or operator stations, it is the country stations that many small-town residents still remember. After all, nearly every town had one. All the jobs the railway had to perform in a small town were there, packed under one roof. They remember the agent's office with its barred window, the large oak desk with its typewriter, telegraph and telephone, and the piles of forms everywhere. Outside, they remember the wooden semaphores perched at various angles, the water tank looming down the track, the farm products piled high on the platform, and the canvas bags bulging with mail resting on the wagon. And they remember the waiting room with its smell of kerosene and the sound of the ticking clock.

A typical agent's office has been preserved in the Bellis, Alberta, station. Photo by the author.

Because so much was packed into the little buildings, the layout was critical. All services had to be arranged within the building so that passengers, freight, and mail were all handy to the agent. And always within reach were the train order crank, the typewriter, and the telegraph key, all indispensable for train movement.

The Agent's Office

The heart of the operation was the agent's office, usually located in the centre of the station. A bay window protruded from the office, out over the platform to allow the agent to see down the track and to keep his eye on the platform. On the desk, set into the bay, was the all-important telegraph key. Here, the information clattered through from the dispatcher's office to let the agent know when a train was on the way. To one side of the office was the ticket window, barred to discourage thieves, where passengers would buy their tickets or just come to chat. On the other side was the entrance to the freight room where express parcels, mail, and freight waited beside the milk cans and egg crates for shipment to the next town. Each section had separate doors on to the platform and usually separate entrances from the street. Behind the office was the door that led to the agent's quarters.

The Port Stanley, Ontario, station displays an early style of order board. Photo by the author.

Station operation depended as much upon what was outside the station as what was inside. The station building was often surrounded by a clutch of smaller structures. Because many early stations lacked basements, a separate shed was added to store the coal or wood that the agent used to heat the building.

In remoter locations where no permanent settlement had sprung up by the track, the station was often a house for the operator and his equipment. In such areas, section houses sometimes doubled as stations.

The Wooden Arms

Another feature firmly fixed in the memories of many Canadians is the wooden order boards, or semaphores, one red and one green, poised at various angles from a pole above or beside the bay window. They gave the locomotive engineer his instructions on whether to stop or to proceed without stopping.

Originally there were no train order boards. Engineers were required to stop at each station and sign for their orders. On some early railway lines a ball placed on top of a pole before the station gave the engineer permission to continue full speed ahead. The term "high balling" originated with this device and has remained in the railway lexicon ever since.

The first boards were, as the name implies, flat boards with white spots painted onto a red background. Oval in shape, the boards pivoted on a spindle and were controlled by a chain that was attached to a lever inside the agent's office. When the board was parallel to the track, it was a "clear board" and the engineer could proceed without stopping. When the board was perpendicular to the track, the engineer must stop. Atop the spindle were red and green glass covers in front of a lamp. When the board was in the stop position the red glass covered the lamp. The "clear board" placed the green glass before the lamp.

With the introduction of the order board, the engineer no longer had to stop the train and enter the station to receive his orders. Instead, he simply slowed the engine while the agent handed them up on the end of a long hoop or fork.

By the 1880s the order board had largely been replaced by the semaphore. Invented by a French schoolboy during the Napoleonic Wars, the semaphore soon became a universal method of long-distance signalling. The early semaphores were two-directional lower-quadrant semaphores. These were eventually replaced by upper-quadrant semaphores, which pointed either up, straight out, or at a forty-five-degree angle. Up meant "go," out meant "stop," and the angle meant "slow."

Ontario's relocated Kleinburg station still has the later style semaphore. Photo by the author.

If by some accident the mechanism broke, the arm would automatically fall into the "stop" position.

At the tiny station of Lorneville Junction, in central Ontario, the order board, located at a distance from the station, mysteriously always ended up in the "stop" position, much to the frustration of train conductors. The mystery was solved when it was discovered that a local pig, fond of sticking his snout into the signal mechanism's grease, was releasing the cog, allowing the arm to fall into the "stop" position. (This delightful anecdote is recounted by Charles Cooper in his history of the Toronto and Nipissing Railway, *Narrow Gauge For Us*.)

The Waiting Rooms

The thing that many Canadians remember most about waiting

Passengers wait in the Carleton Place waiting room with the typical hard benches. Photo courtesy of CP Archives, A-13170.

for the train is the room where they waited. Outside the home, Canadians frequented the station waiting room more than any other room in their communities. They knew its smell, the smell of the wood stove in the winter, or the kerosene from the lamp. There was also the smell of the oil rubbed into the floor; and many knew that the screen doors that would slam upon them before they could flee through the inner door. They knew the sounds … the ticking of the clock, the chattering of the telegraph key and, finally, the distant whistle of the long-awaited train.

No matter how they tried, Canadian rail travellers of the time could never forget the benches. With the square or curved backs, the benches were, as one writer recalls, "the reason you saw so many people walking up and down on the platform waiting for the train." The CPR even had standard designs for benches, one with thin horizontal slats for use at smaller stations, and sturdier benches with wide vertical slats for "the better class stations."

Larger stations provided separate waiting rooms for ladies and men and perhaps still a third for smokers. During segregation in the southern United States, small waiting rooms on the back of the station divided black passengers from white.

While waiting, the passenger could glance at the bulletin board located just outside the waiting-room door where the agent would post the scheduled arrival time. The Railway Act required that the arrival and departure times be written with white chalk. Failure to do so earned the agent a $5 fine plus demerits.

The Mail

Another familiar sight at the country stations was the mail cart. As the train whistle wafted from a distant crossing, the agent would wheel a creaking cart, loaded with grey canvas sacks bulging with the outgoing mail, across the wooden platform to the edge of the track.

Almost as soon as a railway opened its line it assumed mail service from the slower stagecoaches. By 1858 the Grand Trunk Railway was carrying mail between Quebec and Sarnia, the Great Western was hauling the sacks between Niagara Falls and Windsor via Hamilton, the Central Canada carted the loads between Brockville and Ottawa while the Northern moved it between Toronto and Collingwood.

The many gaps that remained in the evolving network continued to be filled by stagecoach and steamer. In 1863, as the gaps filled in, the government introduced travelling post offices. Now the trains could not only carry the mail, but sort it right on the train. Special mail cars were fitted with sorting tables, destination

The mail doesn't always move quickly. These bags are piled up during a mail strike in the 1920s. Photo courtesy of Metro Toronto Reference Library, T 32360.

slots, and even washing and cooking facilities. This speeded up the procedure to the point where a letter could be posted and not only delivered the same day, but, if there was frequent train service, a reply could be received the same day as well.

In 1868, Timothy Eaton, owner of the famous Toronto department store of the same name, introduced the mail-order system. Through his catalogue, a Canadian anywhere could order an item and Eaton's would send it by train. Thus began a Canadian institution that would last over a century.

By 1910 most of the gaps had been filled and nearly every Canadian could send or receive mail by rail. The trains became rolling post offices. Inside the lurching mail cars, sorters pored through the sacks, separating the mail for the next stations. If the train was approaching a flag stop with no passengers to board, the sorters would wrestle open the door and give the mail sack a hefty kick. On occasion, the boot would come too late and the sack would miss the platform and end up in a heap at the bottom of a ditch.

Mail to be picked up was dangled from a hook on a wooden post, a device known as a crane. As the mail car passed the crane, a hook protruding from the mail car door snared the sack. If the mail car was not equipped with a hook, one of the clerks would lean perilously out and clutch the dangling sack as the train eased past. The clerks inside grabbed it and poured its contents onto the table and began their sorting anew.

Many stations had post offices of their own and here the townspeople crowded around waiting to receive the long-awaited letter from home, the *Farmer's Almanac*, or the latest Eaton's catalogue.

Wartime witnessed a tremendous crush of mail. On November 20, 1942, staff at Montreal's Windsor Station ploughed enough mail to fill seventeen mail cars destined for the Atlantic ports, thirteen cars on one train alone. Each mail car could accommodate six hundred sacks of mail.

During the 1950s and 1960s, the dramatic drop in passenger traffic made many of the smaller passenger lines heavily dependent upon the mail contract for revenue. But other ways of carrying the mail were being explored. The Canadian Post Office had started its first air mail service in northern Manitoba in 1927 and by 1948 began air mail delivery to anywhere in the world. Then, in 1971, the Canadian Post Office turned almost all its mail service over to the airlines. A final blow, the loss of the mail turned marginal passenger lines into money-losers, and most were shut down. The mail had found other ways to get through and now the passengers had to do the same.

Freight

Milk cans, egg crates, fruit, and maple syrup containers crowded the darkened freight room beside the agent's office. If there was a greater revenue generator to the railways than passengers and mail, it was freight. Railways moved everything that needed to be moved.

Most stations had a loading platform separate from the station itself from which large items could be loaded or off-loaded. Although in Canada freight sheds were usually part of the passenger station, (these were often called "combination" stations) some communities were so busy that a separate freight building was needed. The English-style stone stations that the Grand Trunk Railway constructed along its Montreal-to-Sarnia line contained no freight facilities, so the freight had to be stored in a separate wooden structure. Occasionally, and especially in the U.S., freight buildings had their own office, and sometimes their own distinctive styles. In fact, some U.S. freight stations were larger and more elaborate than the passenger depots.

In early eastern Canada, the main freight products were lumber and farm products. Near Allandale, Ontario, a wooden railway track linked a sawmill in the great Pine Plains to the small station at Tioga. Horses drew the timber along the flimsy track to the station where it was winched onto flatcars, the longer logs requiring three flatcars. During lumbering's heyday in the 1850s, timber trains would depart the Allandale station every ten minutes, destined for construction sites in Toronto.

In many areas, specialized products dominated. At Grimsby, once the heart of Canada's dwindling fruit belt, the trains might creak away from the platform with seventy thousand baskets of peaches, even in an average season. In 1896, fifteen hundred crates of strawberries left Jordan Station for Montreal within just a two-day period. Prior to its absorption by the Grand Trunk,

Fruit being loaded at the station in Grimsby, Ontario. It was not unusual to ship 70,000 baskets of peaches in a season, or 1,500 crates of strawberries over a two-day period. Photo courtesy of Ontario Archives, 16856-20025.

the Great Western Railway promised delivery of fruit from the Niagara fruit belt to Montreal or Ottawa by six o'clock the following morning.

While in southern Ontario and Quebec, station platforms would regularly be crowded with egg crates, milk cans, salted fish, coal oil, and farm machinery, in northern Ontario, freight was more likely to consist of lumber, stacks of beaver pelts, or ingots of gold and silver.

Occasionally, freight delivery would become something of a community event. One local newspaper reported the arrival of a shipment of farm machinery at the Londesborough station in western Ontario. "A busy scene took place at the station in the delivery of some 25 mowing and reaping machines from the celebrated factory of D. Maxwell of Paris … After they were

all loaded they all made a grand procession to the village hotel where the owner provided a sumptuous repast for the entire company of about 50 people."

Some freight was live and required special treatment. Federal regulations insisted that animals be off-loaded at regular intervals for exercise, watering, and feeding. Local children often earned a dollar or so helping the agent to unload stock and keep them watered.

Probably the most bizarre commodity to decorate the station grounds, if only briefly, was buffalo bones. The arrival of the railways upon the prairies in the 1880s, and the settlement that went with it, decimated the huge herds of buffalo. The great grasslands were strewn with millions of tons of dry and bleached bones of these once mighty beasts — bones that could

TOP: A load of precious silver waits unattended at Cobalt, Ontario, during the town's silver rush. Photo courtesy of Ontario Archives, S 13600. BOTTOM: In Biscotasing in northern Ontario, a pile of furs is ready to ship. Photo courtesy of Ontario Ministry of Natural Resources.

be pulverized into valuable fertilizer. To cash in on this short-lived bounty, the Indians and Metis gathered up the bones and brought them to the stations where they received $5 per ton. Such a sight earned Regina its first name, "Pile O' Bones."

In December of each year, however, the freight ledgers would show a completely different array of items: pails of candies, fruitcakes and biscuits, boxes of silk, bags of oranges, and whisky by the barrel, all destined for Christmas festivities. One such barrel was spied by a group of thirsty residents of Avonlea, in Saskatchewan. To avoid detection they crept along the station platform, unnoticed, and drilled into the barrel with a brace and bit and carried off the contents, some in containers, some in their stomachs.

Hot Off the Wire

One of the sounds many Canadians remember in their local station is the clatter of the telegraph key, for the way stations often contained the only telegraph facility in town. Initiated in 1844, along the Baltimore and Ohio Railway in the U.S., the telegraph was introduced into Canada in 1846 by the Toronto, Hamilton and Niagara Electrical Magnetic Telegraph Company. The Grand Trunk Railway adopted its use in 1856 and by 1860 the telegraph had eliminated the risky guesswork involved in locating the trains. The dispatcher at each divisional point would click out the departure of each train and the station agent in turn would key back whenever the train would pass his station.

As early as 1896, when CPR telegraphers went on strike, the company resorted to the newly invented telephone. However, the company felt that written orders reinforced the personnel hierarchy and discarded the telephone for dispatching after the strike ended. The telegraph was not only vital to the railway for train movement, but turned into a major money-maker as well. By the end of the 1860s two telegraph companies dominated Canada: the Montreal Telegraph Company and the Dominion Telegraph Company. In 1880 the Great Northwestern Telegraph Company was created and provided linkages between Ontario and Manitoba. In 1882 CPR's general manager, William Van Horne, recognizing potential profits, propelled

TOP: Crates of chickens await shipment to a butcher shop. Photo courtesy of CPR Archives. BOTTOM: For a brief period, buffalo bones were gathered by the Plains Indians for shipment. The bones would later be made into fertilizer. Regina's earliest name was "Pile O' Bones." Photo courtesy of Glenbow Archives, NA 4967-10.

the CPR into commercial telegraphy with its acquisition of Dominion Telegraph.

By 1905 the Canadian Northern Railway had forged Canada's second transcontinental rail link and established its own telegraph subsidiary. In 1915 it added to that network by acquiring the Great Northwestern, which by then was bankrupt.

During this period all newsgathering and distribution was controlled by the large telegraph companies. Weather, disasters, stock market quotations, sports or election results reached into

all corners of Canada by telegraph. Commercial telegraphy allowed Canadians to telegraph messages to family, or to send or receive money through money orders, and so the local station became a focus for yet another community function. As the railway stations often contained the only commercial telegraph office in town they were the community's ear to the outside.

In 1918 the CNoR was bankrupt and its assets, telegraph included, were absorbed by the new government railway, the Canadian National. By the 1920s, Canada had two of its own telegraph companies, the CN and the CP. In 1967 they finally joined forces to become the giant CNCP Telecommunications that exists to this day.

Fuelling Stops

Many of the way stations were also fuelling locations. Steam locomotives needed two ingredients, water and fuel. Once the wood-burning era passed and coal became the universal fuel, coal tipples and storage sheds were built at divisional stations. But the distance between the divisional points was too great for engines to travel without refuelling. To supplement the supply, coal docks were placed at many way stations.

But far more common at way stations were the water tanks. Because the steam locomotives so frequently needed water for the boilers, water tanks were located at every other station. To access the water in larger towns and cities, the railway simply hooked on to the municipal water system. In the early days, before piped water was common, the railways erected windmills beside the tank to pump the water to the tank. With the arrival of the coal era, coal-fired pumps were placed beneath the tank, sometimes in a separate pumphouse, sometimes within the enclosed water tank itself. The pumps served two purposes. Besides keeping the tank full, the pumps in the winter also kept the water heated and moving, and prevented the supply from freezing solid.

As railway expansion accelerated during the latter years of the nineteenth century, and as technology changed, many early way stations lost some of their functions and were downgraded. When the CPR and the Grand Trunk took over many smaller

In 1912 the interior of the water tank at Boissevain, Manitoba, also doubled as an office of sorts. Photo courtesy of Provincial Archives of Manitoba.

branch lines during the late 1800s, they increased the train length but reduced their frequency and the number of required station agents. As a result, many of the stations built to house operators were downgraded to caretaker or flag stations. Although they retained their bay windows, they became as silent as the lonely country shelters that they had in fact become.

The Divisional Stations

Divisional stations were the nerve centre for railway operations. Located at intervals of roughly 150 kilometres, these stations were where locomotives were refuelled and maintained, where rolling stock was sorted and made up into trains, and where train crews ended or started their shifts.

Divisional stations provided facilities for coal storage, water changing, and engine maintenance. They also provided offices for staff. Yardmasters oversaw the makeup of trains, dispatchers alerted the agents along the line of their departure, and roadmasters supervised the maintenance of the track and rights or way along which the trains travelled. Divisional facilities might be small on lightly used branch lines, but on the main lines they were often the reason for a town's entire existence.

Divisional points were where many of the railway men lived. To house the train crews, and to encourage family men to work in these often isolated locations, the railways provided substantial housing. They built bunkhouses for crews in transit, and at smaller divisional points the crew were boarded in local hotels or boarding houses, or in later years in a railway YMCA that the railway constructed for rest and recreation.

Even divisional stations might differ in function. Many divisional points developed into huge operations. The CN divisional point at Hornepayne in Ontario still functions with massive yards and buildings that cover more than 150 hectares. By contrast, Manyberries in Alberta contained little more than a small roundhouse and a watershed. Like many of the little branch line divisional stations, it existed solely to service steam locomotives. A few sidings, a coal dock, and an engine house that might contain only a single stall huddled around the small yards. Forty-seven such smaller terminals existed within the CPR network in Alberta and Saskatchewan alone.

During steam days a train might spend an hour at a divisional station while the engine was watered, coaled, and otherwise tended to. To cater to impatient passengers, the railways instituted restaurants.

Some were housed in a separate building occasionally attached to the station by a walkway, others in the station themselves. These early structures were at first simple two-storey

This early CPR divisional station at Fort William, Ontario, has since been replaced. Photo courtesy of CPR Archives, A 16826.

barnlike structures and might contain sleeping quarters for the crew as well. Later on, stations added lunch counters right in the station building itself, and the separate restaurant building eventually disappeared from the station landscape. At the divisional point of Fort Frances, Ontario, the Canadian Northern's original turreted wooden station was moved a few yards away and became a restaurant when the railway replaced it with a larger brick station. In Temagami, Ontario, the original station became a restaurant following the erection of a new, more elaborate, Tudoresque stone station.

In smaller communities the railways would contract out the lunch service to a local hotel or café. The Grand Trunk station at Kingston went further and, according to an advertisement, offered this added feature: "Passengers going east or west by the night trains may avoid much unpleasant inconvenience arising from being disturbed at unreasonable hours by driving to the railway station early in the evening where they can obtain comfortable bedrooms and an undisturbed sleep till the hour of departure for the train."

Then, as snack bar service was introduced right in the coaches, providing the long-awaited inexpensive alternative to the dining cars, as diesel replaced steam and eliminated the need for lengthy stops at divisional points, the lunchrooms were closed and the space was converted to offices for divisional staff.

At Cartier, Ontario, the large wooden CPR station contained the restaurant right in the building, a restaurant that became the roadmaster's office. At Orangeville, the original separate restaurant building was converted to crew quarters and later became the "station" for a new short-line operation. The original station itself was relocated and became a restaurant. Far to the north in Cochrane, Ontario, the much altered CN/ONR station has been expanded to include not only a larger restaurant, but a motel and ticket office for passengers awaiting the departure of the ONR's *Polar Bear Express* to Moosonee, or the *Northlander* to Toronto.

Next up the pyramid were the regional headquarters. More wide-ranging in function than divisional stations, these housed the railway bureaucracy. To administer the complicated business

The CP divisional station at Orangeville (left), with its "witch's hat" roof, later became a restaurant, while the divisional restaurant (right) became a "station" when the original station was moved. Photo by author.

Patrons enjoy a meal in the CPR divisional station restaurant at Smiths Falls, Ontario. Photo courtesy of CP Archives, 25655.

of running a railway, they divided the country into regions, each with its own headquarters. Station plans were often devised in the regional headquarters. Here, too, executives huddled in panelled boardrooms while department heads tallied statistics for the year.

While stations were usually part of the headquarters building, they were secondary at best. The CPR's Windsor Station in Montreal, originally the national head office, the Algoma Central's Bruce Street in Sault Ste Marie, and the Newfoundland Railway's St. John's terminal are all examples of station/headquarters. By contrast, the handsome limestone head office of the Ontario Northland Railway in North Bay

never contained a station, the railway sharing a station with CN elsewhere in town.

Special Stations

Commuter stations

The success of Ontario's GO commuter system and Montreal's SCTUM are really nothing new. More prevalent in the United States, where urban sprawl had despoiled the landscape even in the 1860s, commuter stations began to appear in Canada towards the end of the nineteenth century. In Fredericton, New

LEFT: One of Toronto's suburban stations was this delightful station at Davenport. Photo courtesy of City of Toronto archives, Salmon, 1057A. RIGHT: In 1913 the Toronto Belt Line's commuter station at Moore Park reflected the upscale neighbourhood that surrounded it. The line lasted only months. Photo courtesy of the Metro Toronto Reference Library, T 12185.

Brunswick, workers would cluster in the pre-dawn at the Queen Street station to board the train that would take them to the mills at Marysville. At 8:30 the same train would return to Fredericton filled with restless students for the high school.

During the 1880s and 1890s, when Montreal was becoming a booming port, commuter lines radiated out from the city, north to suburbs like Mount Royal and Roxboro, and west to places like Westmount, Beaconsfield, Valois, and Pointe-Claire.

Suburban lines were initially less successful around Toronto, one a failure nearly from the day it commenced operations. In 1888 a group of Toronto land speculators, anxious to encourage a housing boom around the city, built the Toronto Beltline Railway. Large, even elaborate, stations were built at Moore Park and Lambton Mills while smaller structures appeared in Forest Hill beside Bathurst Street, at Fairbanks beside Dufferin Street, at Lambton Mills near Scarlet Road, and at Rosedale in the Don Valley. Rather than radiate from the core of the city, the line ignored commuting patterns and encircled it. It failed within two years and was leased to the Grand Trunk for freight operation.

Short sections continued as CN freight stubs until the 1970s. Of the six stations, none have survived and only three, Moore Park, Lambton Mills, and Davenport (Bathurst Street), were even photographed. Moore Park burned following the Second World War, Rosedale burned around the same time, while that at Lambton Mills stood as a residence until the 1960s.

As around Montreal, a number of Toronto's main line stations served double duty as commuter stations. Those at Main Street (known as York), Riverdale, St. Clair, Sunnyside, Davenport, two at West Toronto, and two at Parkdale, all served this function.

A brief commuter service on Vancouver Island shuttled wealthy lakeside residents from Shawinigan Lake into Victoria to work. The service was dropped in 1907.

Industrial Stations

Although fewer in number than commuter stations, another form of special station was the industrial station. These were never intended to be passenger stations, nor did they offer the range of functions of the way stations. They were intended purely to control the heavy rail traffic in and out of industrial complexes.

The Clarabelle station near Sudbury was one. Originally a way station on the Algoma Eastern Railway, it became an industrial station when the CPR acquired that line, stubbed it, and turned it into an industrial spur to serve the huge nickel smelters. Because of the enormous flow of traffic, the station became one of the busiest in Canada. In the 1980s the old wooden structure was replaced by one of aluminum, serving only as a shelter for maintenance workers.

In 1912 the CNoR laid out a huge industrial and residential area northeast of Toronto's then urban fringe. It would later develop into the upscale village of Leaside and was one of Canada's first railway-planned towns. But to access the industries, the railway had to obtain running rights over CPR trackage and, in the shadow of the factories, built an industrial station. A functional but solid brick building, CN's Leaside station retained its railway function until the early 1980s before becoming a retail office.

Special Operations

Some special stations were added for specific operational functions. Port Union, Ontario, a small lake port, sat at the base of steep grades in both directions. Engines strained to haul long trains up the hills. To ease the operation, the Grand Trunk built a station and yards to store special helper engines that supplemented the power of the regular engines. While a new GO station stands nearby, the site of the GTR station and yards have been replaced by new suburban development.

Customs Stations

With the world's longest undefended border existing between Canada and the U.S., dozens of railway lines crossed from one

The early CNR industrial station at Leaside is now privately owned. Photo by author.

country into the other. Customs and revenue procedures needed to be followed. All border crossings therefore needed facilities for customs and revenue officers, even through the stations may not be needed for revenue or operational purposes. At many of the prairie crossings, stations literally sat across the invisible line from each other. Solid brick customs stations built by the Canadian Northern Railway occupied opposite sides of the Rainy River, in Baudette Minnesota and Rainy River, Ontario.

Lacolle, Quebec, boasts a unique castlelike station built by the Delaware and Hudson Railway. Being a customs point for incoming U.S. tourists, the company splurged on a chateau-esque stone "castle" that they believed would give their passengers a flavour of old Quebec.

Possibly the widest range of uses found in what was otherwise a simple small-town station were those contained in the White Pass and Yukon Route railway station in Whitehorse, Yukon Territory. Built from Skagway to Whitehorse in 1900, the railway actually crossed into the Canada near a place called Carcross. However, because most travellers were bound for Whitehorse, the custom offices were located there. Possibly to conveniently apprehend miscreant Americans trying to flee into the sanctity of Canada, the RCMP located their offices in the station as well, and backed up their regulations with a jail.

Union Stations

Many Canadians may remember their stations as being "union" stations, stations shared by two or more railway lines. To the railway companies, union stations were as welcome as a shotgun wedding and were in some ways similar.

Fiercely independent and highly competitive, the railway

The early Great Western station at Niagara Falls holds Amtrak for its customs inspection while a VIA train waits to head back to Toronto. Photo by author.

A castlelike border station at Lacolle, Quebec, was intended to give arriving Americans the flavour of the province. Photo by author.

companies preferred their own stations. Through the architecture or the location of their stations they were able to advertise their prominence and their independence. But high land values and the economics of train operations often produced reluctant bedfellows.

As urban Canada boomed in the 1890s, cities grew, railways arrived, and stations soon needed replacing. Skyrocketing land values, or simply the lack of downtown land, forced competing railways to pool resources and build a common station that both could use.

Passenger convenience was another, although secondary, consideration. It was much easier to change trains within the same building than to retrieve luggage and endure foul weather and traffic to reach a separate station to catch a connecting train.

Canada's first "union" station was built in Toronto in 1855. A modest board-and-batten building, it served the Grand Trunk and Great Western Railways. Shortly thereafter, the Great Western moved out and, in 1866, built a station of its own on the west side of Yonge Street. The first Ontario, Simcoe and Huron station was a simple wooden building that lacked even a train shed. The first Grand Trunk was a two-storey brick stub station, small, but at least with a train shed. The Northern, likewise, had a shed, but with a through track rather than a stub. By far the most elaborate of the three first stations was that of the Great Western, with four tracks emanating from beneath Romanesque arches above.

But it would be short-lived, for Toronto was booming. In 1858 a second station opened to replace it, and in 1872 still a third. But even then passengers still had to scurry between seven other downtown stations. Then, in 1876, a large stone station with three domes replaced those seven. Despite extensive additions in 1895, extensions that obliterated its original charm, it too became obsolete.

The great Toronto fire of 1904 cleared several blocks of downtown land for redevelopment. A parcel just east of the station (that had not been damaged in the fire) was ideally situated for a new union station. To build the new station, the GTR and the CPR formed the Toronto Terminals Railway Company. As was often the case, the two companies could agree on very little. While the CPR wanted the station to be a stub station with the tracks at ground level, the GTR wanted a through station with elevated tracks, a design that would reopen Toronto's lost waterfront to its populace.

But the Board of Railway Commissioners approved the GTR plan. As construction dragged interminably on, the CPR, impatient at the delays, stalked out and built its own station, the beautiful North Toronto station, a considerable distance

GRAND TRUNK STATION, TORONTO 1856

TOP: An early painting depicts Toronto's first "Union" station. Courtesy Metro Toronto Reference Library.
BOTTOM: Toronto's next Union station was much more grand. Photo courtesy Metro Toronto Reference Library, T 12190.

north on Yonge Street, and far from what was then the centre of the city. Completed in 1916, the striking stone building with its Italianate clock tower also functioned as a "union" station, with operations shared between the CPR and the Canadian Northern Railway.

After several years of delay, the new union station by the lakefront was finally ready for use, On August 6, 1927, the Duke of Windsor, in what was probably the briefest opening ceremony for a station anywhere, spent thirteen minutes to declare the station open and then boarded a train for his ranch in Alberta.

By contrast, Montreal, Toronto's metropolitan rival, never had a union station. Like Toronto, Montreal was the hub of many railway lines. The Grand Trunk; the Quebec, Montreal, Ottawa and Occidental; the CPR; and the Canadian Northern all had terminals in or near central Montreal, some more than one. Even as late as the 1920s, after the Canadian National Railway had absorbed the Grand Trunk and Canadian Northern Railways, central Montreal could still count nine stations, four of which belonged to the CPR alone.

The Grand Trunk began operations between Toronto and Montreal in 1856 and constructed a wooden station at the corner of St. Antoine and Bonaventure. Prior to building their magnificent Windsor station, the CPR used the Dalhousie Square station at the end of a spur line into the city centre from the Hochelaga station on its newly acquired QMO and O line. (The Dalhousie Square station has managed to survive and today houses a circus company.)

In downtown Montreal, Windsor Station was the stub station for CPR lines west, Viger for those leading east. Following its creation in 1918, The Canadian National still maintained the former Grand Trunk Bonaventure station and the Canadian Northern's Tunnel Station. Around the periphery of the core, the CPR had stations at Westmount, Montreal West, and Mile End, while the CNR stations were St. Henri and Moreau Street.

Although elaborate, the Grand Trunk's Bonaventure station in Montreal was never a "union" station. Photo courtesy of CNR Archives, 44365.

Then, in the 1930s, the CNR began to dig up the ground at the site of the Tunnel Station and proposed a union station for Montreal. With two solid downtown stations already in place, the CPR rejected the idea. A depression and a war intervened and the new station remained just a hole in the ground. Finally, following the war, the *Gare Centrale* opened, but it accommodated only the CNR. Although it is now Montreal's main railway terminal, it never became a union station.

Vancouver's first union station was not even Canadian. In 1915 the Great Northern Railway, an American line, opened a large building to replace an earlier shack. For a number of years it shared the building with another American line, the Northern Pacific. By the 1950s passenger traffic had declined to a trickle and the GNR moved in with the CNR in a grand station next door. Then, in 1964, the GNR demolished the remarkable old structure in order to unburden itself of high land taxes.

Ottawa's first union station was not the better-known structure that stands today as a convention centre, but an earlier station built by the CPR. Designed in its trademark chateau-esque style, the Broad Street building housed both the CPR and the New York Central Railways. Then, after the Grand Trunk

opened its new neo-classical station on the site of the Canada Atlantic Railway station, the CPR shut its Broad Street station and moved into the new building.

Between 1890 and 1920 several Canadian cities gained handsome union stations. A CPR "chateau" replaced two earlier stations in Quebec City, while large "classical" union stations served Thunder Bay, Regina, Halifax, and Saint John, New Brunswick.

Size, however, had little to do with a station becoming a union station. The delightful little wooden station at Jarvis, Ontario, hosted the Great Western's "Air Line" and Hamilton and Lake Erie railways. The Grand Trunk station in Brockville and the Canadian Northern station in Belleville both hosted CPR trains while the Grand Trunk station in North Bay was also the home base for the Ontario government's Temiskaming and Northern Ontario Railway trains. The smallest union station in Canada, however, was that on the London and Port Stanley Railway. About the size of a large outhouse, this "Union" station never served more than one railway line at a time. Rather, it was named after the nearby village of Union.

The "Grand Centrals": Canada's Grand Urban Stations

The most specialized stations of them all, those that occupied the top of the pyramid, were the city stations, the "Grand Centrals" of Canada. Indeed, these were cities unto themselves. In them a person could buy a newspaper, have a haircut, and then relax over a seven-course meal served on china and silverware at tables covered with linen cloths. One could spend a day in them and never see a train.

The operations here were complex. With hundreds of trains huffing in and out each day, tracks had to be allocated, baggage sorted and passengers pampered. An army of personnel, two thousand in Toronto's Union Station alone, bustled along corridors, platforms, and secret passageways to ensure that baggage met the right train, that parcels got to the post office, and that crew members showed up on time. It was a city that never stopped.

One of the busiest organizations to inhabit the urban station was the Travellers' Aid Society. This wonderful organization, an

LEFT: Named after a nearby village, the flag stop station at Union was never a "union" station. Photo by author. RIGHT: North Bay's stone CPR divisional station (right) replaced the first station (left), which gave birth to the town of North Bay. Photo courtesy of CPR Archives, A 1120. BOTTOM: In 1915 thirty cents bought a full meal at the Winnipeg station lunch counter. Photo courtesy of CPR Archives, A 1120.

Canadian Pacific Railway

Winnipeg Station Lunch Counter

LUNCH

BEEF BROTH

BOILED SALMON, PARSLEY SAUCE
HAMBURGER STEAK, SPANISH SAUCE
ROAST BEEF AU JUS
SPAGHETTI ITALIENNE

BOILED POTATOES   STRING BEANS
CARROTS IN CREAM

CHOCOLATE ICE CREAM
RICE CUSTARD PUDDING   APPLE PIE

TEA   COFFEE   MILK

Lunch, consisting of Soup, one Fish or Meat, two Vegetables
one Dessert, one Bread and Butter,
Tea, Coffee or Milk.

30 CENTS

Not Responsible for Hats, Overcoats, etc.

April 30, 1915.   12.00k to 14.00k

Canadian Pacific Railway

Winnipeg Station Lunch Counter

LUNCH

CREAM OF LETTUCE

FRIED LAKE TROUT, TARTAR SAUCE
KIDNEY SAUTE CHASSEUR
ROAST BEEF AU JUS
PICKLED PORK AND CABBAGE

MASHED POTATOES   PARSNIPS IN CREAM
WAX BEANS

STRAWBERRY ICE CREAM
LEMON PIE   APPLE PIE

TEA   COFFEE   MILK

Lunch, consisting of Soup, one Fish or Meat, two Vegetables
one Dessert, one Bread and Butter,
Tea, Coffee or Milk.

30 CENTS

Not Responsible for Hats, Overcoats, etc.

April 29, 1915.   12.00k to 14.00k

offspring of the YWCA and the Women's Christian Temperance Union, helped the hungry and the helpless. On one occasion, staff of the Travellers' Aid spotted a mother with four children waiting to board a westbound train, carrying only a few loaves of bread to feed themselves. Thanks to the network of Travellers' Aids, she was cared for throughout her journey. During the war they helped soften the stark cultural shock suffered by arriving British war brides, and, in the years that followed, they welcomed trainloads of confused immigrants. From a wartime high of one hundred thousand travellers helped, the Travellers' Aid was helping fewer than five thousand annually less than three decades later.

Among the swirling crowds that converged onto the train platforms were pickpockets and pimps. Young girls fleeing the dead-end monotony of rural Canada were particularly easy prey for the bordello runners. These confused newcomers were susceptible to a smiling face and soothing words that led only to a cruel life of sexual slavery. Pickpockets, too, found countless victims, as strange surroundings and jostling crowds distracted arriving passengers from the light fingers that dipped into their purse or pocket. But among the crowd was another army, the railway police and security staff, alert and ready to pounce.

With as many as twelve platforms to sort and shuffle trains, switching was no simple matter. In the sprawling yards around the stations, signal towers controlled the all-important shuffling of the right trains onto the right tracks. Although computer technology has greatly simplified the process, signal towers still puncture the skylines of the railway yards at Toronto's Union Station and in west-end Montreal.

If any Canadian station has changed very little, it is the urban station. Although trains are faster and fewer, Gare Centrale in Montreal and Union Station in Toronto remain as active urban hubs, but with a few new wrinkles. The traveller may still find a meal, a shave, and reading material while electronic voices intone train departures, but they may also shop in a vast underground city of stores and then ride home on a subway, all directly from a station.

TOP: Deep in the Rocky Mountains, vacationers wait at the Mount Robson flag station. Photo courtesy of CNR Archives, X 20165. BOTTOM: An umbrella station, which served passengers travelling the Thousand Islands Railway, has been preserved in downtown Gananoque along with the last of the railway's motive power. Photo by author

Flag Stations

If the urban terminal marked the apex of the pyramid, the flag stations were the base. Passengers travelling on lightly used branch lines, or leaving quiet country areas, were more likely to say their farewells from a flag station than from a busy operator station. Railway companies seldom spent money where it wasn't necessary and areas that didn't need operators didn't get them.

LEFT: Kingston's downtown Grand Trunk station still stands. Today it serves as a restaurant. Photo courtesy of Queen's Archives, PG-K97.s. RIGHT: Many stations were less than grand affairs, such as this early boxcar station in Alberta. Photo courtesy of Glenbow Archives, NA 1753-23.

Because these stations lacked agents, passengers were left on their own to stop the train. To do this they waved a green-and-white flag at the approaching train.

Many places that started with flag stations grew large enough to earn a full operator station. The Prince Edward Island Railway initially designated forty-seven of sixty-four stations as flag stations. Within a few years public pressure and increased business were strong enough to have most these upgraded. Conversely, many operator stations were downgraded to flag stations, the product of railway amalgamation and fewer trains.

Some flag stations were hardly larger than outhouses: unheated cabins with a door, bench, and window. Others had modest freight sheds attached and were heated by small stoves.

Although the small size left little room for architectural imagination, the dizzy days of station building and competition did produce a wide array of pleasing and occasionally elaborate little shelters. Some of the more unusual, and several yet survive, are the little wooden umbrella stations of the Algoma Central Railway, so called because they consisted only of benches beneath a canopy. They were otherwise open to the elements and were built where summer tourist traffic prevailed.

Among those passenger routes that wind through remote regions of Manitoba, British Columbia, Ontario, and Quebec, travellers must still stand beside the simple shelter or the foundation of rubble where the operator station used to stand, and flag down the train. But, on the busiest lines, computers have replaced the little green-and-white flags and alert the engineer to passenger stops ahead.

It has been easier to rescue the little flag station from demolition. Their small size made relocating costs modest and many were hauled away behind a horse or tractor to become a storage shed on an adjacent farm. Several others ended up in local museums where Canadians can still stand and imagine a distant whistle echoing across the forest of the waving wheat fields.

Millet, Alberta, displays a typical station landscape. Photo courtesy of Archives of Alberta, B-A 487.

STATIONS AND THE CANADIAN LANDSCAPE

The Railway Towns

Canada's most prolific town planners were the railways. The shape, the appearance, indeed, the very existence of Canadian communities during the heyday of railway construction were determined by, more than any other single factor, the location of the railway station. During the boom years before the First World War, three national railways extended their tentacles across the largely unpopulated prairies, first choosing locations for their stations and then building the communities around them. In eastern Canada, stations were thrust into the heart of existing communities, altering the urban fabric around them. Towns appeared, towns disappeared, towns were changed forever, all on the whim of a station planner.

Nowhere was this more evident than in western Canada. As part of its incentive to build the railway, the CPR had received 25 million acres from the government to dispose of in whatever manner it wished. One of the most lucrative ways was to carve it up into town lots. Each township received a station and a town.

The CPR's townsite locations were meticulously chosen and rigorously executed. Before construction began, the CPR deliberately selected a southern rather than a northern route for its main line; the northern route would have had to pass through a number of existing settlements; the southern route was largely

uninhabited and gave the CPR almost absolute control over townsite selection, design, and sales.

Although Sandford Fleming, the government engineer for its portion of the CPR, had devised a standard town plan for the prairies with streets radiating from the central railway station, the CPR ignored it and designed its own standard plans. Much simpler, the railway plan consisted of a grid pattern of streets, usually on the same side of the tracks as the station. The Canadian Northern located the towns on the north side of the tracks wherever possible. This would orient the station platform towards the southern winter sunshine, a direction that not only protected passengers from the cold northern winds but also helped heat the waiting room.

Although the routes of the railway lines were well known in advance, the locations of the townsites were not. To discourage the kind of land speculation that would drive up prices for station grounds, the railways left townsite selection until the last possible moment. More often than not, the railways avoided existing settlements and selected bald prairie for their stations and towns. Here they could control the location of the station and not only avoid high land values, but own the townsites outright and reap the bonanza from the sale of the town lots.

While this had the desired effect on speculators, it also caused considerable anguish among existing communities that

The original CPR divisional station in Medicine Hat was typically simple in style. Its replacement was a more elaborate hotel/station. Photo courtesy of CPR Archives, A-175.

the railways deliberately bypassed. In choosing undeveloped land at Portage la Prairie and Brandon for stations and towns, for example, the CPR shunned the established settlement of Grand Valley, and the settlement swiftly shrank.

As the CPR began to construct its southern line through Manitoba, two busy little communities, Mountain City and Nelsonville, eagerly awaited the news that they would soon boast a new station and perhaps even become a divisional point. Nelsonville, in fact, was already incorporated and had a courthouse, a land titles office, a weekly newspaper, several industries, and sixty houses. But, to their shock, the CPR ignored both and located its station between them at Morden. Despite pleas from even the provincial government, the CPR was unmoved. Beaten, the merchants and residents jacked up their stores and homes and moved them to Morden. Today no trace remains of the vanished villages.

Nakina, in remote northern Ontario, was one of the more dramatic examples of a town that had to move. Shortly after the government of Prime Minister Wilfred Laurier completed the National Transcontinental across Northern Ontario, a divisional

town known as Grant was created. Here, the railway built a roundhouse and repair shops, as well as homes for engineers, conductors, and crew. A short distance to the south lay another new transcontinental line, the Canadian Northern.

By 1923 a new crown corporation known as the Canadian National Railway owned both. One of the CNR's first fights was to obtain the lucrative silk contracts from Japan. Success depended upon speed, speed to get the still-living silk to the east coast from the west before it started to deteriorate. But, separate, both the former GTP and CNoR routes were too long. The CNR quickly realized that linking the two lines at their closest point, just west of Grant, would reduce the transcontinental travelling time by four hours — enough to win the coveted silk contracts.

The link was completed in 1923. The CNR then realized that its divisional point of Grant, now east of the busiest portion of the new line, was in the wrong place. At the new junction the CNR hurriedly dumped off a boxcar to serve as a station, gave it the name Thornton Junction, and prepared to move Grant to the new site.

Soon, a parade of houses and stores, balancing awkwardly on railway flatcars, began to slowly wend its way to the newly

LEFT: Crews move the Port Moody, British Columbia, station along the track to a more central location in town. Photo courtesy of CPR Archives, 12850. RIGHT: As in many prairie towns, the Moose Jaw station dominates the end of the main street. Photo by author.

cleared townsite, now named Nakina. The townsite was a standard railway plan, a grid of streets situated north of the tracks with the main street leading straight to the station grounds. The company houses were reconstructed along the main street at the head of which a handsome divisional station replaced the boxcar. A string of false-fronted hotels and stores lined the street behind the station and gave Nakina the appearance of the boomtown that it was.

Soon, the inevitable roads arrived, diesel replaced steam, and the railway pulled out. The old wooden station fell into disrepair. Now, thanks to an Ontario government grant, the station has been restored as a transportation hub, with VIA Rail's transcontinental *Canadian* stopping three times weekly in each direction.

Occasionally the railways failed to dictate the shape of a town around their station. When the CPR sought to build the Crowsnest Pass line through Fort Macleod in southern Alberta, the Board of Railway Commissioners insisted that the railway build its station no further than five hundred yards from the town limit. The railway, however, subsequently convinced the town to shuffle its boundaries so that the station still ended up about three kilometres from the commercial core and, no doubt, the more expensive land.

In 1945 a four-decade battle ended in victory for the Port Moody, British Columbia, business community when the CPR finally hoisted its two-storey station onto flatcars and moved it from its fringe location to the heart of the community. The CPR's crew completed the move in less than seven hours and even turned a blind eye when some of the more daring townsfolk hitched a ride on the slow-moving structure. In the late 1970s the station was moved once again, this time to become a museum.

In the meantime, Lieutenant Governor Edgar Dewdney had been ordered by the federal government to find a new site for the territorial capital on the endless plains of Saskatchewan. At an insignificant siding known as "Pile O' Bones," Dewdney purchased land and pressed the government to place its new offices on it. Meanwhile, the CPR, in keeping with its policy of avoiding private lands, chose a station location three kilometres away. A new town began to bloom around the CPR facility and was given the name Regina. To further confound the hapless Dewdney, the CPR chose, to everyone's surprise, not Regina, but the unlikely raw town of Moose Jaw as a new divisional point. Although Regina grew on the strength of its status as the capital and the fertility of its surrounding farmlands, it never became the railway town that Dewdney and Regina's supporters had hoped it would.

The railways established their divisional points every 150 kilometres or so. Construction booms and soaring land values inevitably followed, and existing towns and landowners vied ferociously for the coveted stations and facilities. Fort Steele, British Columbia, began as a Royal North West Mounted Police outpost. But when the CPR began building its southern main line towards the Crowsnest Pass, rumours swept the town that the CPR had selected it for a divisional point. Instantly the town boomed and land values soared. But the CPR rejected Fort Steele and chose Cranbrook instead. The bubble burst and Fort Steele became a ghost town. It remained derelict and forgotten until 1966, when the government of British Columbia purchased most of the town and reconstructed it as a tourist attraction.

Even before the railway construction crews reached Calgary, it was already a busy trading post. However, once again, to avoid high land costs, the railway located its station more than a kilometre from the fort and its settlement. Despite the howls of protest from the business community, the CPR refused to locate its station any closer and the unhappy merchants had little choice but to move to the station.

The railway further solidified its location by placing its warehouses at the new site, forcing other warehouse owners to follow suit. Then, in 1912, they built the beautiful Palliser Hotel adjacent to the station and the shape of Calgary was forever fixed.

If the CPR's station location had influenced the shape of Calgary, that influence was even more pronounced in Vancouver. Under its original charter, the CPR was to terminate at Port Moody. Van Horne, then CPR General Manager, found the harbour unnavigable and pushed the rails on to a tiny and dilapidated sawmill town named Coal Harbour where he received twenty-five hundred hectares of land from the province. Here, on long wooden piers rising awkwardly from the coastal mud flats, the CPR hastily erected an unimpressive and unadorned temporary wooden station.

The next year the CPR sent in surveyor L.A. Hamilton to lay out the usual town plan with its grid street pattern. Here, the CPR built a new station and added offices, freight facilities, and the first Hotel Vancouver. Until it was demolished in 1914, the grand chateau-esque station, which had replaced the original, visually dominated the main shopping street, Granville, as if to reaffirm that the railway was in control of the city's destiny.

For two decades the CPR's dominance of the West Coast remained unchallenged. Then, in 1905, a new rival, the Grand Trunk Pacific Railway, proposed a brand new town for its own western terminus. On the fog-bound

The CPR's magnificent chateau-esque station dominated Vancouver's growing downtown. The station lasted only eighteen years. Photo courtesy of CPR Archives, A-12537.

Pacific coast, seven hundred kilometres north of Vancouver, the British Columbia government granted the GTP ten thousand acres of land for a station and townsite. The Boston planning firm of Brett and Hall devised a model city of curving tree-lined streets, which the railway christened "Prince Rupert." To attract buyers the GTP widely announced that the new city would have no restrictions on the use of those lots.

In 1909 the lots went on sale. Frenzied selling and reselling pushed prices beyond $10,000 per lot. But, despite the orgy of bidding, the new town remained largely empty. Most of the bidding had been by speculators, buyers who had never intended to even visit the place. When the port of Vancouver proved to be far superior for importing commercial goods, the expected freight traffic never materialized and speculators were left with worthless land.

While the CPR located and designed the townsites across the prairies, the job of selling them fell to a private consortium of British and Canadian investors known as the Canada North West Land Company. Nominally independent, the company was in effect an extension of the CPR's land department and in 1908 was formally taken over by the railway.

The CPR was not the only railway company in the land business. They all were. The hugely lucrative land sales were the fastest way the railways could recover their enormous construction expenditures and the most convincing argument they could place before their shareholders whenever it was time to again expand.

Unlike the CPR, William Mackenzie and Donald Mann, the precocious builders of the Canadian Northern Railways, assembled their land holdings not from the government but by purchasing existing railway charters — charters with land grants included. In less than ten years they could lay claim to more than 4.1 million acres of land, most it prime prairie black soil. By 1906 the duo had created more than 132 villages through Manitoba, Saskatchewan, and Alberta.

The latecomer was the Grand Trunk Pacific. Although it was the darling of the Laurier Liberals, who built most of the line, it received no aid. But by building through virtually virgin territory, the GTP was able to assemble eighty-six townsites at bargain prices. Each town plan was identical. In 1909 one

newspaper headline read, "Towns made to order." "We will put a town here," said the engineer in charge, "there was no ceremony, no one to applaud … These towns-to-be would grow up straight and orderly according to a formula, the parks labelled, the marketplace determined. The main street always runs down to the railway station, 80 inches wide and no building costing less the $1000 can be erected upon it."

Before the town was developed, the station presented a forlorn appearance on the bare prairies. As W.W. Withrow noted in his classic *Our Own Country* (1888), "In some places the station house is the only building in sight. At one such place a couple of tourists came out onto the platform as the train came to a stop. 'Which side is the town on anyhow?' said one to the other. 'The same side as the timber of course,' replied the other. The point of the joke is that not a solitary tree was to be seen on either side."

By controlling the disposition of the land in the town, the railways could control its appearance. Anxious to show to the world the commercial boom that they brought to the prairies, the railways ensured that the lots most visible from the station, along the main street that led to the station, and those that paralleled the track, were all sold for commercial uses. They even endeavoured

An aerial view of the town of Temagami shows how the village grew around the ONR station. Photo by author.

Canterbury, New Brunswick, is a case of the station village outgrowing the original parent village. Photo by author.

to ensure that large hotels were located conveniently just across the road from the station.

As the prairie towns grew, wooden false-fronted stores lined a wide main street that unrolled from the rear door of the station's waiting room. The design was far from accidental. By dominating the main street, the station would daily remind the residents of the railway company's pre-eminence. Conversely, an arriving passenger's first view was of a commercially prosperous main street, a deliberate orchestration by the railway companies to reinforce their own importance in the development and economy of Canada's towns and villages. The tactic certainly impressed W.W. Withrow: "The railway stations through the province of Manitoba gave evidence of life and energy. At many of them are 2, 3 or even 4 capacious steam elevators representing rural wheat purchasing companies and frequently a number of mills … stations succeed each other at intervals of 5 or 8 miles and many of them are surrounded by bright and busy towns."

In eastern Canada, station planners had to contend with towns that already existed. Changes to the landscape, however, were often no less spectacular than they were upon the undeveloped prairies. Factories and warehouses appeared by the track while hotels, stores, and even flower gardens clustered behind the station. More than any other building, the railway station shaped the appearance and the destiny of eastern Canada's small towns.

Until 1853, when the Great Western Railway constructed a new suspension bridge across the Niagara River, the village of Elgin consisted of only a handful of cabins. The instant access provided by the bridge brought 280 town lots onto the market, ranging in price from $150 to $300. In just three years Elgin had boomed into "an enterprising, brisk and lively town with upwards of 100 inhabitants, 14 or 15 grocery stores and 20 saloons and hotels." In 1879 the original wooden station was replaced with "a large brick structure of Victorian gingerbread and ornamental woodwork [whose] massive wood parallel entrance doors made it the envy of the frontier." That little "frontier" village today goes by the name of Niagara Falls, and the station still stands.

Not far away, a similar story was unfolding. In 1873, when the Buffalo and Lake Huron Railway replaced the ferry service across the Niagara River with a new bridge, a new town sprang up on

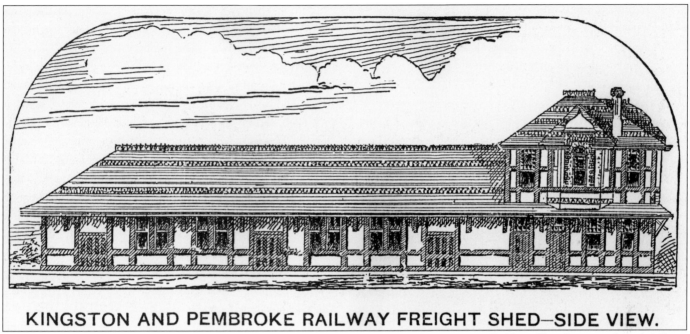

KINGSTON AND PEMBROKE RAILWAY FREIGHT SHED—SIDE VIEW.

While freight stations were seldom a dominant part of the station landscape in Canada, that of the CPR in Kingston, Ontario, was unusually elaborate. Illustration courtesy of Queen's Archives.

the flat shoreline that surrounded the new station. Stores, taverns, and churches crowded the 250-lot town plot. In the words of a contemporary visitor, "Victoria, the new town, is the terminus of the Grand Trunk, the Great Western and the Canada Southern railways. It is contemplated that Victoria will become a suburb of Buffalo [which] can be reached in a few minutes. Victoria already has good hotels stores and neat cottages with unsurpassed facilities for all classes of manufacturing and mercantile businesses."

The town became "Bridgeburg" in 1894 and then amalgamated with Fort Erie. The Grand Trunk station with its conical "witch's hat" waiting room was demolished; however, another of the Fort Erie stations was located to a nearby museum.

A station located apart from an existing village created an equally indelible imprint upon Canada's landscapes: the station village. Most were tiny satellites to the parent village and typically consisted of a hotel or two, a store, a café, and a handful of houses for railway employees.

A few station villages, however, boomed and completely overwhelmed the parent. Canterbury Station in New Brunswick

was one. It developed around the station of the New Brunswick and Canada Railway a dozen miles from the original settlement on the St. John River. Within a decade it had matched the old site in size and then, when the water-powered industries of the decaying old town became outmoded, Canterbury Station became the more important of the two.

Even more dramatic was the growth of Killaloe Station on the Ottawa, Arnprior and Parry Sound Railway in Ontario. As early as the 1840s and 1850s, Killaloe was a small but busy mill village. However, in the 1890s, John Booth and his railway builders chose a route three kilometres north, and the station village quickly outgrew the old mill village. Today, Killaloe Station is simply called Killaloe and claims a population of over six hundred. The older village has shrunk to a tiny clutch of homes huddled around the old general store and mill.

But the impact of the railway station upon the urban landscape can just as easily be overstated. For often there was none. Along branch lines with little activity, stations were mere flag stops. Structures were little more than enclosed shelters, and, if the passengers were fortunate, equipped with a stove. More usually, however, they were unheated and about the size of an outhouse. Here the station remained alone on the landscape, often a solitary silhouette against an open sky.

Station Landscapes

Despite the different shapes that the railways created in towns east and west, the landscapes that immediately surrounded the station were more or less similar. They had to be.

Part and parcel of Canada's station landscape was the water tanks. The steam engines' heavy appetite for water meant that a reliable and frequent water supply was essential. The tanks themselves were steel, a bulbous barrel atop stocky legs and pipes. Throughout most of the country, however, frigid winters could freeze solid even an entire tank of water. To prevent freezing, a protective wooden shell was built around the tanks. Inside the shell a stove and pump kept the water both moving and thawed during the winter. At some eastern Ontario stations the lower section of the shell was of local stone rather than wood.

A rod that pierced the roof of the tank rested on a floating ball and alerted maintenance crews as to the level of the water inside. In the early days of Canada's stations, before municipal water pipes were constructed and extended to the water tanks, windmills beside the tanks pumped the water from a well into the tank. In Avonlea, Saskatchewan, water had to be piped from a lake several kilometres away.

In the early days, coal was loaded from the coal pile onto the coal tenders by a bucket or scoop on the end of a swivel. This awkward process was replaced by the coal dock or tipple. A much more efficient system, the coal was stored in an overhead bin and when the tender was underneath, the operator would

LEFT: The sturdy water tank in Dalhousie, Quebec, is enclosed in stone. Photo by author. ABOVE: Both water tank and station are preserved in Glaslyn, Saskatchewan, completing a typical rural station landscape. Photo by author.

simply open the chute and fill the tender. During the 1920s these dark and dusty towers became an integral part of the station landscape, particularly at divisional stations. Avonlea foreman Jack Dalrymple tried to brighten his dusty coal tower by placing geraniums in the coal dock window.

The most visible and enduring element of the prairie station landscape was the grain elevator. Prairie grain, after all, was why the railways were there in the first place. To avoid the distinctive aromatic unpleasantness of having a steady stream of horse-drawn wagons lining the towns' streets, the elevator companies located their elevators opposite the station and the town. As grain traffic increased, however, the lines of wagons grew so long that they frequently blocked the tracks and disrupted train movement. In response, the railways made land available for elevators only on the same side of the track as the town and station, but at a considerable distance from the town centre.

As pioneer farmers struggled to clear the trees, the sawmill became a common sight beside most stations. But once the forests were cleared, the sawmills closed. As farming became increasingly profitable, the railways began to move farm products to market, and grain elevators, more usually associated with the prairie landscape, became a common sight in Ontario and Quebec.

Stockyards too were a common element of the station's immediate landscape. Towns often vied vigorously with each other for a stockyard at the station. Even where cattle were not raised locally, regulations required that, while en route to market, livestock had to be off-loaded at regular intervals for exercise.

In divisional towns the landscape around the station was heavily dominated by railway structures. Beside the station, sometimes in it, a restaurant provided meals for passengers waiting for the engine to be serviced and for the crews to change shifts. Usually the restaurants were franchised out to private operators, although sometimes they were operated by the railways themselves. In any case, they provided economy-minded travellers with a less

The station skyline in St. Paul, Alberta, is typically dominated by the grain elevators. Photo by author.

An 1890s view of the station and dining hall in Broadview, Saskatchewan. Most divisional stations had restaurants either beside them or in them, offering economy-minded passengers a less expensive, if hurried, alternative to the dining car. Photo courtesy of Saskatchewan Archives Board, R-A 18910-1.

expensive alternative to the more costly dining car.

Sorting yards, roundhouses, engine sheds, and coal tipples dominated the sprawling station grounds. Behind the station, bunkhouses, hotels, or occasionally YMCAs would house train crews awaiting their return shift.

Divisional towns were home to the railway crews. To attract good workers, preferably family men, the railways provided permanent housing. Styles were often reminiscent of the stations themselves. But in all cases the houses could be readily distinguished by their rigid rows and identical designs.

Gardens

One of the most distinctive features of Canada's station landscapes, and one of the least remembered, were the station gardens. The early stations, with their piles of cordwood and muddy grounds, were unkempt and ugly. To soften the unsightliness, the railways began to supply agents with flowers to add to their own vegetable gardens.

Long a practice of station agents in England, the station gardens first appeared in Canada along the Grand Trunk Railway between Toronto and Montreal and along the Ontario Simcoe and Lake Huron (later the Northern) Railway between Toronto and Collingwood. The man who started it all was Fred Cumberland. An engineer from England hired by the OH and S, Cumberland was meticulous in the running of the railway. It was he who insisted that his railway have the best station gardens, and many attribute to him the initial impetus for Canada's station gardens. Bolstered by the unexpected popularity of the gardens, Cumberland hired a gardener at Couchiching Point to set up a permanent green house. In 1868 two of the more popular station gardens, those at Sunnidale and Stayner, cost $436 and $401 respectively.

TOP: A now-forgotten feature of the station landscape was the popular station garden, as seen in this extensive garden at Chelsea, Quebec. Photo courtesy of CPR Archives, 13469. BOTTOM: Uniformed staff stand in front of the restaurant at the Grand Trunk's Allandale Station (now part of Barrie, Ontario). Thanks to Fred Cumberland, whose bust rests in a nearby park, the station garden movement began here. Photo courtesy of CNR Archives, 79095.

Collingwood and Allandale, however, were the most important points on the line, and Cumberland gave them the best gardens. Within two decades of the opening of the Northern Railway, Collingwood had become an important tourist destination. Passengers disembarked here to transfer to Georgian Bay steamers. While waiting for their connections they admired the large gardens or listened to the music from its bandshell.

Allandale, an important divisional point on the Northern Railway, boasted a particularly large and attractive garden. Although the fountain and the flowers have gone, a bust of Cumberland still gazes soberly from what is now a neatly trimmed parkette.

If the Northern Railway was the first to establish station gardens, the CPR was the most ambitious. Like the Northern, the CPR had an economic motive for its gardens. One of Western Canada's pre-eminent developers, the CPR wanted to attract settlers. Promotional literature that featured a photo of a lush station garden made an otherwise arid Canadian West look more fertile than was usually the case. David Hysop, a real estate agent and claims adjuster for the railway, urged, "If you want to show how good the soil is why not have gardens at the railway stations in which flowers and vegetables can be grown?"

For his initiative, Hysop was promptly put in charge of forty-four gardens between Brandon and Golden. Even the surly and cynical CPR president, William Van Horne, caught the garden fever and declared "the station agent with a nice garden is the agent who has a clean station, has a flower in buttonhole, wears his coat, and has well-brushed boots."

Although hugely unpopular for its monopolistic practices and its community insensitivity, the CPR gained many supporters for its gardens. Magazines such as the *Canadian Horticulturist* and the *Canadian Municipal Journal* praised the CPR for its work on station beautification. "The man who has a nice garden," swooned the *Municipal Journal*, "is not the man who spends his time in the nearest saloon, nor the man who has to be discharged for beating his wife. [He is] a decent industrious man who will bring up his children to be the best kind of citizens."

Station gardens were often a town's only parkland and became the focus of the community. Those at Red Deer and Fort

As shown in this 1920s view of the garden at Red Deer, Alberta, the CPR was moving into a less formal style of station garden. Photo courtesy of Archives of Alberta, A-6251.

Mcleod boasted a circular arrangement dominated by a bandshell or a fountain. Broadview, Regina, and Kenora also contained magnificent station gardens. By contrast, simpler gardens might only have the town name spelled out in whitewashed boulders.

To encourage agents to plant gardens, the railways set up nurseries, usually under the auspices of a Forestry Department to manage nurseries. Those of the CPR were at Wolseley (Saskatchewan), Springfield (Manitoba), Fort William, Kenora, Winnipeg, Moose Jaw, Calgary, Revelstoke, and Vancouver. The CNR administered nurseries in Winnipeg and Stratford, Ontario. The forestry departments also oversaw the design and the planting of the station grounds themselves. They established design criteria, circulated catalogues, and subjected the gardens to formal inspection. They also initiated a competition for the best garden, awarding $50 to the winner in each district or division.

The First World War brought with it a temporary lull in CPR's garden beautification program. Hearkening to the federal government's plea for more domestic food production, the CPR ploughed under many of the flower beds and replaced them with less attractive but more essential potatoes.

LEFT: A modern municipal garden graces the landscape at VIA Rail's Brantford, Ontario, station. Photo by author. RIGHT: Both hotel and station continue to cater to the public in Alexandria, Ontario. Photo by author.

The end of the war, however, not only brought more gardens but also more bureaucracy. The CPR's main competitors, the CNoR and the GTP, had just completed their lines when the war broke out. The crippling financial restrictions of the war drove them both into bankruptcy and the Canadian government set up the Canadian National Railway to assume these and other bankrupt lines. Anxious to capture some the CPR's business, the new CNR also set up a Forestry Department and launched a garden program of its own.

In an effort to stay ahead of the CNR and modernize its gardens, the CPR established a floral committee, and encouraged the agents to replace the earlier more formal gardens with a more current concept. The tradition-minded agents, however, largely ignored the new styles and kept to their familiar gardens, formal and usually fenced.

If the end of the First World War fostered station gardens, the end of the Second World War finished them. As cars replaced the passenger train, and modern technology reduced the community's reliance upon its stations, the railways paid less and less attention to the gardens.

Flower beds were replaced by lawns and surrounded by hardy and protective caragana hedges. Then, in response to the greater demand for parking, the lawns were in turn paved with asphalt. Finally, the stations themselves were demolished by the thousands to be replaced by junkyards, modern office towers, or nothing. In other towns, small parks mark the former station gardens, some are dominated by war memorials. Meanwhile, among the many ghost towns of the prairies, the only evidence that there was ever a garden or even a station is the unkempt yet distinctive caragana hedges.

Hotels

But it was not just railway gardens and structures that typified the station landscape. Almost as inevitable as the flowers and the water tanks were the station hotels. Every town had one, sometimes more. Large, small, brick, stone, and wood, they could be found across the street and right behind the station.

In the smaller communities the hotels were typically wood and two, or at the most, three storeys high. Larger communities might warrant a hotel made of brick, perhaps with an elevator. Divisional towns could count on a string of hotels, for here travellers often spent the night while waiting for their connecting train. In the larger cities the railways themselves built large hotels, some of the most beautiful in the country. The Palliser Hotel in Calgary, the Royal Alexandra in Winnipeg (demolished), and the Hotel Vancouver in the city of the same name, were all built by the CPR. The Fort Garry in Winnipeg, the Royal York in Toronto, the Chateau Laurier in Ottawa, and the Bessborough Hotel in

TOP: Passengers travelling to Perth-Andover, New Brunswick, had only to cross the track to reach the station hotel. Photo by author. BOTTOM: The Fort Garry Hotel in Winnipeg was one of many grand hotels built by the railways in Canada's larger cities. Photo by author.

Saskatoon, erected by predecessors of the CNR, are other examples of railway hotels that have achieved architectural acclaim.

The "chateau" period of station architecture greatly influenced many of these hotels, such as the Fort Garry, the Chateau Laurier, and the Bessborough. In a few cases such as McAdam (New Brunswick), Medicine Hat, and the second Moose Jaw station, all chateau-esque, the railways built the hotels right in the stations themselves.

In an era when all travel was by train, hotels were essential. Travelling salesmen, entertainers, indeed, any visitor, relied upon this form of accommodation. "Drummers," as the salesmen were called, often used their hotel rooms to display their latest line of wares to prospective purchasers and encourage clients with gifts of cigars or whisky.

With the elimination of passenger service along most lines, the hotels were either demolished or converted to such other uses as apartments, taverns, or stores. In the ghost towns of Alberta and Saskatchewan, many sit empty, paint peeling, and their shutters banging in the prairie wind.

Names

Less visible, but equally as significant, was the influence that stations had upon community names. In eastern Canada, where the railways often passed near existing towns and villages, the railway companies usually named the station after the town. When the railway created a separate satellite settlement, the company simply added the word "station" to the town name. As a result, there are more than two hundred communities in eastern Canada with "station" as part of their names.

But in western Canada, where the railways created the communities, they exercised a free and often imaginative hand in the naming of their stations. Originally, stations were simply numbered, but as soon as a post office was proposed, a proper name became necessary. Although it was the practice of all railway companies to name stations after their more prominent officials, some went further. During the First World War, employees who had been decorated for their war service were rewarded by having a station named for them. Heskith, Kirkpatrick, Thrasher, and Unwin were all named after decorated railway officials.

Station names have a legacy of their own. In northern Ontario, the CPR named this station after a French artist named Rosa Bonheur. Photo courtesy of CPR Archives, A 16888.

The Grand Trunk Pacific named their new communities alphabetically from east to west, such as Atwater to Zelona and Allan to Zunbro. Acronyms were also popular. Canora, Saskatchewan, was named for the "*CA*nadian *NO*rthern *RA*ilway" while Kenora, Ontario, was named after *KE*ewatin (a nearby town), *NO*rman (the first postmaster), and *RA*t Portage, the community's first name. Near the Alberta–Saskatchewan border, the rationale for the acronym "Alsask" is self-evident; not so, however, for the next station on the line, "Mantario." Apparently the company wished to offend no one.

Humour occasionally influenced the naming of stations. To avoid duplication, the letters of a name might be reversed or rearranged. For example, Leonard became CPR's "Draneol," Ontario, and Sullivan became "Vinsulla." In northern Ontario the CPR named its station at "Bonheur" after a turn-of-the-century female French artist who wore trousers and smoked cigars. Her significance to the CPR, however, remains a mystery to this day.

Not all station names were universally accepted. When the Algoma Central Railway decided to use the Indian names "Ogidaki," "Mashkode," and "Mekatina" for three of their stations north of Sault Ste Marie, Ontario, the *Sault Star* derisively remarked that the names were "devised by a Welshman who talks Russian with the Aberdeen inflection." It added, xenophobically, that the names were "designed to keep the coming Scandinavians at home." Nevertheless, the names were retained and remain in use.

The landscapes created by the stations are vastly different now. The wholesale station demolition of the 1960s and 1970s left a hideous hole in the heart of small-town Canada. Often in place of the sturdy stations and their gardens are vacant and weedy station grounds, dusty parking lots, or unkempt storage yards. The water tanks and the coal tipples are gone, as are most of the cattle yards and many of the grain elevators. The railway houses have been resold, re-sided, and remodelled although the characteristic rows and shapes remain unmistakable. The satellite station settlements at the fringe of the larger towns have now been swallowed by faceless urban sprawl. On the prairies, the wide main streets that ended at the station are still lined with simple storefronts and still end at the railway track, or its abandoned roadbed. But the vacant view down that street now seems strangely empty, for the heart of the community is gone. Sometimes only the name survives.

Uncompleted in this sketch, the first station on the Sherbrooke and Quebec Railway was as simple as they get. Illustration courtesy of CPR Archives, 5397.

"MISERABLE SHANTIES": CANADA'S FIRST STATIONS

3

The First Shacks

"**A**rrived in St. John for a cold collation in the Rail Station house, which was pleasantly cool and decorated with green branches." The date was July 21, 1836, and the occasion was the opening of Canada's first railway station, the St. John terminus of the Champlain and St. Lawrence Railway. Built as a portage railway to shuttle freight and passengers from steamers plying the St Lawrence to those on the Richelieu River, the railway constructed primitive stations at Laprairie and Saint-Jean-sur-Richelieu.

According to an 1835 report by the railway's chief engineer, William R. Casey, they were barnlike in appearance and measured "ten feet by forty feet … substantially built and intended to be finished without unnecessary expense."

Before that, Canada's railways had no stations. The first rail operations were simple industrial tracks. For the construction of the Fortress of Louisburg in the 1720s, horses hauled wagons filled with quarry stone over wooden rails to the construction site. During the 1820s Colonel John By used a short railway to drag quarry stones for the construction of the Rideau Canal at Hog's Back Falls near Bytown (later to be known as Ottawa).

In the 1830s, when the railways in England and the United States began to carry passengers, there were few provisions for their comfort. Like the travellers on stages and canals, railway patrons were forced to purchase their tickets at the nearest inn and there await the train. Early train notices listed street intersections as points of departure. "Starts every morning from the corner of Broad and Race Street" read the ad for the pioneer fast line to Pittsburgh in 1837.

The first building in North America to be called a railway station is considered by many to be that of the Baltimore and Ohio Railway at Mount Clare, Baltimore, and now exists as a museum. Even so, this large brick building at first contained only a ticket booth and had no accommodation for passengers.

Railway builders had no idea as to what a station should be or what it should look like. They were not always referred to as "stations," as some travellers preferred the traditional stagecoach term of "stopping place." Indeed, the Mount Clare station was designed after a toll house.

A classical painting by A. Sheriff Scott depicts the first station of the Montreal and Lachine Railway. Like many of the early North American stations, it was little more than a train shed that resembled a large wooden barn with a track through the middle. It was lit by large windows and capped by a cupola. "The terminal at this end," wrote the *Montreal Witness* on the station's opening in 1847, "though not boasting of much architectural ornament,

A painting by A. Sheriff Scott depicts the opening of the Montreal and Lachine Railway in 1847. The "station" was little more than a covered train shed with minimal facilities for staff and passengers. Courtesy CNR Archives.

will be a very spacious and comfortable building." It was situated at the corner of Bonaventure Street and Rue St. Antoine near the site of the later Bonaventure Station. The M and L too was a portage railway, a ten-kilometre route that simply bypassed the Lachine rapids of the St. Lawrence River.

By the time Canada's first major railway line, the St. Lawrence and Atlantic, was completed in 1853, station planners were paying more attention to the needs of their passengers. Montreal's Longeuil station, on the south shore of St. Lawrence, was described by the *Montreal Gazette* of 1848 as "a large and handsome structure, two hundred and thirty feet in length by sixty feet in width" which, along with the next large station in St-Hyacinthe, contained offices and waiting rooms. Architecturally, however, it was still a train shed, a track and platform under a single roof more closely resembling an engine house than the track-side station that today's Canadians remember.

The first railway in what would become Ontario, the Erie and Ontario, likewise began as a horse-drawn portage line, built to bypass Niagara Falls. Its terminus at Queenston consisted of a primitive shed and warehouse, while that at Chippewa was a

steamboat wharf. After it was absorbed by the Michigan Central, it was extended to both Niagara-on-the-Lake and Fort Erie. It began to promote tourism and added tourist stations at Niagara Falls, as well as several way stations at frequent intervals along its route.

Location, Location, Location

After 1850 railway madness swept North America. By 1870 over seventy railway charters had been approved (although many of them were never started). One of the first problems to resolve was where to put the stations. Railway engineers had to consider the location of wood, water, the existence of towns or villages, the willingness of landowners to sell at reasonable prices, and obstacles like hills and valleys.

Railways could not locate a station on either a hill or a curve. On the upgrade it would have proved almost impossible for a larger train to start, on the downgrade difficult to stop. Furthermore, steam engines required a grade of a half-mile of level track to every foot of grade to allow for acceleration. A grade

A typical "shanty" is the CPR's first station in Wickham, Quebec. Photo courtesy of CPR Archives, 6092.

steeper than fifteen feet per mile was considered unsafe for an approach to a station. Curves were avoided to give approaching engineers ample opportunity to view any unexpected traffic sitting at a station.

Another basic requirement was water. The quantities of water needed to power the huge black boilers were so enormous that a steam engine could exhaust its reserve of water in just thirty-five kilometres.

But perhaps the most important consideration was the location of present or future paying customers. Railways were in the business of making money. And to make that money, especially when railways began to compete with each other, customers had to be pampered. Proximity was the key.

When railways passed through existing towns and cities, stations were located as close as possible to factories and stores. Passengers didn't generate as much revenue as freight and were accordingly relegated to secondary status. It was easier and cheaper to make the passengers come to the train than to take the railway to them.

Quebec's country villages were often close together, located on the many twisting wagon roads that wound across the countryside. To best access these customers, the railways had to locate their stations much closer together than railway operations actually required.

On the unpopulated prairies, the stations preceded the towns. Locations there were determined not by the existing clients but by the anticipated ones. Elevators and stations were therefore located at ten- to twelve-kilometre intervals, the farthest that a farmer could urge his horses over rutted prairie trails in a single day to bring his wheat to a railside grain elevator.

Another player in station location was the Board of Railway Commissioners. Created in 1903 under the new Railway Act, the Board could dictate not only a station's location, but also its design.

In spite of all the engineering standards, the supply of water, or the existence of towns, one intangible factor in station location stood out above all others — local lobbying. Politicians, businessmen, and landowners, all eager to realize a political

Collingwood's first station was a board-and-batten structure still surrounded by the blackened stumps of the newly cleared townsite. It was later replaced by a brick station with a towered entrance. Photo courtesy of Ontario Archives, S 1627.

or financial windfall from a station location, outbid and often outbribed each other to gain a station for their town or their property. The CPR's blustery president, William Van Horne, even boasted that his company would "locate the station where we receive the most liberal treatment."

One example of local influence upon a station location appears in the *Belden's Historical Atlas of Essex and Kent Counties.* Here, near the city of Chatham, a family called Thompson owned a large parcel of land that lay in the path of the Great Western Railway. The family offered the company a free parcel of land if they would locate their station upon it. With the station in place, the family were then able to carve up and sell the rest of their land into residential and commercial lots, a town plot that went on to become the town of Newbury and which would quickly boom to a population of six hundred.

Sometimes the strategy would backfire. To attract a station on the Hamilton and Northwestern Railway to the town of Beeton, Ontario, a local landowner offered free land and the town offered free water. Unfortunately for the residents, whenever an engine began to take on water, a frequent occurrence on the busy line, the taps would go dry.

In Barry's Bay, Ontario, landowner Frank Strafford offered lumber baron John Booth, who was then building the Ottawa, Arnprior and Parry Sound Railway, free land for a station, and awaited the expected windfall. According to Niall MacKay, in his authoritative history of the line, *Over the Hills to Georgian Bay,*

the railway accepted his offer but built the station and water tank literally at his back door. A furious Stafford demanded payment as compensation. In lieu of cash, the railway offered Stafford free water from its supply. But a chastened Stafford was to learn that the frequent requirements of the OAPS engines left him without water most of the time. Both the station and the tank still stand in Barry's Bay although the line has long been lifted.

The conflicts that arose over station location could be furious. In 1883 the CPR needed land along the waterfront at Port Arthur, Ontario. The owners, the McVicars, would agree only if the CPR would locate its station on a different property several blocks from the town's commercial heart. Merchants and politicians, anxious for a downtown station, raged at the CPR, but to no avail. Only when a new station was built more than twenty years later was it located in the centre of the city.

On rare occasions when a railway refused to place a station in a town that requested one, the people would do it themselves. In 1866 Petrolia was at the heart of Canada's first great oil boom. Located eight kilometres from the Great Western Railway line, it lobbied hard for a spur line and a station. The company refused, insisting that the boom would be short-lived and the line would prove a financially poor proposition. Undeterred and rich from its oil revenues, Petrolia proceeded to build its own spur line. So successful was the little line that a grateful and eager GWR quickly took it over.

The railways did not always attempt to locate in or even near the core of existing towns. As a *Globe* reporter wrote of the Grand Trunk Railway line between Montreal and Toronto in 1856: "In no cases do the [stations] approach closely to the villages and, in some, the distance is so great as to be a serious injury to the villages as well as to the railway."

But the railway needed to build a line quickly and economically. Many of Ontario's earliest villages were lake or river ports. A village grew at any river mouth large enough to float a schooner. Those villages with larger harbours deep enough to accommodate steamers, boomed into the towns and cities that the railway set out to serve. However, a lakeshore rail route that passed through each lakeside town would have been serpentine

Woodpiles dominate the grounds around Port Perry's first station. Such piles were an eyesore at stations before coal replaced wood as a fuel. Photo from author's collection.

and would have required long and costly trestles over wide river mouths. The straightest and flattest route, where the valleys were narrower and the rivers shallower, lay inland.

In most cases, the Lake Ontario towns that the GTR bypassed grew out to meet the stations. Towns and cities like Kingston, Belleville, Napanee, and Cobourg all contain stations that were originally well away from the water but which now form part of the urban fabric.

But the rules of railway geography were inconsistent. Some out-of-town station sites remained little more than just a lonely station house and siding and are scarcely discernable today.

Communications

Stations were isolated in another way: before the telegraph there was no communication between stations. Trains operated by a timetable and if a train was delayed, there was no way an engineer could alert station agents, or worse, to alert following trains. To prevent catastrophes, the brakemen would have to set flares ahead of and behind a stalled train. If two trains met, the one closest to the station had to back up.

Timetables were hampered by the lack of a standard time. Each town or village had its own local time that may have differed from its neighbours by a few minutes or by half an hour. To maintain some semblance of order, train engineers were required to stop at each station and sign train orders. Station signals consisted of a simple ball on a pole. The higher position meant the train might proceed, the lower meant halt.

Wood Up

Perhaps the most important role for early stations was fuelling or "wood up." Until about 1873, wood was the main fuel used to fire the early steam engines. If an engine had to haul a heavy load or climb severe grades, the fuel supply was quickly exhausted. Whenever his timber ran dangerously low, the engineer would sound four blasts on his whistle to alert the next station agent that he required wood.

Railways like the Ontario Simcoe and Huron (later called the Northern), which opened in 1853 between Toronto and Bradford, at first contracted with local suppliers to provide the wood. George Brown, founder of Toronto's *Globe* newspaper, began as a wood contractor for the Great Western Railway supplying wood from his seven-hundred-acre woodlot at $1.75 per cord. Before the wood-burning era finally ended, his contract was said to earn $50,000 per year.

Whenever contractors' prices became inflated, the railways switched to buying directly from the local farmers. The farmers would haul the logs to the sawmill nearest the station — often there was one beside it — and there have the logs cut into four- or six-foot lengths. Cordwood piled up around the local station was a common sight on early Canadian railways, and posed a frequent fire hazard.

If, as often happened, the engineer miscalculated and ran short of wood before he could reach the next station, he would engage the male passengers from the train to march into the nearest woodlot and cut enough to continue. Or, should a farmer be foolish enough to leave a woodpile close to the track, the train crew might just help themselves. Because station agents billed the engineers directly for the wood that they used, such pilfering often occurred whether the wood was low or not.

The presence of a wood-up station meant a sure boom to the local economy. Maple and beech were the preferred species and local sawmills might cut as many as six to seven thousand cords of wood in a season. But as the woodlots of Ontario and Quebec were cleared, the supply began to dwindle and trainmen resorted to peat to fuel their fires. By 1873, however, larger and more efficient coal-fired locomotives began operation and by the 1890s had replaced the wood burners.

A New Landscape

The sudden appearance of stations, and a whole new system of transportation, had a stunning and lasting impact upon Canada's pioneer landscape. "It is an interesting thing to see," commented the *Globe* in 1853, "those stations in the middle of the forest with only a few houses in sight … a little building set down by the side of the road for the accommodation of passengers and officials … they are in such glaring contrast to the locomotive and the train which we are accustomed to associate with towns."

When rails first reached Collingwood on the shores of Georgian Bay, it too was little more than a clearing in the woods. Its station, however, appeared to be its grandest building, at least according to the *Northern Advance* in 1855: "[Collingwood is] an opening in the forest … about the size of an emigrant's back wood farm littered with blackened stumps and sparingly sprinkled with hotels and charming houses all dwarfed by the railroad's voluminous passenger depot, freight house and office."

Suddenly, pioneer Canada, used to stage or canal travel that was slow and seasonal, found communities that had been several days distant now lay only hours away. Market access was revolutionized. From miles around, farmers dragged their wheat and other crops to the new stations for shipment. Wagons overflowed from the station grounds onto the streets. Sheds and stables were jammed with whinnying and pawing horses, while dirty and tired farmers jostled each other in the smoky bars waiting for the train. Suddenly the station had become the focal point of not just the town but of the entire community.

Industries, in particular sawmills and grain elevators, vied for trackside space to gain access to the trains that could now so easily carry their products to the booming urban markets. Postal delivery too was profoundly changed. "Every new station increases the business of the post office," observed the *Globe* in 1853, "for a large number of newspapers are immediately demanded in the neighbourhood and we presume that letters were in proportion."

The "Miserable Shanties"

Once station locations were chosen, the next problem was how to build them. The first stations were repetitious patterns built as quickly and cheaply as possible so that the railway could become operational and generate revenue. "American stations," lamented one cynical traveller, "are conspicuous by the absence of accommodation and convenience. They are little more

As with many a temporary station, Calgary's first station was a converted boxcar. Photo courtesy of Glenbow Archives, NA 659-18.

than rough sheds giving shelter while the absence of platforms and railway officials tend to mark the characteristics of these stopping places."

Aside from the early stone stations of the GTR or the "Van Hornes" of the CPR, Canada's first stations, were little better, hastily erected and never intended to be permanent. The *Globe* reporter travelling the newly opened Great Western line between Hamilton and Windsor complained, "One feature did disappoint us very much, and that is the station houses. They are small and shabbily fitted up …" "Miserable shanties," moaned a writer for the *Toronto Colonist.*

Many communities knew only a boxcar as their first station. In the beginning, stations and water tanks were built at every other siding. The remaining sidings were given only boxcars to function as stations until the community grew large enough

to warrant a more substantial structure. Pioneer settlers have recalled arriving in the West, a piece of paper in their hand telling their section number, and finding only a silent boxcar as a station, and behind it the bare and windswept prairie where perhaps a town might grow.

The boxcars contained a tiny bedroom at one end, an office at the other, and, in between, a waiting room with a bench and the ever-present stove. As freight traffic increased, the railway might bring in a second boxcar or retired passenger coaches. Some early Canadian Northern stations were no more than tents with a telegraph key perched upon a packing case.

In their haste to get their trains running, railways often grabbed whatever was handy and converted it into a station. Across the country, stores, hotels, and even private homes were pressed into service as early stations. In Whitbourne,

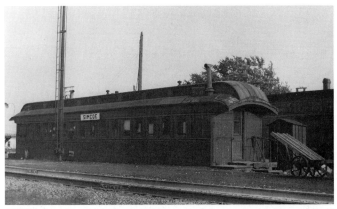

ABOVE: An early station in Simcoe, Ontario, consisted of a retired coach. Photo courtesy of Paterson-George Collection. RIGHT: The Midland Railway's first station in downtown Port Hope was in the rear portion of a main street store. While the tracks are long gone, the apertures remain discernable. Photo from author's collection.

Newfoundland, the first station was located in a hotel. When the Canadian Northern needed a terminal for its line into Calgary, it bought a former school. In Ottawa, the Ottawa, Arnprior and Parry Sound Railway resorted to using a former military building on the Rideau Canal for its terminus.

In Prince Edward Island, every community demanded a station. At first this was granted and the PEI railway could claim to be the nation's busiest with a station every three-and-a-half kilometres. By 1875, sixty-five of these stations were in place; forty-seven of them "flag" stations. Most were made of wood and lacked agent's quarters. Nearly all had been replaced by 1905.

Another early form of the "ready-made" station was the prefab. When the CPR took over its railway from the government, it began shipping out prefabricated stations on the backs of flatcars. As wood was scarce in the prairies, the stations were pre-cut in Winnipeg, shipped, and then assembled on-site.

Not all, however, encountered the bizarre difficulties that awaited the first station in Picton, Ontario. While en route to its location on the back of a flatcar, the engineer realized, in the nick of time, that a farmer had constructed his barn too close to the right of way and the overhanging station was headed right for it. Brakes squealed and the station stopped just short of the barn. The disgruntled farmer, one Crandall, watched helplessly, but not quietly, as the railway workers removed enough of the barn

to permit the station to pass and continue to its site in Picton.

The first stations in what became Canada's major urban centres were, like their country counterparts, wooden shelters. Toronto's first station was such a structure, built in 1853 by the Ontario, Simcoe and Huron Railway on what was then the waterfront at the corner of Front and Bay. City officials, however, had preferred that the railway locate its terminal further east nearer Ashbridge's Bay where smoke and noise would not pollute the city air. Their efforts were in vain. It was replaced a few years later by Toronto's first "union" station. It too was a simple board-and-batten affair shared by the Great Western and Grand Trunk railways. The Northern Railway, as the OS and H had become, built its new station near the foot of Berkley Street near the still-standing Gooderham and Worts distillery buildings.

Montreal's first stations were not even in Montreal, but rather on the south shore of the St. Lawrence River, and were those of the Champlain and St. Lawrence Railway. The first was erected at La Prairie in 1836 (the town has since built a replica) followed

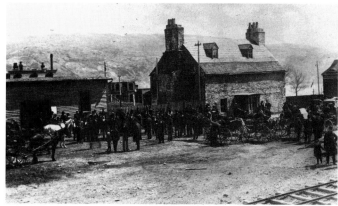

TOP: The Reid Newfoundland Railway's first station in St. John's made its home in a converted military garrison. Photo courtesy of the Archives of Newfoundland and Labrador, c3-1. BOTTOM: Vancouver's first short-lived station was a simple wooden structure balanced on pilings over the town's tidal flats. Photo courtesy of CPR Archives, 11497.

A garland marks the opening of the first station in Charlottetown, Prince Edward Island. Photo courtesy of the Provincial Archives of PEI, 3466/HF72.66.6.30.

by the Longueil station of the St. Lawrence and Atlantic. For a time the St. L and A operated a winter railway across the ice of the St. Lawrence until a bridge was built.

Montreal's first downtown station was that of the Montreal and Lachine Railway on Chaboillez Square and was named Bonaventure after a nearby street. Later assumed by the Grand Trunk Railway, the Bonaventure Station, a wooden building with a veranda on three sides, was described as a "dirty barn" and "a standing reproach to the city and the company." Mercifully it was replaced in 1886 by a magnificent new structure.

In St. John's, Newfoundland, the Reid Newfoundland Railway took over a stone building that had once housed a military garrison known as Fort William for its first station.

Vancouver's first CPR station was a rambling wooden shed supported by wooden poles and perched precariously over the tidal flats. Another early station in Vancouver was that of Great Northern, a ramshackle wooden shed located near Pender and Columbia streets. It remained an eyesore until replaced by a large classical stone building on reclaimed tidal flats in 1915.

Few first generation stations have survived. Built quickly and cheaply to get the railways up and running, nearly all had been replaced within twenty-five years. Booming towns and growing freight and passenger traffic demanded larger stations, new technology required new layouts, and the pressure of competition and community pride placed pressure on the railways to build stations that were more solid and more elaborate. In 1900 Canada was entering its station heyday.

The Ontario and Huron's station at Thornhill typifies the line's early station style. Photo by author.

THE STATION BUILDERS:
THE ARCHITECTURE OF CANADA'S STATIONS

A former editor of a prominent Canadian geographic magazine once offered the opinion that stations all look alike, a generalization akin to assuring an ornithologist that all birds resemble one another. On the contrary, to even an unseasoned station observer, a glance at a railway station's style will often reveal what region of Canada it was in, what railway line it was on, and even when it was built.

Once past the pioneer stage, the railway companies began to focus on the appearance of their stations, which had quickly become the economic focus of the community. An attractive corporate image meant consumer confidence and that in turn meant revenue.

As the end of the nineteenth century approached, stations began to take on a new look. Gone were the wooden boxes, the simple gables and the plain rooflines. In their place came towers, turrets, and arches. Gables and dormers punctured the roofs, cupolas, and finials poked skyward. Station designers from architects to engineers called upon foreign flavours to influence their styles as they tried to outdo each other.

A variety of factors converged at the same time to inspire this station revolution. The close of the nineteenth century witnessed the end of a debilitating economic depression. Canada had suddenly become the favoured destination of land-starved British, European, and American immigrants, and railway expansion was in full swing. Even on many branch lines the original stations were quickly becoming too small. Changing railway technology, even in those early days, necessitated station replacement.

Competition too determined a station's design. A spider's web of competing railway lines criss-crossed Ontario and southern Quebec while no fewer than three transcontinental lines competed for the precious prairie patronage. To attract clients, the railways began a competition that would, for decades, see them try to outdo each other with station styles.

The First Patterns

Among Canada's first station patterns were those of the Great Western and the Ontario, Simcoe and Huron Railways. Those of the OS and H were small, and distinguished by the use of arches over the windows. Simple otherwise, they were board-and-batten buildings with a wide overhang above the platform, but displaying no other embellishments. A subsequent railway executive was reported to have said of the original station at Aurora that "the architect who planned and built it should be in either the asylum or the penitentiary." Three of these old stations survived into the 1970s at Holland Landing, King City,

LEFT: The Ontario and Huron's 1853 station from King City, now at a museum, is said to be Canada's oldest surviving station. Photo by author. ABOVE: Throughout the 1850s, the Grand Trunk adopted an English-style pattern for its stations between Montreal and Sarnia. The Ernestown station, shown here in steam days, now vacant and vandalized, still survives. Photo courtesy of CNR Archives, 38316.

and Concord. Only that from King City survives, now located in a museum ground and billed as "Canada's Oldest Station."

Canada's first truly distinctive stations were those of the Grand Trunk Railway. Early Canadian travellers scorned the cheap standards of railways operating in the United States. This cheapness was often reflected in the small, simple wooden look-alike depots that proliferated along the Yankee lines. The last thing Canadians wanted was an American-style railroad, and they feared that in the Grand Trunk that was what they would be getting.

Anxious to reassure a Canadian public that was skeptical of its plans, the Grand Trunk promised a "first class English railway" and hired the firm of Peto, Brassey, Betts and Jackson to build between Montreal and Toronto a series of decidedly English-looking stations. Their prototype came from an 1842 book by English station architect Francis Thompson and recalled in a print of an 1840s station at Kenilworth, England. By building in stone and incorporating into the design a series of Roman arches, Thompson wished to evoke in the minds of the traveller the solidity and durability of Roman public works and, subliminally, confidence in the railway.

These buildings were usually constructed of stone, although a few used brick, and were distinguished by a row of arched French doors, the larger stations having up to seven arches on the sides, and the smaller stations with five. Most were wide enough to accommodate a pair of arched French doors at each end. Other features that set them apart from other stations of the time were the lack of freight shed and bay window.

The *Brockville Recorder* gushed over the sturdy little structures, praising them as being "of the most solid and substantial masonry that in no way belied the promises of the company as the character of the works along the line."

LEFT: The Grand Trunk's Cornwall, Ontario, station, now demolished, was an enlarged version of its English stone pattern. Photo courtesy of CNR Archives, HL 145. RIGHT: The Great Western's Merritton station displays that line's typical small-town pattern. Photo courtesy of St. Catharines Historical Museum.

Although the string of stations were at first nearly uniform, changes were inevitable. Adoption of the telegraph meant that a bay window was needed. Some were added in wood, others in brick; all, however, severely disrupted the tidy and solid appearance that the first uncluttered row of arches. Even the arches themselves, which originally reached down to ground level, were partially filled in with stone to create windows.

When the GTR began to plan its extension west of Toronto to Sarnia, A.M. Ross, the GTR's chief engineer, suggested that less costly timber stations should be considered instead of the fine stone stations that graced the original line. However, the outcry was so vociferous that the GTR was forced to spend more on stations that they had wished. Nevertheless, when the contractor, Gzowski and Company, had finished, Walter Shanley, chief engineer of the new line, was moved to admit that "the Grand Trunk buildings here [meaning on the original Toronto–Montreal line] are very well built, better than anything we can show [on the Western line]."

Not all communities received such attractive stations. Many had to be content with simpler wooden buildings. These were often wide structures with shallow roofs, board-and-batten siding, and erected in smaller centres of along lightly used branch lines. Of the few that survive, most have gained new life as stores or restaurants.

Buoyed by the enthusiastic response to their stations in Ontario, the GTR station builders applied the same principle in Quebec. Anxious to soothe the anxieties of French Canadians travelling on an unabashedly English railway, the GTR offered them a sense of comfort through a familiar style. Department of Public Works architects T.S. Scott and Pierre Gavreau looked to current Quebec domestic architecture and built between Quebec City and Rivière-du-Loup a series of sturdy brick stations with distinctive ski slope or mansard roofs. And so, by a deliberate use of familiar styles, the GTR dispelled the fears of English Canadians over an American-style railway and those of French Canadians over an English railway.

Most of these charming stations survived until the early 1970s, when reduced passenger travel and the advent of Centralized Traffic Control made them redundant and most were demolished. English-style stations at Ernestown and St. Mary's Junction, neither in passenger service, were spared the addition of an incongruous telegrapher bay in the 1890s, and retain their original appearance. While the Ernestown station sits vacant and vandalized, that in St. Mary's is being restored by the local historical society. Others at Napanee, Belleville, and Port Hope still see passenger service, while that at Kingston is now a fire-ravaged shell, its future uncertain. Similar stations at Prescott

Preserved off-site in Andrew, Alberta, is one of the CPR's most common small-town styles, formerly found in many western towns. Photo by author.

These early stone and brick GTR stations were built to last. Those that survive have outlived several revolutions in station styles, changes in technology, and the decline in passenger service. Indeed, they are truly Canada's oldest stations.

The Great Western Railway employed a small range of early patterns as well. The most common rural station was two-storey with front and end gables. All are now gone. Larger towns received brick stations, storey-and-a-half, with a small gable above the bay window. Survivors remain in Ingersoll and Tillsonburg in Ontario. Larger urban stations drawn from the GWR's pattern book were designed by the GWR's architect Joseph Hobson, and consisted of large two-storey brick buildings with hip gables at the end and often a gable above the bay. These were constructed at Hamilton, London, and Niagara Falls. Only the latter survives.

Masters of the Pattern Book: The CPR Stations

While the Grand Trunk's original stone and brick stations survived, usually without successor stations until most were demolished after 1960, the CPR's first stations were remarkably short-lived. In June 1875, sod was turned in west Fort William, commencing the construction for the Fort William–Winnipeg section of the railway. As the private CPR syndicate began to work westward from Fort William, the Canadian government began its portion eastward from Port Moody. (The government had already completed a section from Sand Point near Ottawa to near North Bay.)

One of the CPR's first station builders was the firm of Lamay and Blair. But after building just four of their contracted eight stations, at Buda, Nordland, Linkooping (later shortened to Linko Station), and Savanne, all in northwestern Ontario, the firm was fired for their poor work and replaced by Moses Cheverette, who added stations at Kaministiquia and Finmark. Most were crude log cabins and possessed no architectural embellishments whatsoever.

The first standard station plan was devised by Sandford Fleming, government engineer for the western portion. One-and-a-half storeys in height, the stations were constructed of

and Brighton still stand as well, that at Brighton now a popular private museum known as *Memory Junction*. The original GTR station at Georgetown, now a GO station, was greatly altered in 1904 with the addition of a new roof and a turret.

Between Quebec and Riviére-du-Loup, samples of the Quebec style linger at La Pocatière and L'Islet, while that at Montmagny was given a mansard roof when taken over by the Intercolonial Railway. All remain station stops on VIA Rail's daily Montreal–Halifax *Ocean* train. A string of well-maintained wooden stations also line VIA Rail's route of the *Chaleur* between Matapédia and Gaspé.

LEFT: The wide roof of the Spuzzum, British Columbia, station displays one of CPR's earliest western patterns. Photo courtesy of CPR Archives, A 1508. RIGHT: By far the most common of the CPR's early patterns was nicknamed the "Van Horne" after its president who launched it. Nearly all are gone now. Photo, 1900. Photo courtesy of CPR Archives, A 17086.

board and batten and were noted for their steep pitches and wide eaves. These were built by Andrew Onderdonk in the mountains of British Columbia and by Chevrette in northwestern Ontario at places like Vermilion Bay and Kenora, where a small turret was added.

Between Sand Point and Nipigon in Ontario, the government had constructed a number of simpler board-and-batten structures. Some were single storey, and those requiring agent's quarters were a storey and a half. All, however, lacked the wide overhanging eaves that typified Fleming's buildings.

Prior to taking over the government-built portion of the line in 1885, the CPR syndicate inspected their new stations-to-be. Of the twelve built along the Fort William to Winnipeg section, Van Horne declared the six built by Lemay and Blair and Chevrette to be totally unfit for use as stations. On the western section, inspectors noted that many of Onderdonk's stations were already in poor repair. Green lumber had been used and was wearing so badly that the plaster was falling away. Others used by Onderdonk's agents had been poorly maintained.

Finally, in 1884, the CPR devised a standard plan of its own. Inspired by Van Horne himself, the CPR's engineering department created a simple two-storey plan with agent's quarters on the second floor, and waiting room, ticket office, and baggage room on the ground. There were no eaves. To build them as quickly as possible, the CPR sent building plans ahead to local contractors

The station style appeared at virtually every new station site between Winnipeg and the Rockies and at those locations between Sand Point and Fort William, where the government had not previously completed stations. The style was nicknamed the "Indian Head" style or the "Van Horne" style, after the first place it was built, and the man who promoted it. This style was used even in places that the railway knew would shortly become large centres and require larger stations: Regina, Moose Jaw, Medicine Hat, and Calgary all could claim "Van Hornes" as their first stations. (Calgary's first station was in fact a temporary boxcar used until a "Van Horne" replaced it.)

Other first generation patterns used by the CPR included a storey-and-a-half structure with a wraparound overhang, a curious two-storey boxlike building with a mansard roof, confined largely to western Canada; and a two-storey station with a front gable used in larger centres such as Westfort (Fort William) and Strathcona (Edmonton).

The Second Generation Stations

Between 1870 and 1890 the GTR similarly embarked upon a spate of new station designs. Across southern Ontario and Quebec, the railway gobbled up a number of short lines, many of them financially troubled, a strategy that allowed the GTR to block competitive intrusions into their profitable market areas. Their main conquest came in 1882 when it merged with Canada's first major railway, the Great Western, and its 1280 kilometres of track.

The Grand Trunk retained many of the Great Western's larger stations (those at Niagara Falls, Ingersoll, and Tillsonburg, Ontario all still stand), and indeed many of its station architects

such as Joseph Hobson. In 1882 he became the GTR's chief engineer and, using the gothic revival style of his GWR Woodstock station, custom-designed replacements for the outdated GWR stations in Chatham, Windsor, and Sarnia. His new stations were distinguished by their steep roofs and prominent hip gables on the front or the ends. As a result, the Grand Trunk's stations in southwestern Ontario sported a distinctively Great Western flavour. Surviving examples of these include the VIA Rail stations at Woodstock, Sarnia, and Chatham.

With the depression over in 1895, the GTR introduced a special new station plan to replace stations on the old short lines that had either deteriorated or were no longer large enough for the growing communities that surrounded them. Because the GTR did not need to provide living quarters for agents, the station was only a single storey. It did, however, possess a variety of architectural embellishments in the wood trim and in the small decorative gable that punctuated the roofline over the bay window and over the porch (port-cochère) at the end.

Limited almost exclusively to Ontario, and known as the "stick style," these stations numbered in the hundreds. Several survive, most having been relocated to parks or museums. Those still in place include Newmarket, Maple, and Aurora, the latter two used by Ontario's GO train commuter service, as well as former stations on site at Haliburton and Kinmount.

LEFT: The Great Western's chief architect, Joseph Hobson, designed some of Canada's most pleasing stations, such at this VIA station, which is still in use today at Woodstock, Ontario. Photo by author.
RIGHT: The Grand Trunk's most popular branch line station pattern, once numbering in the hundreds, still survives in Newmarket, Ontario. Photo by author.

The West: A Portfolio

Mowbray, Manitoba

Banff, Alberta

Melville, Saskatchewan

Prairie scene

Edmonton (Strathcona), Alberta

Field, British Columbia

Dauphin, Manitoba

Rowley, Alberta

Like the CPR, the GTR recognized the need to provide agent's quarters if it was to attract family men, considered the most reliable by nineteenth-century Canadian standards. While in most of the larger towns the company found separate housing for its agents, in many smaller communities they provided quarters in the stations themselves. The most common design consisted of a gangly two-storey station usually with a dormer over the front and hip gables at the ends of the roof. These were usually found in southern Quebec, between Barrie and North Bay (with examples at Huntsville, Bracebridge, Burk's Falls, and Coldwater, the latter surviving on a nearby property) and in a few places along the Toronto–Montreal line (e.g. Darlington, Collins Bay, and Dorval; none survive).

While the GTR used a wide variety of patterns and many custom-built stations, there were two other patterns that were almost as common as that at Aurora. One, found almost exclusively in southwestern Ontario, is clearly distinguished by an end waiting room with an octagonal, almost conical roof. Nearly ubiquitous on some southwestern lines, survivors are now few and can only be found in Burlington, Jarvis, and Thamesville.

After the turn of the century, the GTR added another re-placement style. Much simpler, it had no embellishments other than the bay window and hip gables at the ends. The exterior woodwork was equally plain. Although it too was common, almost

Where the Grand Trunk needed quarters for its agents, they built the style once found at Dorval, Quebec. Photo courtesy of CNR Archives, X 37315.

none survive on site, although good examples can be found near the site of the buried St. Lawrence Seaway town of Aultsville, and in Wanstead, neither far from the original station grounds, and in Casselman, near Ottawa, which serves as a VIA station.

Turretmania

As the nineteenth century drew to a close and competition among railways intensified, the station builders added detail and decoration to draw customers. One of the most numerous was a style created by the GTR. With a gable over the bay and a turret on the corner, it became the GTR's most attractive turn-of-the-century pattern. Used as their main replacement station in southern Quebec, it was built in several southwestern Ontario communities as well. Prominent among the survivors are the St. Bruno and Acton Vale stations in Quebec, and Glencoe in Ontario, all preserved, and the two-towered Goderich station in Ontario, now privately owned.

No line was spared from turretmania. One of the more unusual variations was the "witch's hat" style adopted by both the CPR and the GTR. This style involved a circular waiting room enveloping the entire end of the structure with a conical roof above. Purely decorative, it was used by the CPR primarily at divisional points such as Orangeville, Lindsay, and Goderich in Ontario, Mont-Sainte-Anne in Quebec, and Saint John in New Brunswick. Another was added at Parry Sound to break the string of western-style stations that stretched between Bolton and Sudbury, while a smaller version appeared at Eganville, Ontario. Those at Parry Sound, Ste-Agathe, and Goderich survive on site, while that in Orangeville was moved offsite and converted into a restaurant.

The GTR added "witch's hats" of its own at Chesley, Fort Erie (both demolished), and at Uxbridge, which is now a museum and terminus for the York Durham Heritage Railway. A small but heavily altered "witch's hat" station survives on the abandoned former London, Wellington and Bruce line in Blyth, Ontario.

Smaller turret plans appeared almost at random throughout Ontario and Quebec. Survivors from CPR lines include

Turrets and towers were commonplace during the heyday of station building. The plans for the Berlin, Ontario, (now Kitchener) station were particularly elaborate, although the ornamentations have long since been removed. Illustration courtesy of the National Archives of Canada, NMC 99084.

Streetsville and Milton (both relocated as houses), while survivors from GTR lines include those at Don (Toronto), and Craigleith. Perhaps the most elaborately decorated of the small turret stations was that at Smithville, Ontario, on the former Toronto, Hamilton and Buffalo line. Here, an inordinate amount of detail was incorporated into the woodwork under the gables. It has been moved a few metres from the track and now houses a local archives and tourist office.

It was, however, on the individually designed stations that turrets flourished. Here, the railways found added incentive to embellish their stations. Some stations were ports of entry to the country or the province, locations where the railways felt that a traveller's first impression called for something extra. Stations at Georgetown, Prince Edward Island, and Placentia,

Newfoundland, were given turrets for that reason. In Quebec, the Delaware and Hudson recreated a miniature "French" castle for their border station at Lacolle. In 1888 Nova Scotia Central Railway architect Vincent Griffiths added a particularly imposing turret to the Bridgewater, Nova Scotia, station. Although turrets were proposed for dozens of other stations all across Ontario and Quebec, cost-cutting resulted in simpler styles.

Towers were another symbol of railway dominance in turn-of-the-century urban Canada. Originally introduced by the GTR along its main line to Chicago, it quickly caught on in towns and small cities across southwestern Ontario as well. Notable among surviving towers are those at Brantford and Guelph in Ontario, and the CPR's short-lived North Toronto station (the building still stands as a liquor store but as a station it

Where the Grand Trunk and the CPR wanted to attract additional attention to their stations, they added a feature known as the "witch's hat" to its waiting-room roofs. This example still stands in Goderich, Ontario. Photo by author.

lasted less than two decades). Other stations lost their towers due to deterioration or high maintenance costs such as at Kitchener and Stratford, both in Ontario.

Distinctly Canadian: The CPR's Chateaus

The most distinctively Canadian style was that introduced by the CPR and known as the "chateau" style. Ironically, it began with the arrival of New York architect Bruce Price in 1886.

Inspired by CPR president Van Horne's love of Scottish baronial and French chateau styles, Price designed stations that were distinguished by high-peaked roofs, turrets, and sturdy bay windows. The style was incorporated into custom-designed and plan-book stations alike. Some of Price's early stations included those in Woodstock, London, and Galt. He was also assigned the mighty task of designing the CPR's headquarters, the handsome Windsor Station in Montreal. But his Chateau style gained its greatest prominence with his magnificent Place Viger, a combination station/hotel in east-end Montreal.

So wide was the acclaim for this distinctively Canadian style that the Canadian railway architects incorporated it into many early railway hotels such as the Royal York in Toronto, the Chateau Laurier in Ottawa, the Chateau Frontenac in Quebec City, and the Fort Garry in Winnipeg.

Then, in 1895, the federal government imposed on imported architectural plans a 2 percent tariff calculated on the ultimate value of the completed building. The cost-conscious CPR

LEFT: The three elaborate towers on the street side of Ontario's Petrolia station reflect the heady years of Canada's first oil boom. Photo by author. RIGHT: Now a Montreal municipal office, the CPR's "chateau" style of station is at its best at the Viger Station. Photo courtesy of CPR Archives, A 19703.

immediately switched to Montreal architect Edward Maxwell, who became Canada's most prolific station designer. Adopting Price's Chateau style, Maxwell created Ottawa's Broad Street station, Vancouver's second station, and the station hotels at Moose Jaw and Sicamous, all long gone, as well as the surviving station at New Westminster, British Columbia.

In 1906 the CPR created the office of Chief Architect and, under the directorship of H.E. Prindle, added the magnificent Gare du Palais station in Quebec City, and the massive McAdam station hotel near the Canadian border in New Brunswick. Both still stand.

The CPR incorporated the chateau style into their station plan book with stations at Lethbridge, Edmonton (Strathcona), Saskatoon, Kenora, and Red Deer, all surviving, and at Kamloops and Cranbrook, both since replaced. (When that at Cranbrook proved too small, the CPR crew tried jacking up the top floor in order to add another storey. But the roof, balancing precariously on the jacks, began to sway and then crashed down upon the workers. Somehow no one was killed, but the CPR never again tried to use that method to enlarge a station.)

With their steep roofs and sturdy central towers, the chateau-style stations pushed Canada and the CPR in particular to the North American forefront of station architecture and inspired many imitators. Under the guidance of its own architect, Ralph Benjamin Pratt, spirited away from the CPR, the CNoR constructed elegant chateau stations at Port Arthur, Saskatoon, Dauphin, and Edmonton. Only those at Port Arthur and Dauphin survive.

The CNoR incorporated the chateau-esque style into smaller stations at Belleville, Port Hope, and Smiths Falls on its now abandoned Toronto–Ottawa line, and in Sudbury using the Smiths Falls pattern. The two stations at Port Hope and Smiths Falls yet survive while that at Belleville was subsequently transferred to the CPR and, naturally, demolished. The one in Sudbury fell victim to an urban "renewal" scheme and was likewise demolished.

More Patterns

By the dawn of the twentieth century most of Canada's pioneer railway lines had been absorbed by the GTR, the CPR, or the Intercolonial Railway of the Maritimes, and had replaced most of the earlier simpler stations of the original roads with patterns of the new owners. There are, however, many areas in eastern Canada where the distinctive styles of the regional lines lingered until recent times, and linger still where stations have preserved.

In the province of Quebec, a small number of the former

TOP LEFT: The oft-forgotten Canadian Northern Railway offered attractive patterns. This now demolished example at Belleville, shared with the CPR, was also found at Cobourg and Port Hope. Photo courtesy of the National Archives of Canada, PA 12554. TOP RIGHT: Wide, shallow roofs with extended gables were typical of the CPR's antecedent stations across Quebec. Photo courtesy of CPR Archives, A 12798. BOTTOM: The Dominion Atlantic Station at Yarmouth, Nova Scotia, the pattern common on that line. Photo courtesy of CPR Archives, A 1745.

Quebec, Montreal, Ottawa and Occidental stations have managed to survive between Quebec City and Montreal and again between Lachute and Hull. Identical in style and without variation, these were attractive storey-and-a-half structures noted for their oversized eaves and gables. Divisional stations such as those at Hull, Hochelaga (Montreal), and Lanoraie were distinguished by their double gables. Similar styles were found on the Roberval and Saguenay line, on the Dominion Atlantic line in Nova Scotia (where the last survivor at Weymouth was demolished in the 1970s), and on the Quebec, Montreal and Western Railway, which wound its way into the Laurentian Mountains north of Montreal. Among the few survivors of this style are stations at Prévost and St-Fabien.

Throughout eastern Canada, the Intercolonial Railway produced a vast array of station patterns, which some researchers estimate numbered at more than fifty. Much of this remarkable variety was due to the ICR's long period of railway building and its several takeovers of local lines. Started in 1858, with a line from Halifax to Truro, it expanded into New Brunswick in 1860 and into Quebec in 1874, where it absorbed a section of the Grand Trunk line.

Many of Canada's oldest stations can yet be found in Nova Scotia and New Brunswick along the former Intercolonial line.

One of the most common styles in Nova Scotia is still evident at Orangedale. A large two-storey style with several dormers punctuating its mansard roof, the station was designed by Walter Shanley while he was working for the Halifax and Cape Breton Coal Company. The building is now a museum and displays a small diesel engine, boxcar, and replica of the agent's ticket office. The style was repeated in northern Nova Scotia and across Cape Breton between 1889 and 1900. Other examples stood at Iona, Grand Narrows, River John, Scotsburn, and West Bay Road, although none survive.

LEFT: The last of the Intercolonial Railway's two-storey country stations at Orangedale, Cape Breton Island, is now a museum. Photo by author. RIGHT: The oldest surviving station in the Maritimes, at Rothesay, New Brunswick, featured the pattern employed by the European and North American Railway. Photo by author.

A style found on the ICR's predecessor lines, particularly the European and North American, and on the Halifax and Cape Breton Railway and Coal Company, dates from the 1860s and consisted of a storey-and-a-half building with a small dormer on the second story and a hexagonal bay window. Examples survived into the 1970s at Avondale, Merigomish, James River, and Bras d'Or in Nova Scotia.

Another distinctive style was built along the Tatamagouche line by the ICR in 1887. Constructed of brick, the structures were simpler than those of the Orangedale style, but were two storeys in height with high, narrow gables. Survivors linger at Pugwash and Tatamagouche. Meanwhile, the Maritimes's oldest station is that at Rothesay, New Brunswick. An unembellished two-storey structure, it was built by the European and North American railway in 1859 and survives on its original site as a private business. An identical structure built in 1860 at nearby Salisbury was demolished by the CN in the 1970s.

Because of their status as ports of entry, special stations were designed for Pictou and Lunenburg. Both survive.

The early patterns of railway stations in Prince Edward Island and Newfoundland portrayed a distinctive domestic flavour of the Maritimes. Most resembled houses of the period and were constructed of wood. In 1874 the Prince Edward Island Railway had just completed its line across the island and along it had placed sixty-five stations, forty-seven of which were mere flag stops, most with waiting rooms and small freight shelters under the same roof.

As business increased and public pressure for better stations mounted, many of the flag stations were upgraded and the original structures were replaced with two-storey mansard-roofed buildings, a style found nowhere else in Canada. The second story housed the agent's quarters. As the supply of local housing increased, the railways no longer supplied quarters for their agents, and most of these were replaced by more functional single-storey stations, using a style similar to that found on former Intercolonial lines in northern New Brunswick and eastern Quebec. The only recorded survivor is the former Kensington station, relocated to become a residence. It in turn was replaced by a beautiful station constructed of local boulders. It survives and is now a national historic site. A second boulder station was constructed at Alberton, also in 1905, and it too survives as a tourist centre.

Newfoundland too boasted distinctive station buildings. Commenced in 1881, the railway was eventually completed by John Reid and was known originally as the Reid Newfoundland Railway. Less striking than the way stations in Prince Edward Island, those in Newfoundland were unembellished two-storey wood frame buildings with a simple dormer piercing the roofline. In the larger communities where housing was more plentiful, the

TOP LEFT: The Intercolonial line's Tatamagouche Station is still around, a pattern unique to that line. Photo by author. TOP RIGHT: The Newfoundland Railway's most common pattern was a simple houselike structure found in most of the island's small communities such as in Princeton. Photo by author. BOTTOM RIGHT: Similar to the Van Horne, except for the two-storey bay window, the Bay of Quinte Railway's pattern has left a string of surviving structures in central Ontario, including that shown here at Stoco, circa 1899–1900. Photo courtesy of Lennox and Addington County Museum, N–39370. BOTTOM LEFT: Even small flag stations could demonstrate a flair for style. Both the castlelike style and the name, Ypres, celebrate the First World War battle of the same name, and marked the junction with the branch line to the army's Camp Borden. Photo courtesy of the National Archives of Canada, PA 71077.

railway used a single-storey structure. Perhaps the island's most attractive station is the old mansard-roofed building at Avondale, which was in use as a station as early as 1883. Today it has been restored as a museum.

In the late 1980s, in both PEI and Newfoundland, the CN abandoned the lines and tore up the tracks. In both places, however, several former stations have found new private or public uses.

Ontario, like Nova Scotia, proved to be another hodgepodge of station styles. As the nineteenth century closed in on Ontario, the GTR assembled a vast network absorbing small lines that

optimistic railway companies had built. Most of the original lines built their own identical stations, usually single-storey with end gables, a bay window, and little else in the way of architectural distinctions. These stations were soon replaced by GTR styles, as they had proven inadequate for the boom that overwhelmed them, or, cheaply built, had rotted where they stood.

The Central Ontario Railway and the Bay of Quinte Railway are exceptions. Both lie close to each other in central Ontario and indeed cross each other. Both were constructed during the 1880s from ports on Lake Ontario deep into the hinterland and were later absorbed by the CNR. Although long abandoned, they retain several original stations.

Both used pattern books, and the smallest sample of the COR style was a single-story wooden structure distinguished only by a large eave that extended over the platform. Surviving examples have been relocated from their original sites at Frankford, Bloomfield, Coe Hill, and Marmora. Only one example of the larger station with agent's quarters survives at Bancroft as a museum and tourist office. (A two-storey concrete passenger terminal, now derelict, at Maynooth Station, is a later CN replacement.)

The BoQ survival rate is even more remarkable. Between Deseronto and Bannockburn, a nearly unbroken string of six original stations have survived on site, little altered since 1942 when the line was abandoned. Although inspired by the CPR's two-storey Van Horne style, the BoQ stations, with their hexagonal bay windows that extended to the second floor, were distinctive from any other two-storey station in Canada. Complete with their original exterior stucco finish, their freight sheds, and trademark narrow cement platforms, the survivors include the stations at Stoco, Queensville, Erinsville, Marlbank, Tamworth, and Newburgh.

Southern Ontario was the only region of Canada to be strongly influenced by American station designers. Southwestern Ontario sits like a wedge between southern Michigan and upper New York State. During the 1860s and 1870s this region provided an easy shortcut for American railway builders looking for connections between borders. Soon, new American-owned lines crossed the area, including the Canada Southern (later the New York Central), the Canada Air Line, and the Toronto, Hamilton and Buffalo (later the CPR) and on them were simple American style "depots." Small, wooden, and punctuated by only a front gable or perhaps a small tower, these were repeated in most towns and villages, but some outstanding exceptions broke the monotony. Elegant stone stations were placed in Essex and Kingsville in far southwestern Ontario, and a delightful, small turreted station in Smithville, as well as a richly embellished structure in Ridgeway. All survive in new uses. Outstanding major terminals were built at St. Thomas (standing but abandoned) and at Windsor (demolished).

One of the CPR's most common country station styles was used mostly in smaller communities. That from Locust Hill, Ontario, now resides in the Markham Museum village. Photo by author.

The CPR Gets Back Into the Act

In 1897 the CPR produced its first new station design in fifteen years and in less than two decades went on to produce a plan book with twenty-one different designs. After building fewer than seventy new stations between 1886 and 1896, the CPR went on a binge of station construction, adding or replacing more than 758 stations over the following eighteen years.

One of the CPR's earliest contracts was with the firm of J.W. and E.C. Hopkins of Montreal, who designed the stations for the Perth–Vaudreuil portion of the Ontario and Quebec Railway. In marked contrast to these larger more varied stations, those west of Perth were a string of utterly uniform "Van Horne" stations identical to those that had been built on the transcontinental line a few years earlier. Broken only by the yet standing Peterborough station, this string of identical stations stretched all the way to Toronto. Although a few were replaced because of fire, most survived until the 1960s and 1970s when the CPR demolished all except those in Smiths Falls (now a theatre and VIA stop), Havelock (a restaurant), Tweed (recently removed), and Peterborough (a government office).

Several communities throughout the Ottawa Valley were given similar attractive stations built from local stone. Such

LEFT: The CPR demonstrated a flair for the Oriental in what it called its "Chinese pagoda" style. Used only in western Canada, the sole survivor is here in Virden, Manitoba. Photo by author.
RIGHT: A smaller version of the CPR's Chinese-style stations stands in the tiny prairie town of Empress, Alberta. Photo by author.

structures appeared in Perth, Almonte, Arnprior, Renfrew, Carleton Place, and North Bay. Sadly, rebuffing strong protests from the communities in which they sat, the CPR demolished all save those in Carleton Place (now a day care) and North Bay (now a community facility).

Aside from the early "Van Hornes," the CPR's most common way stations were a storey-and-a-half style, known as pattern 2A, which contained agent's quarters, and the smaller "Swiss Cottage" style, which did not. Generally, larger brick stations were placed on the busy main line between through Ontario and Quebec. Some included a decorative hip gable above the operator's bay (e.g. Oshawa; Ontario; and Sherbrooke, Quebec), others, although brick, lacked architectural frivolities entirely, for example, Streetsville, Bowmanville, and Cobourg (all demolished). Even divisional stations were simply extended versions of this plan (Woodstock and Galt). Special designs were incorporated into stations at Windsor (demolished) with a turret, and at Chatham (relocated) with an interesting arch. Other early designs saw limited use. Attractive brick stations were designed for Yorkville, (North Toronto), Guelph, and Peterborough, but saw no application outside of these places. "Yorkville" station was later replaced by the monumental North Toronto station, Guelph was disassembled (and never reassembled), while that at Peterborough

has been restored by the Chamber of Commerce. Tudor-style stations were added at West Toronto and Trenton, but both are now gone.

Although the CPR's patterns were largely pleasing, they did create one that was stark and unappealing for the stations of the Sault Ste Marie branch in northern Ontario. These were typically long, low, and wooden, with end gables and a flat dormer barely peeking through the roof over the bay window. No effort was made to add anything to these buildings to make them the least bit attractive. But, whenever they needed replacing, the CPR would pull something a little more elaborate out of its pattern book. Eventually, the nicest station on the line was that built at McKerrow. All of these buildings are now demolished.

Prairie Patterns

If any part of Canada is associated with pattern-book stations, it is the prairies. The railways created the towns, and the stations dominated them. Because the CPR has been there the longest, it can claim the greatest variety of station patterns. Very quickly, the ubiquitous "Van Hornes" were replaced by what the CPR called its "Western Line" stations. Between 1895 and 1914, the CPR devised more than twenty attractive station plans. Some were

LEFT: Found almost everywhere along the Grand Trunk Pacific line, this simple style in Dunster, British Columbia, has now almost vanished. Photo by author. RIGHT: VIA Rail's Canadian stops at Sioux Lookout, Ontario, where the National Transcontinental Railway erected one of its more fanciful divisional stations complete with a pair of Tudoresque gables. Photo by author.

mere elaborations upon the Van Horne, (different size gables being added to the front) while others invoked an international flavour including a "Chinese" pagoda style, (a sample still stands in Virden, Manitoba) and a "Rheinish" gable style. The most common style, however, was that which the CPR called the A5. A simple operator station with agent's quarters, it was erected by the hundreds across the prairies and even along the Sudbury to Bolton branch of the CPR in central Ontario.

Nearly all the CPR's more interesting stations were designed by CPR architect, Ralph Benjamin Pratt. Pratt, who had been noted for implementing the CPR's "chateau" style in local stations (and was responsible for designing the long-lost Broad Street station in Ottawa), was, in 1901, spirited away by the Canadian Northern Railway. William MacKenzie and Donald Mann, the duo behind the CNoR, wanted nothing but the best, and Pratt promised the best design in stations. Indeed, during his sojourn with the CNoR he created Canada's most distinctive and widely used station, the pyramidal Class Three. Although the basic plan was a simple, boxy two-storey affair, Pratt placed upon it a high, pyramidal roof, a feature that could be seen at great distances across the flat prairie landscape. The distinctive roofline quickly became the Canadian Northern's trademark from British Columbia to Nova Scotia. Several survive as museums or as private homes. In Ontario it predominated along the CNoR lines between Toronto and Parry Sound, and between Port Arthur and Rainy River.

So flexible was this trademark feature that it was incorporated into its divisional stations and even into the large stations such as those at Edmonton, Saskatoon, Dauphin, and Port Arthur, of which the latter two still stand. Due to Pratt's influence, the former three were nearly identical to the Broad Street station in Ottawa.

The last of the three major lines to cross the prairies was the Grand Trunk Pacific (or the National Transcontinental as it was called in eastern Canada). It drew from an even narrower range of patterns than either the CPR or the CNoR. Perhaps its most pleasing and distinctive style was the storey-and-a-half style with a bell-cast roof and an octagonal bay window that punched through the eave to become a second-floor dormer. Known simply as plan "A," it was created in 1910 by the GTP's chief engineer, K.B. Kelliker, and comprised nearly two-thirds of the GTP station roster. A simpler version more common in Ontario and Quebec saw the octagonal window replaced with a square format. Its larger stations were two-storey boxes with no distinguishing features.

Some interesting exceptions are the divisional stations still standing in Melville, Saskatchewan, and Sioux Lookout, Ontario, both of which feature large front gables at both ends of the second storey. That in Sioux Lookout is further enhanced by Tudor-style woodwork within the gables.

LEFT: The old and the new: The CPR's first station at Spences Bridge, British Columbia, was a crude log shack. Photo courtesy of CPR Archives, A 1448. RIGHT: The new Spences Bridge station, a post Second World War style, is in marked contrast. Photo courtesy of CPR Archives, A 732.

When the newly created Canadian National Railway took over the GTP and the CNoR, it devised standard plans of its own. One that it borrowed from the GTP was the two-storey box that it used to replace older CNoR stations in northern Ontario, and which it enlarged and built on the Noranda branch of the CNR in northern Quebec. This massive pattern was repeated nowhere else in Canada. Otherwise, the CNR's patterns were for the most part smaller and simpler, their single-storey style being embellished only by a gable over the bay.

Before the Second World War changed Canada's station styles forever, the CNR introduced three new patterns, largely in the Maritimes. One was a modification of Pratt's pyramid but with a less exaggerated roofline. Examples of this were at Saint Quentin, New Brunswick; Musquodoboit, Nova Scotia; and Borden, Prince Edward Island. The second style altered Pratt's station roof, replacing the pyramid with interesting hip gables (a throwback perhaps to the very first designs tried by the CNoR), with examples at Grand Falls and Plaster Rock, New Brunswick, and St-Félicien, Quebec. The third was much less interesting and consisted of a two-storey structure with a front gable. Examples of this style were found at Londonderry, Nova Scotia, and St. Leonard, New Brunswick. All three were combination stations with large freight rooms and waiting rooms for passengers.

A New Era

Following the Second World War, the world entered a new era. As if rejecting the war and the debilitating depression that preceded it, Canadians cast aside the old order with all its trappings and eagerly grabbed on to anything new. Televisions, automatic household appliances, and the family car all moved from being luxuries to becoming necessities. With the new age came new architecture. It too cast aside the frivolities and trappings of the pre-war styles and emerged with what has been called the "international" style of architecture.

Although this style, which originated in the Bauhaus school of architecture, was known in Europe and the U.S. before the war,

The post Second World War years brought with them a new approach to stations as shown in the CPR's Terrace Bay station. Photo by author.

Canadians waited until after the war before incorporating it into their stations. Characterized by expanses of glass and steel, and flat roofs, it was a total rejection of the Victorian, the classical or the "beaux arts" styles that dominated less than a decade before. The new architecture also rejected national distinctions in favour of international uniformity.

Canada's station builders fell into line and abandoned the old styles. One of the earliest of the new-era stations was the CNR station at Midland, Ontario, a building that actually used the stone base of the earlier structure. The CPR too introduced a new-era style with single-storey stations at places like Field, British Columbia; Pendleton, Ontario; and St-Basile, Quebec. When a string of modern pulp mill towns was created along the north shore of Lake Superior in the early 1950s, the CPR responded with its new international station style, building a string of such stations at Marathon, Red Rock, and Terrace Bay in Ontario, as well as at Thurso and Asbestos in Quebec.

Meanwhile, in the Maritimes, many of the old Intercolonial stations were nearing their one-hundredth birthday and the CNR embarked upon a replacement program. To implement the change, the engineering department in the late 1940s created a new and flexible pattern characterized by a single storey and a simple gable over the waiting room or bay window. Despite some variety in the massing and in the rooflines, aesthetics were cast aside in favour of utility. Then, in the 1960s and 1970s, in conjunction with CN's new logo and corporate image, the railway again replaced many of their New Brunswick stations with a string of international-style stations. Magnificent old ICR stations at Campbellton, Bathurst, Newcastle, and Moncton were removed and replaced with featureless boxes. Many were subsequently renovated by VIA Rail after CN no longer required them.

Most of Canada's railway lines followed suit. The Algoma Central added the new flat-roofed styles at Wawa and Frater, the Pacific Great Eastern (later to become the British Columbia Railway) added new flat-roofed stations at Prince George, North Vancouver, and Shalalth.

When the St. Lawrence Seaway flooded the original route of the Grand Trunk Railway between Cornwall and Cardinal, a series of five new international-style stations were built on the new alignment. Of the former GTR stations, only those from Moulinette and Aultsville survive, now in new locations. Of the new structures, only that in Cornwall still provides passenger service.

Despite the spate of new styles, stations were still stations. Mail and milk cans still waited in the freight shed, passengers still paced the platforms, and the agents still cranked up the order board and hooped up the train orders to the engineer or the brakeman. But this too was about to change.

The 1960s brought with it the end of the traditional station and the introduction of functionally specialized stations. The most visible were the new passenger stations. More reminiscent of airports than train stations, these stations were almost all glass, and almost all waiting room. Gone were the bay window and the agent. In their places were glass walls and uniformed ticket agents who stood smartly behind airport-like counters. Nearly all were located in suburban areas far from the cramped and congested downtowns, and, to attract the car-oriented consumer, there was always ample parking.

Opened in 1967, the new Oshawa, Ontario, station was, according to CN's press releases, "a prototype of functional bright stations to serve medium size communities." The style was created by S. Reznicek, CN's senior architect, and appeared in other places such as Saskatoon and Kingston, Ontario.

The CNR's Oshawa, Ontario, station was one of the few new station styles added in the 1960s. Its suburban location and appearance reflected the new symbiotic relation between rail and road. Photo by author.

Smaller communities were not so lucky. What the CN press releases failed to mention was that many magnificent and historic way stations were being razed by the hundreds, even where passenger service still existed, and replaced with tiny glass and aluminum "bus" shelters.

In 1973, to accommodate continuing passenger service in the remote northern Ontario town of Chapleau, the CPR brought in on a string of flatcars its new structure, consisting of nine prefabricated sections, moved them by sleigh to the new site, and placed them on cement posts. A few months later the old divisional station was demolished.

Prefabricated structures became the order of the 1970s. With most station functions gone or fast going, there remained little need for anything more than a shelter for maintenance crews. Their foundations rotting, their paint peeling, and their upkeep and insurance costs growing, the old stations became impossible to justify. Through the 1970s and 1980s they were removed by the thousands and replaced with prefabricated trailers, transported on trucks rather than rails, and moved onto the old station site.

Suddenly, station grounds that had once possessed an architectural treasure, a joyful focus for the community, had acquired all the ambience of a construction site. Even new divisional stations were concrete blocks or, later, aluminum shacks. Two of the more hideous examples of modern divisional station styles were the CPR station at Victoria, British Columbia, and the CN station at Jonquière, Quebec (where the previous attractive brick station had been torn down to make room for a parking lot). Happily, these have subsequently been replaced by new VIA stations, which display a more traditional form.

Revival

Indeed, VIA realized that station design still had a role to play in attracting passengers. The revivalist era of station styles had begun. They devised three basic patterns that varied in size according to passenger numbers but that incorporated imaginative lines, traditional rooflines, and stylish wooden benches. In two cases they designed special stations that recalled the early days of station architecture, the E and N terminus at Victoria, British Columbia, and the passenger station at Capreol, Ontario. The latter was designed by a Sudbury architect and

TOP: When architects went to the drawing board for a new VIA Rail station in Capreol, Ontario, in the 1980s, they went back to the station's stylistic roots. Photo by author. BOTTOM LEFT: The Ontario Northland Railway's new $4 million station for North Bay incorporated modern glass facades with a more traditional roof line. Also used as a bus station, the station is linked by tunnel to a large shopping mall and contains displays of Cree craftwork. Photo by author. BOTTOM RIGHT: Ontario's new GO commuter station for Agincourt hearkens back to Canada's earliest station styles. Photo by author.

includes a vaulted waiting room, a traditional roofline, and the brackets from the former wooden Canadian Northern divisional station where VIA had been the sole tenant.

More recently, VIA Rail began upgrading existing 1970s stations by adding a retro-style hip-gable roofline and a faux tower. These can be seen in places like Oshawa, Kingston, and Oakville in Ontario and Sainte-Foy in Quebec. VIA demolished the six-storey CN office tower in London, Ontario, which housed a small dingy waiting room, and replaced it with a modern station that boasts such traditional station features as a steel-beamed waiting room reminiscent of the train shed, along with decorative pillars and a tower.

In Ontario, the most recent stations erected by GO Transit display a distinctively traditional style, even though the massive parking lots that surround them testify that the car era is not soon likely to end. The Ontario Northland Railway, after flirting with modernism in its New Liskeard station, returned to revivalism with traditional-looking new stations at Engelhart and North Bay, all of which are stops for the *Northlander* train.

Following the swearing in of new federal transport minister, David Collenette in the late 1990s, Canada's rail passenger service gained new life (since stalled by a string of indifferent ministers). With the recognition of climate change and global warming, rail travel is nevertheless increasingly being seen as part of the environmental solution. And, as it does, station styles are coming full circle. Station architects have rediscovered the beauty and elegance of an era that once seemed doomed to extinction.

The Canadian Northern Railway served Calgary by moving into what was a school. The building still stands, most recently as a ballet school. Photo courtesy of Glenbow Archives, ND 8-307.

URBAN MONUMENTS: CANADA'S CITY STATIONS

5

Canada's finest stations were her urban stations. In many medium-sized cities they were the most stunning structure in town. In contrast to small town and rural stations, they were special stations built for special reasons.

In some places they were the points where a number of railway lines converged. In these places it was simple economics that dictated the railway line or lines should build marshalling yards, regional headquarters, and sometimes, when that rare spirit of cooperation prevailed among rival railroads, they would build union stations.

In other places, urban stations were built just because the size of the city warranted a grand building. Inter-rail rivalry and civic pride often teamed up to force the railways to bring in their best architectural talent and build a monument to their supremacy.

Other centres were important points of entry. Here, visitors or immigrants arriving in Canada would catch their first glimpse of their adopted country and the railways wanted that first glimpse to impress them. In some instances that dominance was reflected in the height of the building, with high pyramidal roofs or towers, while in other instances it was the size of the entrance, reminiscent of triumphal Roman arches or the great pillars of Greek temples. Railways envisioned their stations as the gateways to urban Canada. Whatever the reason for building an urban "palace," the operative word was "grand," for the railways fully intended to dominate the townscape as they dominated the economy.

One of the early influences on North American urban station styles was the Union Station in St. Louis, designed by Theodore Link. Its high-peaked roofs and looming clock tower utterly dominated downtown St. Louis. This influence was particularly evident in the 1895 extension to Toronto's second Union Station, as well as in the smaller but no less appealing Grand Trunk station in Brantford, Ontario, designed by the firm of Spier and Rohns and built in 1905.

Then came the Chicago Exposition of 1893, which inspired a new wave of station styles. The invention of the steel beam had suddenly made possible the construction of massive flat-top buildings, many examples of which were displayed at the exposition. Steeply pitched roofs were no longer needed to create the impression of size. With it came a new wave of classicism. To the station builders, the flat rooflines called for Greek columns and Roman arches and gave them a new dimension for their grandeur — the gateway. Suddenly the stations began sporting Doric arches or classical columns, some of which stretched five storeys high. They were the new statement, the grandest entrance to urban North America.

The third phase of urban station design was the office tower. Again, a partial response to construction technology, corporations

The CPR's Vancouver station was well lit during its heyday, and remains busy today. Photo courtesy of CPR Archives, A 1264.

began to express their dominance in height rather than beauty. Called "modernism" by some architects, ("brutalism" by others), the style consisted of office towers of concrete, or glass, and aluminium, with the station hidden, almost as an afterthought, at the ground level. Calgary (CPR), Edmonton (CN), and London (CN) were examples. Nothing about the outward appearance of the building cried "station."

Although embraced by urban politicians and corporate executives with skyscraper mentalities, "modernism" was roundly scorned. The population had become cynical over the depersonalized profiteering that motivated modern corporations, especially those that ran the railways, and with the office towers that epitomized them.

This wave of rejection has led to the latest phase, postmodernism, or revivalism. While few new urban stations have been built during this phase, it has initiated a resurgence in urban station preservation. Grand urban stations, many scheduled originally for demolition, have been preserved and millions have been spent on their restoration. Washington D.C.'s Union Station, New York's Grand Central Station, Windsor Station in Montreal, and Union Station in Toronto, have all been preserved and rescued from modernist madness, simply because the public had had enough.

Canada's newest "urban monument" is the newly opened VIA Rail station in London, Ontario, with its exterior tower, and an interior that is a tribute to the ancient train shed. Photo by author.

Toronto

The first of Toronto's large urban stations was built by the Great Western in 1857. Although not that company's largest urban terminal in Canada, its elegance was unsurpassed in its day. The prominent use of rounded arches and the emphasis on the train barn reflected a distinctly American influence, not surprising since that railway was American. However, when the Grand Trunk built Toronto's next grand urban palace in 1875, the Great Western joined in and abandoned its station to eventually become a farmers' market, a use it retained until it burned in 1952.

The GTR's new union station replaced a small board-and-batten building and was quickly proclaimed the grandest urban station on the continent. Although that may have been an overstatement, the station was indeed a grand structure. Constructed of stone and dominated by domes and Roman arches, it contained waiting rooms, offices, and a three-track train shed.

But within two decades Toronto had outgrown it. New rail yards and train sheds were added to the southern main entrance and completely obliterated the beauty of its original facade. A new entrance and offices were added to the north side but they too proved inadequate. By 1900, Union Station had again

Sprawling yards added to the front of Toronto's 1873 union station obliterated its elegant features. Photo courtesy of the National Archives of Canada, PA 87429.

become obsolete. An extension was built on the north side but it also proved inadequate.

The great fire of 1904 that destroyed much of downtown Toronto provided the Grand Trunk with the opportunity to lease one of the available sites and, in conjunction with the CPR, began to plan a new Union Station. The Board of Railway Commissioners approved the plans and ordered the GTR to have the station ready for 1908. However, the GTR's dispute with the CPR over track elevation forestalled commencement and, when the CPR stalked out in 1912, the GTR commissioned the Montreal architectural firm of Ross and MacDonald to devise plans for what would be one of the grandest railway stations in North America. Although construction was almost complete in 1919, political wrangling over grade separations delayed the opening until 1927, and even then it wasn't entirely complete. For two more years passengers were required to walk from the new concourse to the old platforms.

The culmination of what architects call the "beaux arts" style, the new station featured a row of soaring Greek columns. Inside, the cavernous waiting room was designed to bring to mind the great hall in the Roman baths of Caracalla. Bas-relief on the outside above the columns displays scenes of industrial Canada, dominated, naturally, by the railways. Etched on the inside are the names of Canada's major cities, once railway destinations all.

Although the acrimonious dispute with the CPR delayed Union Station's construction, it did have one beneficial result, another architectural gem, the CPR's North Toronto station. Unfortunately it was in the wrong place at the wrong time.

Anchored by Union Station near its foot, Yonge Street was Toronto's main drag, a bustling strip of shops, cafés, and theatres. Development was thinner north of Bloor Street. Houses, fields, and ravines interrupted the wall of commerce. A few shops huddled around the main crossroads of St. Clair, Davisville, and Eglinton.

When the CPR opened the Ontario and Quebec Railway in 1884, it crossed Yonge Street at Summerhill, where the

LEFT: Opened in 1927 after more than a dozen years of construction, Union Station's grand hall was inspired by the Roman baths of Caracalla. Photo by author. RIGHT: Toronto's first "North Toronto" station was a CPR standard way station, and was named "Yorkville" after the nearest village. Photo courtesy of CPR Archives, A 20990.

railway built a small station on the west of the street, designed using the same pattern seen on today's Peterborough station. It named the station "Yorkville," the nearest village at the time. In 1916 the Yonge Street skyline was dramatically reformed upon the opening of a spectacular new limestone building that was Italianate in design and dominated by a fifty-metre clock tower. Impatient with the delays plaguing the GTR's new union station downtown, the CPR built the handsome new station, to be shared with Canadian Northern. Designed by the Toronto architectural firm of Darling and Pearson, it contained bas-relief motifs on the outside while three arching windows that stretched the full fifteen-metre height of the waiting room shed ribbons of light that reflected on marble of brown and green. As Yorkville no longer existed as a municipality, the CPR renamed the station "North Toronto."

Despite its great beauty, the station was a failure. When it opened in 1927 the new Union Station could more than handle increased passenger traffic, while a change to a train at the CPR's North Toronto station meant a long and inconvenient trip along a crowded Yonge Street. By 1930 passenger service at the North Toronto station remained at fewer than ten trains per day (compared to 150 at the new Union station) and the station was closed. In July of 1940 the station was reopened as a beer store, later to become a liquor store, a function that it retains today.

As part of area redevelopment, Marathon Realty, the CPR's real estate wing, and the Liquor Control Board of Ontario have restored the grandeur of the aging building, including opening up the long-enclosed ceiling of the waiting room.

Montreal

CPR's first Montreal station was anything but grand. The Dalhousie Square station, which it had inherited in east end Montreal from the Quebec, Montreal, Ottawa and Occidental Railway, was a solid but simple structure, noteworthy only for its high-arching windows and use of stone and brick.

It was soon superceded by Bruce Price's chateau-esque Viger Station and hotel, built in 1896. Here, Price's use of high-peaked roofs, dormers, gables, and turrets made the Viger Station one of Montreal's more elegant buildings. When the Viger station opened, Van Horne, making much of its French "chateau" origins, grandly dedicated it to *"la gloire de la race canadienne-française."*

Montreal's most famous station, however, was the CPR's Windsor Station and headquarters building. Designed by Bruce Price in 1886, the building was opened in 1889. Van Horne proudly proclaimed in six-foot letters that it "Beats All Creation:

Opened in 1916 as a "union" station and renamed North Toronto, CPR's Yonge Street landmark has been restored, its three-storey waiting room finally opened up. Photo by author.

The New CPR Station." An 1897 CPR guidebook described the station as having "a rare combination of elegance, comfort and architectural beauty, undoubtedly one of the handsomest buildings in the city and a fitting illustration of the enterprise of the CPR." Edward Maxwell later designed extensions to the station along the Rue de la Gauchetière that nearly doubled the size of the building. Today, with the CPR headquartered in Calgary and commuter trains now stopping a short distance west, the Windsor station houses restaurants and offices that have little to do with its railway heritage.

Shamed in part into action by the design for the Windsor Station, the Grand Trunk began in 1886 to replace its much-criticized Bonaventure station. In 1888 their new Victorian-style

structure opened for business. Victorian arches and cast iron around the tower roofs showed that the GTR meant business. Inside, the GTR showed off a vaulted waiting room and an elegant dining room. But the beauty did not last. In 1916 a fire gutted much of the upper structure. Rather than rebuild, the financially strapped railway simply removed the magnificent towers and turrets. In 1943, most passenger train service was removed to the new Gare Centrale. Designed by the CNR's chief architect, John Schofield, it was a large but very plain representation of the early "modernist" style with its flat roof, straight lines, and ordinary windows. Now the main station for VIA Rail's passenger trains, and many of Montreal's commuter trains, it lies buried beneath the Queen Elizabeth Hotel on one side and the new CN

"Beats all creation" was how the CPR's William Van Horne described the new Windsor station in Montreal in 1889. Although trains no longer call, it remains one of Canada's grandest stations. Photo by author.

headquarters on the other. Only a small portion of the original exterior is visible along a side street. Following another fire in 1948, what remained of the Bonaventure station was replaced by a new freight and express complex.

Canada's third major railway line, the Canadian Northern, was soon to be heard from. In 1917, the railway that MacKenzie and Mann had built piecemeal from short lines across Canada made its grand entrance into Montreal. On Rue de la Gauchetière, just across the square from the Windsor station, they began erecting what was by comparison a utilitarian-looking station. Passengers entered through a classic opening of five arches and into a main waiting room with seats of oak, and then into a men's smoking room or a separate women's waiting room. The main concourse and platforms were located on the lower level.

But the CNoR was by then on the verge of bankruptcy and soon afterwards became part of the government-operated Canadian National Railway system. This station too was eventually replaced by the Gare Centrale.

Quebec City

Another of Canada's most magnificent stations sits in the heart of Quebec City; it is the Gare du Palais. Although clearly chateau-esque with its turrets, arches, and steep roof, it was designed, not by the masters of the chateau, Price or the Maxwells, but by a

LEFT: Montreal's Bonaventure Station, built by the Grand Trunk, offered one of Canada's most elegant waiting rooms. Photo courtesy of CNR Archives, 43552. RIGHT: Montreal's Gare Centrale remains a busy terminal although most of it now lies buried beneath skyscrapers. Photo courtesy of CNR Archives, X 31079.

later CPR architect by the name of H.E. Prindle. Built in 1914 as a union station, it replaced an older CPR station (a former Quebec, Montreal, Ottawa and Occidental station) that stood adjacent to it, and the Grand Trunk station that stood several blocks away.

Other stations in the Quebec area were the National Transcontinental's "bridge" station, a divisional station built in that company's standard pattern. The site is now occupied by VIA Rail's "retro" style Sainte-Foy station. Across the river sits the former Intercolonial's Levis station, a massive two-storey building with steep rooflines. Although it was renovated by VIA and the city of Levis, CN has removed the tracks, and passengers must now board at the Charny station outside of the town. The Levis station, however, still fills a transportation role as the terminus for the ferries, which shuttle across the St. Lawrence River. The Gare du Palais, after a period of disuse, has been extensively renovated, celebrating many of its original heritage features, and is once more VIA Rail's terminus in this historic city.

In addition to its railway role, the station has become a community focus again, hosting events and exhibits such as those associated with Quebec's four-hundredth anniversary celebrations.

Ottawa

Before 1912, when Ottawa finally got a grand urban terminal that befitted its status as the nation's capital, it was a city of scattered nondescript little stations. The Canada Atlantic (a line later absorbed by the Grand Trunk), the New York Central, the Canadian Northern, and the Bytown and Prescott railways all used small wooden stations or recycled buildings. In 1881 when the CPR opened its Broad Street station, Ottawa had its first architect-designed station courtesy of the CPR's Edward Maxwell in his trademark "chateau" style. Finally, in 1912, the Grand Trunk opened its new "Central Station" on the site of the former military store that had been used as a station by the Canada Atlantic Railway. It too was part of the "beaux arts" wave that was sweeping North American station building. Passengers entered into a high-ceilinged waiting room through classical columns that stretched four storeys high. In 1920, when the CPR closed its Broad Street station and moved in with the then CNR, Central Station became a "Union Station."

Ottawa's current VIA station more resembles an airport

TOP: The CPR's Gare du Palais in Quebec, shown with an ice train, has been refurbished and remains the city's rail terminal. Photo courtesy of the National Archives of Canada, PA 175333. BOTTOM: VIA's modern Ottawa station was modelled more as an airport terminal, and lies well away from the city's downtown core. Photo by author.

terminal than a traditional railway station. Located so as to be convenient to cars and not the downtown, it was part of a major urban redesign undertaken during the 1960s by the National Capital Commission. It is, however, easily accessible by public transport and well landscaped, somewhat reminiscent of the old station gardens. Inside are a barbershop, snack bar, and VIA's first-class Panorama Lounge. The former Union Station went on to become a conference centre. Although the exterior has remained unaltered, the interior is off limits to visitors, who are sternly reminded of that fact by stone-faced security guards.

Vancouver

Until the mid-1960s Vancouver was the only city in Canada that could count three massive classical stations. That of the CPR, designed by Barrott, Blackadar and Webster of Montreal, sported a row of gleaming white columns in front of a large red office building. In the waiting room were models of Canadian Pacific steamships and scenic oil paintings in the frieze. Built in 1914, this station replaced one of Canada's most magnificent but shortest-lived chateau stations, designed by none other than Edward Maxwell. It was demolished in 1914, just sixteen years after it was built to make way for the new station.

The two other classical stations stood side by side. The Great Northern station was designed by Vancouver architect Fred Townley and built in 1915. A union station, for it housed the Northern Pacific Railway as well, it was distinguished by two arched entranceways.

Meanwhile, next door, Canadian Northern's architect, R.B. Pratt, was turning his skills to the classical mode, designing a station that, although it contained only one arched entrance, was equally attractive. The building featured lunch counters and a dining room, as well as a barbershop, drugstore, and YWCA Travellers' Aid office. In the 1950s, the Great Northern transferred its passenger traffic to the CNR station, and in 1964, to avoid high land taxes, demolished its classical station.

Today, the CPR station contains a retail complex and serves as an entrance to Vancouver's ferries and commuter trains. The CN station still serves VIA Rail and Amtrak passenger trains.

Hamilton

Hamilton, Ontario, lost two early monuments, that of the GTR (a former Great Western station) and the original

The CNR's classic Vancouver terminal gives the city a second magnificent station, one at which trains still call. Photo by author.

Italianate Toronto, Hamilton and Buffalo station, but gained in their place two perhaps equally appealing monuments, the neo-classical station of the CNR and the art deco station of the TH and B.

The TH and B's art deco style is unique to stations in Canada. Designed by Fellheimer and Wagner, it was built in 1933. Modified from a more elaborate design, the six-storey tower housed headquarters for the company. The wider two-storey base displays curved wraparound windows. The waiting room impressed passengers with modern terrazzo floors and central lighting fixtures. Passengers entered from the street and boarded the trains from the second level.

The Hamilton CNR station was one of a series designed by CNR architect John Schofield. It was built in 1930 and features a neo-classical facade punctuated by Greek columns and portico, while bas-relief above the entrance shows railway scenes.

Both buildings have gained new life. After the CPR abandoned the TH and B station, it was restored to much of its original grandeur and now offers GO Train and regional bus service. The CN station, after briefly providing GO train service, was fixed up for a Hollywood film, *The Long Kiss Goodnight*. Then it was acquired by LIUNA (Labourer's International Union of North America), which restored the waiting room, and converted the facility to a banquet hall and offices. Statuary now decorates the wide front lawn.

TOP: *Classic pillars and red brick distinguish Vancouver's CPR station. Photo by author.*
BOTTOM: *Hamilton's original Toronto, Hamilton and Buffalo station was a grand turreted building, but was replaced with a bold new art deco building when grade separation was needed at the level crossing. Photo by author.*

At the same time as the TH and B station was being replaced, so too was Hamilton's CNR station, sporting a more conservative neo-classical look. Photo by author.

place on the third. It is not known whether or not management intended part of its corporate headquarters for that use. The railway fell under the umbrella of CNR in the 1920s and closed for good in the 1980s. After VIA Rail and CN had moved out, the building became a farmers' market.

Charlottetown

Built by the Prince Edward Island Railway in 1907, Charlottetown's two-and-a-half-storey station of local sandstone replaced a much earlier and much simpler single-track train shed located near the corner of Water and Weymouth streets. The new building, which measured a more substantial fifteen-by-fifty metres, and constructed of local sandstone, was located near the original. It contained waiting rooms, ticket offices, and a newsstand on the first floor. The offices of the roadmaster, yardmaster, and other officials were on the second, while union meetings generally took

Pictou

While many of Canada's larger cities managed only modest pattern-book stations, some smaller places warranted larger and more impressive buildings. One of Canada's more delightful stations stands in the relative backwater of Pictou, Nova Scotia. Here, in 1904, in this industrial waterside city, the Intercolonial Railway built their most playful station. Three curving Elizabethan gables figure prominently on the windows of the second storey, an almost

LEFT: Charlottetown's red stone station may be train-less, but remains a landmark heritage building. Photo by author. RIGHT: Halifax's neo-classical terminal was built when the first was destroyed in the Halifax explosion of 1917. It remains a terminal for VIA Rail's Ocean Limited. Photo by author. BOTTOM: St. John's Railway terminal is still grand and is now a museum. Photo by author.

identical twin of the English station at Ambergate. There is no apparent reason for such an elaborate station in such a relatively small city other than the city's role as a major seaport.

Halifax

Built by the Canadian National Railway after it took over Canada's bankrupt lines, the Halifax station falls easily into the neo-classical category. Its Greek pillars and stone walls gaze soberly over an otherwise uninteresting Halifax street. It retains its railway role as the Atlantic terminus of VIA Rail's *Ocean Limited*.

It replaced an earlier Intercolonial station built in 1877 by Halifax builder Henry Peters and was described as "the finest and most striking upon the Intercolonial Railway System." The original station contained offices, waiting rooms, and living quarters for the agent and was heated by steam and lit by gas. This station met a grisly fate, being destroyed in the tragic Halifax explosion of 1917.

St. John's

In contrast to its near namesake (Saint John, New Brunswick),

St. John's, Newfoundland, has retained its original urban palace. Designed in the French Second Empire style and built by W.H. Massey, the station replaced the one-time military building that had served as the Reid Newfoundland Railway's first station.

Here the station builders used local stone and created arches, steep mansard rooflines, and high, narrow gables. Although the trains don't run in Newfoundland anymore, the station still offers a railway adventure, housing the Railway Coastal Museum, with several displays. Adjacent to the station is a "train park" with heritage train equipment, and marking Mile Zero of the Trans-Canada Trail.

Saint John

In 1858, the European and North American Railway built Saint John's first grand station, a large wooden Romanesque structure. It lasted until 1884 when the Intercolonial Railway replaced it with a stone building that, with its steep roofline and prominent tower, was reminiscent of the 1895 addition to the former Union Station in Toronto.

Designed by architect J.T.C. McKean, it consisted of brick and stone and measured thirty metres by forty metres. Three storeys high, it housed waiting rooms, offices, and a dining hall, with the agent's quarters on the second floor.

This in turn was replaced in 1932 by a CNR station, a union station that incorporated the classical lines that the railway was using in station like those in Edmonton and Saskatoon. This building lasted until 1978 when, despite efforts by local citizens to save it, the CN demolished it and replaced it with a simple glass shelter, designed to provide only a waiting area for VIA Rail passengers. Newer CN facilities were built nearer the outskirts of the city. Today, VIA no longer calls, and Saint John can claim no station at all.

Thunder Bay

Thunder Bay originally was two cities, Port Arthur and Fort William. A major grain trans-shipment site for the CPR and the Canadian Northern, as well the later Grand Trunk Pacific, both Fort William and Port Arthur contained a half-dozen stations. The most striking was that designed by R.B. Pratt and built by the Canadian Northern in 1905. Its two steep pyramidal roofs displayed the chateau-esque roofline that even the CNoR's smaller stations displayed, while beneath the gables, the CNoR added concrete wheat sheaves, a tribute in this non-agricultural area to the western wheat growers who supported them. Its size and its unique design, however, set it completely apart from anything the CNoR had done before or after.

TOP: Saint John's second station, that of the Intercolonial, was even grander than the first, a three-storey wooden gothic building. It was followed in the 1930s by a neo-classical station, which in turn was demolished for a small glass building. Photo courtesy of the New Brunswick Museum. BOTTOM: Fredericton's CPR terminal was not a large building, but elegant in its own way. Photo by author.

Meanwhile, on the other side of town in Fort William, the CPR reigned supreme. This was in fact the site of the ground-breaking for the CPR as it built its transcontinental line west from this point. Then, in 1910, when the Grand Trunk Pacific rolled into town, the CPR moved out of their two smaller pattern-book stations and into a single large flat-roofed building that it shared with its rival. (At this point the GTP was not a through line but rather a branch line from its main line further north.)

The Canadian Northern's Port Arthur station sports twin pyramid roofs beneath which concrete wheat sheaves are a tribute to the early railway's western customers. Photo by author.

In Port Arthur, the CPR also operated two stations, one an attractive but smaller brick building built in 1907 directly across the track from that of the CNoR. The building was dominated by a massive tower that was out of scale with the smaller waiting room and offices. All of Thunder Bay's original CPR structures have been demolished, although the "union" station in the Fort William area still serves the railway. Port Arthur's CNoR station is no longer in railway use but remains a stunning centrepiece for Thunder Bay's renovated waterfront.

Winnipeg

Virtually all lines to the west passed through Winnipeg. Often called the "Chicago of the north" (perhaps we should call Chicago the "Winnipeg of the South"), Winnipeg owes its existence to the railways. The railways, in turn, built stations here that are among the classics of the country.

In 1888 the CPR built in Winnipeg the largest station in western Canada. According to a contemporary traveller, the "large and handsome station was worthy of a metropolitan city like Winnipeg," but within a decade even that building was due to be replaced by a larger chateau-style station. Haggling over the price of land delayed construction long enough for the CPR

to change its mind and opt instead for the current trend in station architecture, the beaux-arts style.

In 1904 the new large red brick building with its Greek columns, and designed by the Maxwell brothers, replaced the old station. Adjoining the station, the CPR added the Royal Alexandra Hotel. The hotel has been demolished, but the station survives. In 1993 it was designated as a provincial heritage site and today contains the Winnipeg Aboriginal Centre.

Winnipeg did, however, end up with a chateau station, if only for a short time — the Northern Pacific's Winnipeg Hotel. Seven stories high, and bearing the steep roofs that typified the chateau style, it was designed by architect C.E. Joy, who incorporated the station on the ground floor. The building was short-lived, burning in 1899.

In 1911 the CNoR built what it called its Fort Garry union station in conjunction with the GTP. It was designed by the New York firm of Warren and Wetmore and used an oversized archway to emphasize the railway's role as gateway to the city. The four-storey limestone building sits at the end of the tree-lined Broadway Avenue. Capped by a dome, the marble waiting room soars more than twenty-five metres and contains the provincial coats of arms in gold leaf. The architects used natural light to illuminate both offices and waiting room alike. Because Winnipeg was a major immigrant distribution point, the railway incorporated special food and bath facilities for immigrants on the basement level, although immigrants were at all times firmly segregated from first-class passengers. While most of the building space is now government offices, the public areas have been restored to their original appearance as VIA Rail still operates two trains through the station, the transcontinental *Canadian*, and the popular service to Churchill.

Brandon

Brandon was one of those cities that earned its grand stations through the size and vitality of the city alone, for it lacked the specialized railway functions that fuelled places like Winnipeg and Fort William/Port Arthur.

LEFT: Of Winnipeg's two grand stations, both neo-classical, that of the CPR has become a native drop-in centre. Photo by author. RIGHT: Winnipeg's former CNR station remains a stop for VIA Rail's Canadian *and for its Churchill train. Photo by author.*

In 1911 the CNoR built a stub line from its main line into Brandon, where it built an impressive brick station with a hotel attached. Nearby, on the CPR main line, a small neo-classical station replaced an earlier Van Horne station.

The track to the CN station was lifted in 1970 and the place is now a popular lounge. The CPR station saw daily passenger traffic until 1990, when the Conservative government of Brian Mulroney stripped the country of much of its badly needed rail service and left the Brandon CPR station without passengers for the first time eighty years.

Regina

In 1892 CPR architect Edward Colonna designed a single-storey red brick station for Regina, one that was distinguished by a squat but prominent tower. Like so many other stations of the period, it quickly proved too small.

Regina's attractive union station, which reflected the Italian Renaissance mood that swept the railway world after the turn of twentieth century, was designed by the CPR and the CNoR in 1911. The GTP operated a smaller station nearby until 1920 when it was absorbed into the CNR monolith. This station was extensively renovated in 1930, an alteration that removed the Italian Renaissance appearance and replaced it with the then current art deco style. Only the trackside entrance retained the earlier style. Passenger service ended with the Mulroney-era cuts to VIA Rail. The building has been further renovated and today houses the Regina Casino.

Saskatoon

Saskatoon has gone through a surprising number of stations. The earliest was built by the CPR in its chateau style, a copy of those in Strathcona and Kenora. The Grand Trunk Pacific in 1913 added a two-storey wooden station, and the Canadian Northern used the architectural wizardry of R.B. Pratt to design one of his chateau stations, a style nearly identical to that used in Dauphin.

Both these old structures were replaced in the 1930s when the CNR built a simpler flat-roofed station of brick and concrete. Although the classical details were gone, the strong entranceway continued to reflect the railway's obsession with "gateway." But even this station was demolished in the 1960s when CN added its modern-era station on the outskirts of the city. The CPR station, however, still survives.

LEFT: Regina's "union" station has become a casino. Photo by author. RIGHT: The chateau-esque touch of Canadian Northern architect R.B. Pratt is evident in Saskatoon's second Canadian Northern station. Photo courtesy of Saskatchewan Archives Board, R-A 20879-2.

Edmonton

Like its sister cities on the prairies, Edmonton went through several generations of stations. Here, too, the talents of R.B. Pratt created for the Canadian Northern Railway a chateau-style station that was a near duplicate of the CPR's Broad Street station in Ottawa. The Grand Trunk Pacific used the station as well.

In March 1928, the CNR opened, to much fanfare, its new station. CNR architect, John Schofield, chose to combine utility and beauty and came up with a "simple but dignified front," according to the *Edmonton Bulletin*. The main floor contained a large waiting room illuminated by skylights and, off to the side, a dining room and restaurant. "Edmonton may well be proud of her new station," crooned the *Bulletin*.

Meanwhile, the CPR, denied entrance into Edmonton, had at first to content itself with its chateau station in Strathcona on the south shore of the river. Finally, in 1913, with the long-awaited bridge finished, the CPR built a classical station in downtown Edmonton. Costing $200,000, the station contained, in addition to the usual ticketing and waiting room, a special immigrants' waiting room tucked into the basement. "The new station, yards, depot and freight shed proclaim the company's faith in the future importance of Edmonton," lauded the *Bulletin*.

Despite the praise of the day, both Edmonton stations have been demolished. The CN station was replaced in 1966 by the modern office tower known as the "CN Tower," and that of the CPR came down in 1978 despite the earnest efforts of the local citizenry to save it. Ironically, the oldest of them all, that in Strathcona, still survives.

Small-Town Monuments

Many of Canada's smaller towns and cities contain urban monuments of their own: the beautiful red sandstone office and former station of the Algoma Central Railway in Sault Ste Marie; the Ross and MacDonald creation for the CPR at Trois-Rivières, Quebec, with its surprisingly minuscule entrance; and the E and N (CPR) station at Nanaimo, British Columbia, built in 1920 and likely designed by a divisional engineer by the name of R.A. Bainbridge.

The former Penn Central station in Windsor (burned) and the one-time Michigan Central station in St. Thomas, both in Ontario, are elegant examples of American railway architecture. The two-storey stone station in North Bay, with its wide-arched windows, has presided over the CPR yards since 1903, while the CN/ONR union station in Cochrane remains that town's most prominent building and its historic raison d'être. Likewise, the station in Churchill,

Ontario: A Portfolio

Temagami

Barrie

Kenora

Biscotasing

The *Northlander* approaching Toronto's Union Station

Hearst

Parry Sound

Sudbury

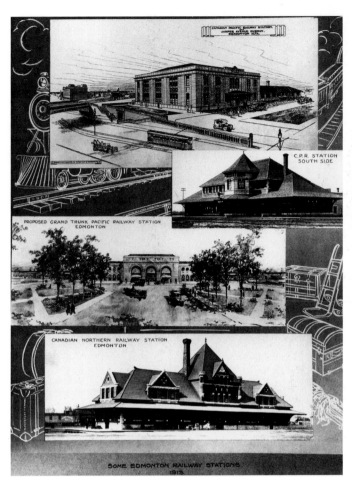

LEFT: In a 1913 montage of Edmonton's stations, only that shown as "South Side" or Strathcona station has survived. Courtesy of Provincial Archives of Alberta, A 4690. TOP RIGHT: Long gone and largely forgotten is the London, Ontario, terminus for the London and Port Stanley Railway. Photo courtesy of Metro Toronto Reference Library. BOTTOM RIGHT: Since this early view, Cochrane's "union" station, shared between the Temiskaming and Northern Ontario Railway (now ONR), and the National Transcontinental (now CNR), has added hotel rooms and a new restaurant and remains a busy terminal for the ONR's Polar Bear Express and the Northlander. Photo courtesy of the Ontario Ministry of Natural Resources.

Manitoba (1942), although not old, has, with its steep roof and hip gables, captured fully and eloquently the chateau lines of Canadian station architecture of a half century earlier.

The CPR's former London, Ontario, station, designed by Bruce Price in 1887, and with a mixture of chateau and Tudor styles, is the sole survivor of the era when London could claim five stations including its original Great Western station and the ornate but long-forgotten Michigan Central station (built as a terminus for the London and Port Stanley Railway).

Having weathered redundancy and threats of demolition,

many of Canada's monumental urban stations survive. Despite periodic and politically motivated rail cutbacks, many are still gateways for arriving train passengers. Those in Halifax, Quebec City, Toronto, Winnipeg, and Vancouver still cling to that function. Although it was largely for corporate self-glorification, the railway station builders at least gave Canadians a sense of grand arrival, of importance and self esteem as they walked through the looming archway or the towering columns, and found the city at their disposal. It is value that today's transportation architects would do well to emulate.

A night operator transcribes train orders. Photo courtesy of CPR Archives, M 5276.

THE MASTERS OF THE STATION: THE RAILWAY STATION AGENTS

At Work in the Station

They once numbered in the tens of thousands and were the most influential men (only a few were women) in small-town Canada, more prominent than bankers and politicians and the envy of the clergy. According to others, the agents were surly and self-serving, more concerned about rules, forms, and freight receipts than they were about the comfort and convenience of passengers. But revered or reviled, the railway station agent, like the stations he manned, has vanished from the roll call of Canadian communities.

Before construction began on the Great Western Railway in 1851, Canada's railways consisted of only a handful of portage railways: the Erie and Ontario, the Montreal and Lachine, and the Champlain and St. Lawrence. Because these lines served only to transport passengers and a bit of freight from one waterway to another, agents' roles were quite simple. As with the stagecoach and canal operations that preceded them, their first jobs were to ticket passengers and collect express charges, and drum up business for the railway. But, unlike stagecoaches and steamers, trains operated along a single track and a new function was added: making sure that trains didn't collide.

Before the telegraph and before standard time, that wasn't easy. No two communities had the same hour on their clocks at the same time, and trains operated as best they could, according to a simple timetable. All trains were required to stop while the engineers entered the station to sign the train order forms. If the train ahead had been late, the agent held up the train at hand until he assumed the previous train was clear. With no telegraph or other form of inter-station communication, he simply held his breath and hoped he was right.

However, by 1855, the Grand Trunk and Great Western Railways had become Canada's first trunk lines, and the telegraph was making train operations simpler and safer. Relaying train orders soon became the agent's most important function. As orders would click in from the dispatcher in the divisional station, the agent had to carefully write them down. Because this task took up such a large portion of the agent's time, sending and receiving telegraph messages became almost second nature. It was not uncommon for an agent to send a telegram with one hand while at the same time writing a letter, carrying on a conversation, or even reading a book.

Still, he kept order out of the chaotic comings and goings of trains, and made sure that the distances between them were safe. Early on, when engines were smaller, and trains therefore shorter and more frequent, this became a tricky juggling act, especially on busy main lines. In the fall, when grain and farm products had to be shipped or perish, trains puffed past main line stations often

A typical agent's office in the Canadian Northern's station at Boissevain, Manitoba, 1912. Photo courtesy of Archives of Manitoba, N 360.

at twenty-minute intervals. Therefore, a mistake of mere minutes meant the difference between life and death. On December 26, 1902, the crack passenger train, the *Chicago Flyer*, blinded by an early blizzard, roared through the Watford, Ontario, station without receiving orders. Ahead, manoeuvring to get onto a siding in Wanstead and out of the way of the onrushing *Flyer*, was a slow freight train. Had the *Flyer* stopped for orders it might have averted disaster. Instead, it smashed into the freight, killing the engineer, fireman, and thirty-eight passengers.

Another bane of the agents was the hated silk trains. In 1924 the newly created Canadian National Railways won the coveted silk-run contract. The job was to get Japanese silk from Vancouver to New York before the living cocoons, worms, and mulberry leaves that made up the valuable shipment, began to deteriorate. Spurred on by the high cost of insuring the shipments, the CNR pulled out all the stops to get the shipments across the country as quickly as possible. As the trains stopped only briefly at divisional points, the agents had to clear the track ahead for the high-balling

LEFT: When time permitted, an agent might relax by watering his station garden, often his pride and joy. Photo courtesy of CNR Archives, X 50363–2. RIGHT: Family members often chipped in to help with the mail, one of the agent's least favourite tasks. Photo courtesy of Queen's University Archives.

silk train. All freight and passenger trains had to be safely on sidings well in advance.

In 1924, one silk train roared across the continent, from Vancouver to Prescott, a distance of 3500 kilometres in just eighty-one hours and ten minutes. By the end of the Second World War, nylon had largely replaced silk, and the silk trains became a fading memory for the agents who had handled them.

Train ordering was just one of the agent's many duties. Lorne Perry of the CNR writes, " They had to be masters of many trades. They handled and remitted money, collected accounts, ordered supplies, tended the garden, handled telegrams and money orders and kept track of goods awaiting pick-up or shipment."

It is not surprising, then, that the railways were often accused of heaping too much work on the solitary agents. In 1908, when the Post Office tried to urge the railways to add mail-side delivery to the lists of agents' duties, their union, the Order of Railroad Telegraphers, complained that "they are being overworked … every agent west of Fort William was urged to assume the mail-side delivery." This with the "manipulation of gates and at some distance from the office were great a multiplicity of duties." Extra duties were heaped on the agents with no increase of

staff. "Just at the time that the responsibility in handling train orders is greatest, the excessive burden of the numerous duties also occurs." Complaints by employees were routinely countered with threats of dismissal.

In 1960 the Board of Transport Commissioners (formerly the Board of Railway Commissioners) listed no fewer twenty-eight separate duties that the agent must perform when handling grain alone. These included sending daily wires of empty grain cars needed, filling out forms, billing and sending cars, sending daily revenue reports, preparing switch lists and way bills, and keeping track of which cars went to which elevator. If this wasn't enough, the agent had to tally most of the daily paperwork each month, not only for his home station, but for unmanned flag stations as well.

Passenger bookings were another of the agent's more important tasks. When railways expanded into the tourist business with hotels and steamships, the agent became a travel agent and made bookings that might be a simple one-way fare to the next town, or a worldwide excursion that included several steamer and train connections.

In addition to all that, the agent solicited freight business, the railways' most important source of revenue. In towns where

Freight waiting shipment from the CPR station at Olds, Alberta, 1904. Soliciting and shipping freight consumed most of an agent's time. Photo courtesy of Archives of Alberta, A 4646.

more than one railway existed and competition was fierce, it was a task that required particular tact and salesmanship. He supervised the loading and unloading of shipments and made sure the bills were paid. Not all freight shipments were easy. Clayton Cook of Newfoundland, an agent's son, remembers the cattle. "Should there be a shipment of cattle," he recalls, "[my dad] would have to, in addition to his station duties, feed and water the cattle and clean the mess." That job might last until the cattle train was ready to move the animals on to their destination, or until the owner came to claim them, "sometimes for several days" according to Mr. Cook.

When railways entered the commercial telegraph business, the agent became responsible for sending and receiving messages and money orders. Because the agent was a banker of sorts, the railways provided the stations with safes, bars on the ticket windows, and sturdy locks. The rule books were firm; no one was allowed into the ticket office for any reason.

In addition to all their other duties, many agents were postmasters as well. When the mail train arrived, the agent would sort the letters and the magazines, and then pass them to the small but eager crowd waiting anxiously for the news from the old country, or the latest mail-order catalogue. In Canada,

only those communities too small for separate post offices were given post offices in the stations. However, in Newfoundland, during the Depression, the small post offices were given to the agents all along the line, a chore that lasted until Newfoundland's confederation with Canada in 1949.

Railway rule books reminded the agents not only of their duties but also of their role in the community. "The local agent is the railway's front line contact with the public," notes the CNR rule book. "To many he is the railway." As a result, much of the rule book was devoted to station appearance: "Stations should always be kept clean and tidy. A clean tidy station creates immediately a favourable impression on our passengers and patrons … The waiting room should be kept free from dust and rubbish. Frequent sweeping and dusting and a periodic washing of the floors should be carried out." Even the least appealing of an agent's household chores were spelled out in detail. "Particular attention should be directed to keeping the toilets as clean as possible. These places should be frequently washed, adding a small quantity of suitable disinfectant [Phenolic Emulsifiable Disinfectant was recommended]. Attention should be paid to the toilet bowls; sometimes these become discoloured and very repulsive looking, often giving off an objectionable odour."

That the waiting room of the North Toronto station remained spotless was due to the railway agents' rule books on cleanliness. Photo courtesy of City of Toronto Archives, James, 930.

Nevertheless, the agent was like a king ruling over a small domain and played a key role in the everyday life of the community. In some communities the agent held the best-paid position in town and might well share the local spotlight with such vital individuals as the grain elevator manager, the mayor, the pool hall operator, or even the preacher. If the town was located on a busy line, one that had several telegraph wires, the agent was their source of news. Clayton Cook recalls how his father, agent at Princeton, Newfoundland, would copy all the news from the wire and place it on a special bulletin board for members of the community to read.

Whenever a special sports event occurred, the agent became the announcer, long before radio. Donald Leslie, agent at Troup Junction in British Columbia, recalls in his lengthy and eloquent memoirs the night of the world boxing championship fight between Jack Johnson and Tommy Burns in Australia. "It was suggested … that I should copy the fight story off the press wire handing [it] out the window round by round and that one of the men would announce it as the account came in. Before radio, this was standard procedure for all major sporting events such as the World Series and always at election times." As expected, excitement soared as the fight neared its climax, the

crowd favourite, Burns, losing. "The audience solaced itself with assorted beverages, but the announcer was too busy announcing so he could not participate and he tried to catch up when the fight finished and swallowed too much in too short a time … he fell off one the moored barges into deep water instead of stepping into his boat and we had quite a session getting him aboard."

In 1909 telephones were finally introduced to the railway stations. Bowing to pressure from the Peoples Telephone Company and the Caledon Telephone Company, the Board of Railway Commissioners required the railways to allow telephone companies to install phones in the stations. But as the agent was the only person permitted to use the phone, and the station phone was often the only one in many small towns, it was just one more job for the overworked agents. Many resisted. In 1911 the *Renfrew Mercury* complained that the K and P agent at Calabogie, Ontario, was demanding payment to answer the phone, while in Quebec, the Bonaventure and Gaspé Telephone Company raged that agents were refusing to answer the phone at all. But gradually the telephone was accepted and soon became a vital news link to what was still the "outside" world.

Not all the news was welcome. During the wars the agent, often having the only telephone in town, was called upon to relay the news of a son or husband killed overseas.

If the agent was the news link, he was often the emergency link as well. Mrs. Ollie Bertie of Taber, Alberta, recalls the role that the station in her hometown of Beaver Brook, New Brunswick, played: "If there was any emergency we depended on the station master. The phone in the office was strictly a railway phone. You could talk only to other station masters on it. In any kind of emergency the station master in Beaver Brook would have to get in touch with the station master in whatever town you were calling [who] he would have to make the call for you."

Clayton Cook notes that his father saved more than one life. Whenever a villager would fall ill he would arrange to have the section foreman transport the patient on his track motor car to the nearest doctor.

Sometimes there was no time to travel to the doctor or to wait for one. As a result, many small-town babies were born in the local station, with the agent or his wife performing midwife

Dominion Express agent for the Port Moody station, J.P. Phelan, stands third from the left, along with other Dominion Express employees. Photo courtesy of CP Archives, A 7632.

functions. One former agent claims to have delivered, over the years, fourteen babies before a doctor could arrive.

Throughout the country, young men aspired to be agents, even though many were not old enough. Many young boys spent their free summer hours down at the station helping the agent load and unload freight, and learning to read the semaphore. Then, when they were old enough, they would hire on. Most began as clerks, working their way up to telegraph operator, and then finally bidding on the coveted job as full-fledged agent.

E. Stanley Johnson wrote in the CPR *Staff Bulletin* in 1943 how he hungered for a railway position. "'You're only fourteen!' exclaimed the agent. 'That's pretty young for a form clerk.' 'Well,' said I, 'for one thing, there's nobody else around here can do it. For another I'm mighty quick at figuring.' … There was a CPR rule that no man could become a train order telegrapher until he was nineteen … but finally came my birthday. Nineteen years old! It was the most glorious day of my life and I celebrated it by setting out on the road as a telegraph operator."

Donald Leslie, when applying for a job as station agent, was a little less scrupulous. "I was asked how old I was and I countered with the question 'How old must I be?' Eighteen was the required minimum to hold the position of railway agent so

I deducted three years from 1894 and appeared on the staff records as having been born in 1891."

One of the youngest of all was Hugh Neilson who, as telegraph operator in the Great Western Railway station in St. Catharines, Ontario, left a remarkable diary of station life in 1861. "After having been on the job for a month," he noted in his diary, "I will be 14 years old on the 18th of this month."

At busier stations, a special night operator was often used to man the telegraph while at others a full-time telegraph operator was on duty even during the days to relieve the agent.

Other than memorizing the rule book and spending hours on the telegraph key, there was little training for station agents. The biggest hurdle was waiting in line for a vacancy. "Employees bid on jobs," remembers Lorne Perry of the CNR, "according to seniority, so the lonely night jobs were for the newcomers. Prized jobs were for those with the opportunity for commission in addition to salary, for telegraph, money orders, express."

Although the position was coveted, the life of an agent could be crushingly dull. "Life at Troup [Junction] was dull, really," recalls Donald Leslie. "I had been used to hearing intelligent conversation at home … Now I had no one at all except for a brief moment or two when the two trains went through and a freight train at two or three day intervals." He sought ways to fill those empty hours. "At night I played telegraphic chess with the night operator up at Kaslo, but neither of us was very good at it."

Hugh Neilson of St. Catharines complained often in his diary of having little to do. "I have been lying on the sofa nearly all day sleeping," he wrote on one particularly day, "not much doing."

But on a main line like that of the Great Western through St. Catharines, life did not stay dull for long. "Have been busy in the office today," writes Neilson the very next day, "lots of specials and pilots coming and going … trains all very late … train west didn't come until 9:45. It was late when we went to bed."

Whenever a dignitary passed through, all hands were put on alert. "Father got a message today saying we must be on hand with operator to make arrangements for a special passenger train with the Honourable John Ross, Inspector of Public Works, going to Toronto." Then he adds sardonically, "That will be another thin dollar for me this month."

The hours were long. Neilson opened his station at six-thirty in the morning and remained on duty until eight o'clock at night. Bad weather or extra traffic sometimes kept him until midnight. Sundays were the only holiday, and paid vacation was unheard of.

Pay for full-time agents stood at about a dollar a day, and from that they had to pay the railway $5 a month for accommodation. Divisional stationmasters in charge of a large staff received $75 month. To earn this they worked ten hours a day for six days a week. With monthly pay, overtime pay did not exist.

To help compensate for the lack of overtime pay, agents earned commissions from handling Dominion Express Company work, selling land for the company's Land Department, sending commercial telegrams, or, as one agent in Lindsay, Ontario, did, teaching telegraph school.

The agent's job was not all rosy. J.A. Hamelin, former night operator at Fort Macleod, Alberta, provides this rare insight into the less pleasant aspects of station work. Testifying at the hearing of the station's regular operator, he laments, "A night operator has to work twelve hours every day... I worked all the night before last and yesterday there was a big dance at the hotel, (hotels were almost invariably right behind the station) which was full of people dancing and making noise, and consequently I could not sleep, and then I had to get ready for another twelve-hour shift... I have been working nearly every day for three years, Sundays and all."

A risky task that many agents dreaded was hooping up train orders to an oncoming steam engine in the black of the night. Substituting for off-duty agents was another unpopular task, one that was made more onerous in the 1950s when the forty-hour work week replaced the sixty-hour week, requiring more substitutions than ever before.

Then there was the hated ritual known as "bumping." This occurred usually during downsizing whenever an agent with more seniority bumped a more junior agent from his station and replaced him. The agent who was displaced could in turn bump an agent still more junior, and set in motion a domino process that could upset an entire division.

TOP: An agent prepares to "hoop up" train orders from the boxcar that served as the Lindsay Junction station to a slowing passenger train. Note the semaphore in the "halt" position. Photo courtesy of the Public Archives of Canada, C 12196. BOTTOM: Hooping up in more modern times at the Matheson, Ontario, station. Photo by author.

Writing in a special edition of *The Coupler*, BC Rail's employee publication, Don McKinnon recalls how he bumped a local shipper working on contract, a move that proved somewhat unpopular with the shipper's fellow villagers. "In 1947 the railway decided to open the Pemberton station and I bid on the position and got it. At that time the railway had a contract person handling the shipments. He was a nice gentleman and was performing the job well ... it didn't go over well with the people in the valley. It wasn't really difficult or unpleasant, it was just lonely."

Generally, however, the railways rewarded loyalty. A CPR agent in Tweed, Ontario, when too old to continue with his heavier duties, was transferred to a larger station where, for the same salary, he carried out lighter, more specialized duties. At Kaladar, Ontario, the CPR broke from practice and paid an agent the $250 that he had missed in wages while attending to family problems.

Disputes between agents and maintenance crews were not uncommon. While agents were responsible for interior maintenance, the maintenance workers looked after the exterior. "There was a man fell through the platform," complained Elgin Ontario agent M. Boses to his divisional superintendent. "Although he was not hurt he might have been. I have repaired it temporarily but if they [the maintenance crew] do not repair platforms I have no lumber to repair them … Please see what can be done and oblige."

Stubborn supervisors occasionally made an agent's life unpleasant. When Hugh Neilson planned to visit his sister in Kansas he had to secure permission from his superior, one Dwight, but found that getting it took longer than he had anticipated: "Telegraphed to Dwight asking if he had received my letter and if he could grant my request." Two days later, the despairing Neilson wrote, "This was the morning I expected to leave for Kansas, but as I have heard nothing from Dwight and no one sent in my place, I couldn't leave." He finally received his leave, but his troubles didn't end there. After he returned, his replacement, O'Donohoe, departed, leaving a few unpaid debts. "O'Donohoe went west today on Day Express. It seems he didn't pay all his board at Knapps. He owes one week yet and it's doubtful if they will ever get it."

Receiving his own pay presented Neilson with additional problems. "Smith [his paymaster] is going to fetch up [my $24] today sometime. I guess he is afraid I or my father will speak to Dwight about it … he is going to pay me regular after this month."

Agents had to adhere strictly to the rule books, and any deviation meant the agent could receive demerit points. According to the *Educational Bulletin* for the southern Ontario district of the CNR, dated April 1937, more than fifty-five employees, including agents, received demerit points. Some of the infractions included, "Failure to punch ticket 'baggage checked,' five points; delay to correspondence, five points; responsibility for passenger missing train connection, five points; error in billing, ten points." By contrast, only eight individuals earned merits. But according to one former agent, no one was ever fired for compiling too many demerits.

More serious problems, such as drunkenness, were dealt with more severely. Marty Young, agent at Nokomis, Saskatchewan, remembered the night in 1907 when the RCMP awakened him to check on his night operator. He hurried down to find a waiting room full of people and the operator asleep. "I ticketed as many as time would permit," he later recalled. "I was about to try and awaken the operator when he staggered to his feet and said he was going to bed … The next night he came in drunk and out for trouble … I told him to go home and sleep it off … he refused so I pointed to the door and began taking off my coat. After a brief bout I ejected him and as he was being propelled through the door he grabbed the wall phone and took it along with a spot of plaster." The story, however, has a happy ending. "The next night he came on duty in good fettle and from that night on he was as good as any man I ever worked with."

The economic depression of the 1930s brought the agents some unexpected problems — hobos. Desperate for work, they would illegally ride freight cars from town to town hoping for a job. On cold nights they would sleep in the baggage room of the nearest station, sometimes with the unspoken approval of the agent. Many agents sympathized with the hobos and some would bring them a meal in exchange for light labour. Ernie Boyd of Ompah, Ontario, remembers his agent father allowing one itinerant to bed down in the Lavant, Ontario, station waiting room one Christmas. In exchange, the traveller, who had some magical talent and played violin, performed for the local community Christmas party.

Although the job of agent was an almost exclusively male domain, many women filled in during the Second World War when many agents enlisted to fight in Europe. The arrival of the ladies evoked different reactions among the remaining males, and often resulted in the playing of jokes. At the station in Ignace, Ontario, the veteran male employees seemed cordial enough to the new female workers, until the ladies opened their desk drawers to find them filled with young snakes.

Break-ins were infrequent, but during the 1920s a rash of break-ins plagued a number of stations in and around Toronto. The agent at Don station rigged a rope from the door to the telegraph so that the night operator along the line would be alerted of a break-in. Shortly thereafter the booby trap caught the culprits and the agent received ten merit points.

Another station operator, however, was fired for his inventiveness. American inventor Thomas Alva Edison was just fourteen when, like many other youngsters, he fell in love with the railway. By sixteen he had become night operator at a southwestern Ontario station. Because the nights saw few trains, night operators were required to show they were awake by sending to the dispatcher every half hour the code word "six." But the youthful inventor devised an apparatus that automatically tripped the telegraph while he napped. To his shock, he awoke to find that a train order had arrived, he had missed it, and the train had passed. A frantic call to the next operator saved what might have a disastrous wreck. Soon after being called before the supervisor, Edison returned to his native Michigan and left railway life behind him.

Sometimes agents found themselves in the middle of larger disputes. In 1891 when the Toronto, Hamilton and Buffalo Railway purchased the older Brantford, Waterford and Lake Erie Railway, the directors of the latter line became impatient with the former's late payment. To hasten repayment of the debt, they seized a locomotive at West Brantford and decided next to take the station. When the agent tried to defend the building, the BW and LE directors made him a "general manager" of their own line on the spot. He then retreated back into the station to ponder his unexpected new authority. Eventually the TH and B assumed and operated it under the CPR until the 1980s.

Not all stations needed full-time agents. Many needed only caretakers. Their job was simply to open or close the station, light the waiting-room stove and handle the freight and mail. They could not, however, ticket passengers or relay train orders. In 1910 the Board of Railway Commissioners, which oversaw all railway matters, decreed that any station with earnings less than $15,000 a year did not require an agent. While this forced the railway to hire operator agents at some previously unmanned locations where earnings exceeded $15,000 a year, it also meant that they could demote some full-time agents to caretakers at others.

The duties of the caretaker agent were, according to a later CNR staff bulletin, "to see that the station building was

Flag stations like that of the Toronto, Hamilton and Buffalo at Mount Pleasant, Ontario, relied on caretaker agents, or agents from nearby stations. Photo courtesy of Ontario Archives, S 2257.

kept clean, heated and lighted for the accommodation of the passengers and to take care of freight shipments." Originally, the order stipulated that caretaker agents could not sell tickets. However, the howl from the railways and passengers was so great that the commissioners routinely exempted caretakers from that prohibition.

The decline in revenue during the Depression heralded a flood of requests from the railways, asking the Board of Commissioners to downgrade agents to caretaker status. Within two years, more than four hundred agents were downgraded. Clearly, the demotions were a hardship, for salaries tumbled, too. To alleviate the problem, the railways often allowed the former agents to continue to inhabit the station and paid them higher wages than those they paid to newly hired caretaker agents. In addition, the railways allowed them to continue to earn commission on telegraph, express, and ticket sales.

The Kingston and Pembroke line north of Kingston, Ontario, was a case in point. After the CPR purchased the line it demoted many of the operators to caretakers. Hilda Geddes's father became caretaker of the Snow Road Ontario station. Although the station had been an operator station before the CPR takeover, and retained the operator's bay window and ticket office, Geddes's father conducted the railway's business from his general store.

The interior living conditions at the Bellis, Alberta, station have been preserved in the Ukrainian Heritage Park near Edmonton. Photo by author.

Clyde Forks was another K and P caretaker station. Here, a renovated boxcar served as waiting room and freight shed. According to Mel Easton, K and P historian, the caretaker was an elderly lady named Sarah who lived in the village a kilometre away. At train time the villagers would "wheel" her on the freight wagon down to the station where she would light the stove and check for freight. Because the station had no telegraph, notice of freight shipments, usually wood from the mill, had to be phoned to the operator at the Lavant station sixteen kilometres away.

After the Second World War, life for full-time agents became a little easier. On September 1, 1949, agents in the U.S. finally obtained what other workers already took for granted, the forty-hour work week. Almost two years later, after heavy bargaining between the Order of Railroad Telegraphers and the management of the CNR and the CPR, Canadian agents received the same. Suddenly, dozens of communities all across Canada found their beloved agents weren't so beloved anymore. Station doors that had been open evenings and weekends were locked. Letters and telegrams flooded the Board of Transport Commissioners warning of economic collapse in the small communities. A way of life was swiftly approaching its end.

At Home in the Station

Although it is now a way of life that is almost forgotten, many Canadians were born in, lived in, and died in railway stations. Occasionally they partied in them, and some even married in them. To attract steady and reliable family men into agent positions, the railways incorporated into many of their station plans accommodation for the agent and his family. This was usually necessary in new or remote communities where housing was scarce. Most such station plans called for a large second storey on the building. Through the back door of his office the agent could retreat to his combined dining/living room. The kitchen was located beside the back door, while three or sometimes four bedrooms would be situated upstairs.

Railways like the Grand Trunk, which passed through or close to existing towns, placed their agents in separate houses, and had no living quarters in the stations. When the CNR took over the operations of Canada's bankrupt lines, their new station plans seldom included living quarters, except, again, for those in remote locations.

Although by today's standards living conditions were difficult, by the standards of the day they were better than most. Ed Holmes recalls his life at the station in Keewatin, Ontario. "Our living quarters were heated by two stoves … a big coal and wood range in the kitchen and a 'self feeding' heater in the living room. The upstairs bedrooms went unheated, absorbing what heat came from the pipes that led from the downstairs to the roof, or through vents in the floor." Coal was supplied free by the railways.

Amenities that today are taken for granted were slow and inconsistent in arriving. For Ray Gilchrist, now of Lethbridge, Alberta, electricity arrived as early as 1922, while for Bernice Sanderson of Avonlea, Saskatchewan, plumbing did not come until the 1960s. Some couldn't wait that long. "I remember my mother telling me a story," reminisces F.A. Howard-Gibbon in *The Coupler*. "She wasn't too keen about moving into the Williams Lake (British Columbia) station, especially when she discovered the privy for the railway station outside down beside the tracks. It was one of those bisexual jobs, one side for the ladies and one side for the gents. It was for the patrons of the railroad, and, incidentally, to serve for the station agent and his family. 'I don't want to have to go downstairs and across the yard all winter long to go to the bathroom,' she complained, so they put a bathroom in."

Often the agents' families simply outgrew the crowded quarters. When the family of the caretaker agent at St-Lazare, Quebec, began expanding, the CPR severed off a piece of the waiting room to create a third bedroom. By his retirement in 1942, his family numbered eight and the station had been significantly enlarged.

Despite living within metres of thundering trains, those who lived in stations did not see the station life as a dangerous existence. It was not, however, without some risks. In the days of wood-burning locomotives, a stray ember might land in the woodpile and ignite a blaze that could quickly engulf the station. Indeed, one early station burned down the day it opened. Faulty wheels or twisted tracks occasionally launched a train into the side of the station. The agent at Franz, Ontario, barely escaped when a train ploughed into his office. The little wooden station at Rogers Pass, British Columbia, was nestled below the snow-covered peaks of the mountain. In January 1899, the snow suddenly shook loose, roared down the mountain side, and smashed into the station. The agent and his young family were killed instantly; only the servant girl survived.

Trying to sleep only a couple of metres from a busy railway track was not for insomniacs. Trains that rumbled through, often several times a night, set dishes rattling and plaster falling. Should a road crossing be located nearby — and there usually was — the deafening blast from the engine's whistle would roar through the bedroom windows.

Winter brought its own problems. No sooner might an agent sweep off the platform following a snowstorm than the plough train would dump the snow right back onto it, sometimes hurtling chunks of frozen snow right through the windows.

During the 1920 and 1930s, the railways tried to alleviate the bitter winter cold by adding insulation. For the CPR it was insulbrick, while for the CNR it was stucco. Then came electricity, generally in the 1920s, and finally indoor plumbing. The latter was usually the last amenity, with some station agents relying on the outdoor privy until well into the 1960s.

For kids such as Ed Holmes, the station presented unusual opportunities for play, play that might worry most parents. "Growing up in Keewatin's station poses grave concerns for one's

While an agent's job isn't normally dangerous, this collision outside the Collins Bay station, near Kingston, Ontario, came too close for comfort. Because of the death of much livestock, it became known as the "sheep wreck." Photo courtesy of Queen's University Archives.

parents in particular. With Portage Bay and a lot of water on one side, and a very busy railway right of way on the other side, my mother must have spent the greater part of each day running back and forth from one window to another to make sure we hadn't drowned or been run over by a train."

Games were unlike those for any other youngster. "A friend of mine and I were walking on top of a number of cook cars on a siding east of the station," recalls Holmes. "We happened to look down a ventilator on one of the cars and there below on a stove was a pot of prunes [also called CPR strawberries] boiling away… We gathered up a number of clean white egg-sized stones from the roadbed ballast and dropped them unnoticed through the ventilator into the pot below. We didn't wait around for the gang when they returned to the cook cars for supper."

Helena Campbell, now of Simcoe, Ontario, recalls that in her station home at Wellwood, Manitoba, "Five days of the week when no trains passed through, we children and our playmates utilized the station areas, the waiting room, the freight sheds,

Isolation could be hard on an agent's family in isolated postings such as Canoe Lake in Algonquin Park. Photo courtesy of Algonquin Park Museum, # 73.

and the extensive platform. All the children in town played with us there."

For families in isolated stations, life was probably not unlike that experienced by Alice E. Takacs during her childhood in a section house near Manyberries, Alberta. "We lived in wilderness and isolation. Our friends were the gophers, antelope, and rattlesnakes. Evenings were special. Our family would gather around the Marconi and listen to our favourite programs, Lux Radio Theatre, John and Judy and Wayne and Schuster … At ten in the morning everything would stop for the Happy Gang."

As with the station agents, the railway supplied most of their needs. "Every other Monday the train would bring us our water supply for two weeks placed in a cistern," adds Takacs. "On Tuesdays, in a specially made wooden box, two quarts of milk would arrive from Manyberries … In the dirt basement we would store our canned foodstuffs. In quart sealers we would have such items as beef, pork, peas, carrots, beans, and pickles."

Living as they did in the station building, families became part of station operations. Helena Campbell relates, "Mother had learned telegraphy too … as a child we were all taught the call for Wellwood so we could alert Daddy, who might be in the garden, that he was wanted on the wire. Daddy also rigged up a telegraph line between the office and the living quarters.

Mother used to call him to meals or tell him that so and so was heading for the station [She had a view of the town from the living room area]."

This familiarity often meant that generations of families became railway families. Clayton Cook's three sisters received work with the Newfoundland Railway and Telegraph and with the Canadian National Telegraphs, all because they had learned telegraphy while living in a station. As a child, Ray Gilchrist of Lethbridge earned $5 a month from the CPR for cleaning the chimneys of his father's station and filling the semaphore lamps once a month.

Many marriage vows were exchanged in stations. The terminal supervisor in a CPR divisional station in northern Ontario met his future wife while she was working in the restaurant of a nearby divisional station. Ed Holmes's wife, Nonie, assembled her bridal bouquet from the flowers that were growing in the Keewatin station garden, while both Helena Campbell and her sister were married in the large CPR station at Virden.

Life in a station was not always easy. "Cooking was a bit of a problem," recalls Donald Leslie. "A general store in Nelson made up a parcel for me every week with sugar, pepper, salt, butter, bacon, bread, potatoes, tea, eggs, and condensed milk. … those were the days before refrigeration other than the old ice box and I had none … I built a meat-safe arrangement with fly-screen sides which I kept in the creek under the railway bridge … The earth oven was really a five-gallon coal oil can on its side with space for a fire underneath it … It took me a little time to get on to controlling the heat but after awhile a roast could be cooked deliciously."

While most station accommodations were adequate, many stations might be little more than shacks. Donald Leslie describes his station at Troup Junction as "perhaps 6 by 10 with a partition dividing off the one bunk bedroom from the 'office,' which held a small kitchen table, a caboose pot-bellied mushroom-topped coal stove and a shelf table for the telegraph instruments and train register, and I think that was all."

Another problem was isolation, which struck agents in northern Ontario the worst. With no farmland around, the many

Agents oversaw many community functions, including this marriage at the station in Sandon, British Columbia, 1904. Photo courtesy of Vancouver City Archives.

stations attracted neither settlers nor villagers. They remained isolated in a silent forest, an existence made tolerable only by the arrival of trains, communication with other agents, or the visits of the dental or school cars. The few residents of the isolated community of Metagama in northern Ontario formed an Arts and Letters society and endured the long and lonely isolation by organizing concerts and carnivals.

The Twilight of the Agents

The years that followed the Second World War changed forever the role that the station agents played in Canada's communities. TVs and telephones replaced the agent's telegraph key as the link

VIA Rail's Superior *halts at the remote Metagama station in northern Ontario where, in early years, the isolated residents occupied their time by forming an arts and letters society. Photo by author.*

with the outside world. Residents of Canada's small communities began to see less and less of their agent.

With the advent of the forty-hour work week in the 1950s, station hours became like those of any other business, and the station lost its role as a community drop-in centre. When longer hours were required, substitute agents manned the building. By 1960 the agent was no longer a key member of the community, but rather had become just another railway employee.

By the early 1970s the agents were no longer handling local freight and mail. Their role had been reduced to train inspection and train-order handling. A few continued to live in the station, but most lived out, for the buildings had become outdated and difficult to heat. Maintenance slipped and many became fire traps, expensive to insure.

By the end of the 1970s with Centralized Traffic Control (CTC) universal, stations had become redundant and agents by the thousands were given their notice. While most agents retired, many were given jobs as dispatchers in the large central offices or as terminal supervisors at divisional stations. A few agents remained in local stations to handle specialized tasks. An operator remained in the Medonte, Ontario, station as late as 1991 to operate the signals at a diamond. Oliver Engel, former agent at Petersburg, Ontario, followed his closed station to the pioneer village at Kitchener to become its guide. Today, however, even the term has been dropped from the railway lexicon.

There are still dispatchers, there are still roadmasters and engineers and section foremen, but the railway station agent has, like the steam engines and the stations, become just a memory.

Children, likely those of the agent, pose on a hand cart before the Grandes-Piles station in Quebec. Photo courtesy of CPR Archives, A 21216.

THE STATION AS A PLACE TO PLAY

For many Canadians, their small-town station was a place to travel, to socialize, or to work. It symbolized their town and was their gateway to the outside. But for other Canadians, the station was a focal point for recreation, a place to play.

By the 1850s the Industrial Revolution had swept England's small towns, overwhelming them with its smoke and its row housing, and thrusting upon the workers long, unrewarding hours in dreadful factories or mines. Many tried to blot out their environment with an alcoholic stupor. Thomas Cook, a temperance advocate, took one of the Industrial Revolution's own inventions to provide an alternative to booze. That invention was the railway. In the 1850s he began organizing Sunday rail excursions for city workers. These outings, usually to the sea, proved an enormous success and launched Thomas Cook into the travel industry, where his name remains prominent in travel over a century later. And so, railways entered the tourism business.

Canada's Excursion Stations

Ontario's first railway, the Erie and Ontario, entered the tourism business early. Originally a horse-drawn portage railway around Niagara Falls between Chippawa and Queenston, the line added steam engines and was soon extended to Niagara-on-the-Lake and Fort Erie. In 1855 the line published ads that claimed it had "the most attractive route to the tourist in North America." It connected with steamers to Toronto and offered onward connections via the Ontario, Simcoe and Huron Railway to steamers between Collingwood and Sault Ste Marie, or Lake Superior.

Most Canadians, however, preferred local excursions. From its very sighting by Samuel de Champlain, the foaming cataract at Niagara Falls was a popular excursion destination. "There is but one Niagara Falls on earth and but one great railway to it," boasted the Michigan Central Railway, which had acquired the Erie and Ontario. By the brink of the Falls the railway built the six-sided Falls View station, designed to resemble a summer house, and landscaped it with a lawn and flowers. As the railway literature boasted, "Falls View [station], which as the name indicates is a splendid point from which to view the great cataract … thousands of beauty lovers and grandeur worshippers will journey over the only railway from which it can be seen." The Michigan Central added two other tourist stations, at Clifton Hill and Wesley Park, both now part of the City of Niagara Falls.

Ontario's many lakeside stations became popular for Sunday school picnics. The Great Western station at Port Dalhousie was one. "We arrived at the [station] ground in somewhat of a jam,"

It looks like a warm day for this couple sheltering under an umbrella near the Stanley Junction station on the Port Arthur and Duluth Railway west of Thunder Bay, a rail line that has long vanished. Photo courtesy of Thunder Bay Historical Museum.

recalls one reveller. "One loco brought down the cars filled within and, on top, water was in great demand … a great many baskets were very quickly emptied of their contents … to the great comfort of all." In 1901 the Niagara, St. Catharines and Toronto

The Empress of India excursion steamer has docked at the wharfside station in Port Dalhousie, Ontario, whose amusement park often attracted vacationers from Toronto across the lake. Photo courtesy of St. Catharines Museum, N 1586.

Electric Railway added not only a station at Port Dalhousie, but an amusement park as well. Steamers brought excursionists across the lake from Toronto to the popular little station.

In 1876 the Hamilton and Northwestern Railway built a line along Lake Ontario's longest sand spit, the beach that divided Lake Ontario from Burlington Bay, and built a station that became one of the area's most popular excursion destinations. Close and cheap, Hamilton Beach attracted steel plant workers from their hot and smoky refineries. They tumbled from the trains and into such beachside taverns as the Wells, the Sportsmans Arms, the Grey House, and Dynes Hotel. Others built small cottages. Although the station has been demolished after serving many years as a private home, the tracks have been lifted, and most of the hotels replaced, the Dynes Hotel remains a popular local cocktail lounge while the cottages have been converted to permanent homes.

North of Toronto, the sandy beaches and clear waters of Lake Simcoe drew sweating city dwellers to stations at Bond Lake, Keswick, Willow Beach, Jackson's Point, or Sutton on the Toronto and York Radial Railway, or to stations at Port Bolster and Maple Beach on the Canadian Northern.

One of the most popular of Canada's excursion stations was that on Lake Erie at Port Stanley, Ontario. Ever since the London and Port Stanley Railway opened its line in 1853 it had been popular with land-locked Londoners seeking a waterside escape that was close and cheap. And Port Stanley lay less than an hour away. Although the line was originally opened to haul farm products and lumber to the port and bring coal back up to London, it had, by 1915, carried over 28 million passengers to the beach. Later, as the big-band era swept the continent, evening excursions were added to hear the bands play at Port Stanley's Stork Club while the reflection of the hazy summer moon shimmered in Erie's waters.

Although the line was short, it proved so popular that the Michigan Central, which operated it for a time, added an attractive red sandstone station in downtown London opposite that of the GTR.

By 1957 Londoners had turned to cars to carry them to other beaches, and passenger service on the London and Port Stanley ended. But, unlike other railway lines that died and disappeared, the LPS has been revived as the Port Stanley Terminal Railway, and once again transports tourists. Although the London station has long been demolished, excursions run between the Port Stanley station and St. Thomas. En route it pauses at North America's smallest "union" station, a flag station that served the village for which it was named, "Union."

Excursion stations were not peculiar to Ontario. Victoria Beach, a Canadian Northern station on Lake Winnipegosis, offered Winnipeggers much-needed relief from the hot, dry prairie summers. Vancouver Islanders climbed onto the coaches of the Esquimalt and Nanaimo Railway to visit seaside stations at Nanaimo or Qualicum. Goldstream Station near Victoria attracted excursionists who crowded the station grounds to hear Victoria's Fifth Regiment band fill the summer air with brassy military marches.

The CPR and the Hotel Era

"If we can't export the scenery we'll import the tourists," thundered William Cornelius Van Horne. As CPR's vice president in 1884, he was in charge of scenery. A capitalist in the American tradition, Van Horne was fully prepared to turn

The Mount Stephen House station hotel was the CPR's first attempt to attract tourism to the remarkable scenery through which it passed. Photo courtesy of Metro Toronto Reference Library.

the overwhelming mountain scenery through which the CPR was obliged to pass, into tourist dollars. Van Horne's perception and initiative led to Canada's greatest hotel-building era (true hotels, not the prefabricated look-alikes that dominate our highways today).

Like the CPR's first stations, its first hotels were born of necessity; they were simple in appearance, and had little to do with scenery. Because the railway dining cars were too heavy for the CPR's engines to haul through the mountains, they were left behind. In their place, to provide for the hungry and well-heeled diner, the CPR built a string of station hotels.

The first of these were the Mount Stephen House at Field, the Glacier House at Rogers Pass, and the Fraser Canyon House at North Bend, all similar in layout, and designed by Thomas Sorby. A fourth was erected in Revelstoke. Although the stations were intended to be restaurants with a few rooms added on, Van Horne discovered that the tourists were staying on to enjoy the scenery before proceeding.

Van Horne then hired the world's best architects to build more and better hotels. Working in the chateau-esque style, which would set Canada apart in the world of station architecture, Bruce Price, Edward Maxwell, and Frances Rattenbury added the Empress Hotel at Victoria, the Hotel Vancouver in Vancouver,

Mountain scenery like this made the Glacier House Hotel one of the CPR's most popular station resorts. Photo courtesy of CPR Archives, A 1679.

line was downgraded to branch status, and Algoma Mills became just another wayside station.

But it was the new combination station/hotels that set the CPR apart in the railway recreation business. The station hotels at Glacier House, Field, and North Bend were enlarged, while others were added in British Columbia at Cameron Lake and Strathcona on Vancouver Island, and at Belfour and Sicamous in southern B.C. Hotels were incorporated into the stations at Medicine Hat; Moose Jaw; Montreal (Viger); and McAdam, New Brunswick. Built in the imposing chateau-esque style, these buildings incorporated rooms upstairs and elegant (and expensive) dining rooms at ground level as well as waiting rooms for passengers, and facilities for the agent.

By 1890 the CPR was well into the tourist business and was promoting the mountains of Alberta and British Columbia as the "Canadian Alps." Of all the mountain stations, that at Glacier House became the most popular. Built initially as only a dining room, the Glacier House had a mere six rooms for overnight accommodation. But looming high above the little hotel was the mighty Illecillewaet Glacier which, as one visitor put it, "pours seemingly out of the sky in a magnificent ice cascade and descends into the valley towards the hotel as a massive fissured tongue."

No wonder that, in a day when wealthy Victorian tourists were taking to nature, space at the Glacier House was quickly in high demand. In 1892 the CPR added a thirty-two-bedroom annex and, in 1906, a second with more than fifty. With its glacier, its mountain-climbing, and its meals, the Glacier House had become one of Canada's premier tourist attractions. Unlike the other station hotels, the station was not in the hotel as such, but rather was a small log shelter located a few metres away.

Just as the snow-capped mountains had brought about the success of the Glacier House, the mountains destroyed it, for that area of the Rogers Pass was the worst avalanche area in the mountains. When, in 1910, the same peaks unleashed a torrent of billowing snow upon sixty-two hapless CPR crewmen, the CPR chose to head under the mountains and bypass the deadly valley where the Glacier House stood. By 1916 the CPR's engineers had finished the famous Connaught Tunnel, the world's longest double-track tunnel.

the Banff Springs and the Chateau Lake Louise hotels in the Rocky Mountains, the Palliser in Calgary, the Royal Alexandra in Winnipeg, and the Chateau Montebello and Chateau Frontenac in Quebec.

What might have been Canada's first station hotel was never built. In 1880, with the CPR's proposed transcontinental line on hold, the railway chose a remote lumber town named Algoma Mills on the Sault Ste Marie line as a steamer terminus. To take full advantage of Lake Huron's north shore scenery, Van Horne instructed Sorby to design what was intended to be the CPR's first recreational hotel. Although the foundation was laid, the two-storey hotel was never built, for John A. Macdonald's Tories were re-elected and revived the transcontinental route. The Sault

Tourists journeying on the CPR's Atlantic trains often booked into the luxurious McAdam station hotel while waiting to transfer onto trains to take them to the grand CPR hotel at St. Andrews by-the-Sea in New Brunswick. Photo by author.

Glacier House was suddenly no longer accessible by train. Although visitors now had to reach the hotel by buggy, it remained open for another ten years. Then, in 1926, the CPR closed the hotel forever and, in 1929, demolished it.

On the opposite of side the continent stood another of the CPR's great station hotels. A remote lumber town in New Brunswick, McAdam became, almost by accident, a key railway junction. Here, tracks of the St. Andrews and Quebec Railway crossed those of the European and North American Railway as they carried well-heeled tourists to the popular resort town of St. Andrews by-the-Sea. After the CPR took over both lines in 1889 it needed offices, crew quarters, and more space for passengers, many of whom required accommodation while transferring trains.

CPR house architect H.E. Prindle turned to a style originated by the CPR's "chateau" specialist, Bruce Price and designed a massive stone station hotel that, while in keeping with the railway's tourist image (it was nearly identical to other station hotels at Moose Jaw and Medicine Hat), was out of all proportion to the tiny lumber town. It did, however, help lure tourists to the CPR's Algonquin Hotel in nearby St. Andrews. On the main floor travellers could snack at a lunch counter, or dine in style at linen-covered tables in the dining room. On the second floor they could settle into one of seventeen comfortable rooms while awaiting overnight train connections. On the third floor, twenty-eight young women, employees of the hotel and dining room, crowded into their tiny staff quarters, subject to a rigid 10:00 p.m. curfew.

In the 1960s the hotel was closed to commercial traffic. Train service declined from sixteen a day to less than ten a week while yard staff dwindled from 650 to just 35. Today, the grand building is a national historic site, although trains no longer call.

LEFT: The CPR's station hotel in Sicamous, British Columbia, now gone, was squeezed between the tracks and the lake. Photo, 1900. Photo courtesy of CPR Archives, A 18353. RIGHT: The Strathcona Hotel on Vancouver Island remained a popular private hotel until the CPR acquired it in 1916 and added a station in it. It later became a girls' school and was demolished in 1969. Photo courtesy of CPR Archives, A 19542.

Price's trademark chateau style also appeared on station hotels at Moose Jaw and Medicine Hat, which, like that at McAdam, were primarily layover stations. In Montreal's towering Viger station hotel, Price was at his best. In 1896 he designed a magnificent urban station hotel that ranked with the Chateau Laurier and the Chateau Frontenac as being among the grandest urban railway hotels in eastern Canada.

The Sicamous station hotel was squeezed between the CPR main line and the waters of Lake Okanagan. Originally designed by Price in 1888, it was finally completed in 1897. An addition in 1910 nearly doubled the size of the building and obliterated most of its chateau turrets and roofline. It was finally demolished in the early 1960s.

A popular destination for Vancouver Islanders was the Strathcona Hotel on Shawinigan Lake. Designed by a Victoria architect named McClure, the Strathcona Hotel was operated by the Shawinigan Lake Hotel Group until it was taken over by the CPR in 1916. The CPR added station facilities and operated it as a station hotel. Its thirty-two rooms, and fifty acres of landscaped lakeside lawns with croquet and tennis facilities, made it one of the most popular destinations for west coast vacationers. In 1927 the railway sold it to a private girls' school, and it continued to function as a combined station and girls' school until it was demolished in 1969.

The CPR's other station hotels suffered various fates. The Glacier House was demolished in 1929, the Field House became a YMCA and survived until the 1950s. The station at Moose Jaw was replaced by a larger office and waiting room in 1922, while those at Sicamous, Belfour, and Strathcona were simply demolished when the CPR tired of the tourist business.

Three of the most magnificent, however, have survived. That at Medicine Hat continues to provide divisional office space for the CPR, in Montreal, the Viger Hotel was converted into municipal offices, while the stone station hotel at McAdam, New Brunswick, is now slated to become a museum.

Log Stations

The rustic appeal of log construction has long been a tourist lure. With the burgeoning trend to take nature vacations in the 1890s, log stations became part of the railways' efforts to

The fine log station built by the CPR for its Chateau Lake Louise is now a restaurant. Photo by author.

attract visitors to their lines and their hotels. As William Van Horne advised his officials, who were discussing how to replace the boxcar that had served as Banff's first station, "Lots of good logs there," he reasoned. "Cut them, peel them and build your station." Where the railway line was close to the hotel, the station facilities were in the hotel itself, or in a small nearby structure. If the hotel was some distance away and out of sight, the railways wanted to ensure that the first thing a disembarking passenger saw had high visual appeal, and that was usually the station.

When the loop line to Glacier House was replaced by the more distant Connaught tunnel, the station that was opened to serve the hotel was constructed of log and named "Glacier." Similarly, the CPR erected log stations to serve their hotels at Banff and Lake Louise. While the station at Banff was replaced by an equally appealing frame station, that at Lake Louise was replaced by another, larger, log structure. The original log station from Lake Lousie (named Laggan) now rests in Calgary's Heritage Park, while its replacement still stands.

Ontario and Quebec, with their lake-studded vacation lands, accessible at first only by train, also claimed a large number of log stations. Two of the best known were the Joe Lake station built along the Grand Trunk line in Algonquin Park to serve the Algonquin Hotel, and the now relocated Montebello station

LEFT: Log construction was used by many railways to complement their wilderness tourist destinations. The CPR built a log station to serve its Chateau Montebello in Quebec. The waiting room offered a massive stone fireplace. The hotel still operates while the station was relocated to become a tourist information centre. Photo by author. RIGHT: A log exterior was added to Canada's most northerly station at Whitehorse in the Yukon on the White Pass and Yukon line to enhance the community's tourist image. Photo courtesy of Parks Canada.

built east of Ottawa to serve the CPR's magnificent and still-functioning Chateau Montebello.

Canada's most northerly log station was that of the White Pass and Yukon Route in Whitehorse, Yukon Territory. Part of a community revitalization effort, log siding was added in the 1950s to a station that replaced the original, which had burned in 1905. Although the White Pass and Yukon trains no longer travel this far, a tourist train operates from the station along a short section of track.

While the log stations had the most appeal, other hotel stations used standard patterns. That erected by the Grand Trunk for its Highland Inn in Algonquin Park incorporated a style common throughout southern Ontario. The National Transcontinental station built at Minaki for the Minaki Lodge used a pattern found in seven other NT stations in northwestern Ontario. Only that at Minaki survives and is today a gift shop.

Steamer Stations

Steamer stations were special lakeside stations where travellers could transfer quickly from train to steamer. In Ontario, a string of large lakes, known as the Muskokas, lay temptingly close to Toronto and other growing cities. Their (then) clear waters, their (then) peaceful bays, and their (then) tree-lined shores all appealed to city dwellers tired of the noise, the crowd, and the smell of nineteenth-century urban Canada.

As early as the 1870s the trains of the Northern and Pacific Junction Railway began hauling wealthy urban tourists to the lakes. At such lakeside towns as Gravenhurst, Huntsville, and Burk's Falls, the NPJ constructed sidings to the steamer wharves where a fleet of steamers waited to carry the happy throngs off to the several hotels that, in the pre-cottage era, offered the only comfortable form of lakeside vacation.

Then, when the Grand Trunk took over the NPJ Railway, and when the CPR and the Canadian Northern built new lines along the west side of the Muskoka Lakes, more steamer stations appeared. The Canadian Northern constructed steamer stations at Bala Park and Torrance on Lake Muskoka, and at Barnesdale on Lake Joseph, while the CPR added structures at Bala and at Barnesdale as well.

Most steamer stations were little more than shelters. A small, enclosed area provided an office for the operator and foul weather waiting space for the passengers. For the most part, however, the steamer stations were distinguished by their large, canopied, open waiting areas. Only that at Muskoka Wharf in

The attractive steamer station at Muskoka Wharf allowed vacationers to transfer from trains to the fleet of Muskoka Lakes steamers. Today, steamer service again operates, while a facsimile of the early station has been added. Photo courtesy of Metro Toronto Reference Library.

Gravenhurst, designed by architect Joseph Hobson, could claim to be of any size or to have architectural embellishment.

Because the steamer stations were seasonal, the railway often had a second station at such locations for use in the winter. In addition to its station at Muskoka Wharf, Gravenhurst had a year-round station on the main line in the centre of town. The CNoR had separate winter stations at Barnesdale and at Bala Park, while the CPR had a winter station, in its standard style, at Bala. Burk's Falls had a large two-storey pattern-book station on the main line, while a simpler steamer station huddled by the Magnetawan River. At Huntsville, the main line station stood just across the track from the steamer station. Steamers with names like the *Armour*, the *Sagamo*, or the *Segwun* would depart the wharf stations after meeting the train from Toronto, and puff off, their decks jammed with bags and crates, and alive with milling passengers, destined for camps, cottages, and hotels.

Muskoka's steamer stations were vital for the area's permanent settlements as well, many of them just barely out of the pioneer stages. Villages like Rosseau, Port Carling, and Port Sandfield on the Muskoka Lakes, or Cecebe, Magnetawan, and Ahmic Harbour on the Magnetawan River, all depended upon the steamers for groceries, hardware, and supplies.

Following the First World War, trains of the CPR and the new CNR began to make fewer and fewer calls at the steamer stations, preferring instead the cheaper alternative of dropping passengers at the main line stations. More and more people were buying cars and cottages, and following the crude roads that led to them. The popularity of the grand hotels and the steamers declined drastically.

The years that followed the Second World War saw the steamer stations disappear completely. Cottage fever swept Ontario, roads were paved and everyone suddenly owned a car. Cottage-bound urbanites were prepared to endure five-hour traffic jams in return for the flexibility of driving their own car to their own cottage.

In 1954 the CNR, which had been collecting $1,000 a year from the navigation companies for use of its Muskoka Wharf station, shut down the station completely. In 1959 the building

One of Ontario's most popular excursions was that of the CPR's Great Lakes cruise ships, which met the Toronto train at the Port McNicoll station. Photo courtesy of CPR Archives, A 15376.

was demolished. A replica that houses a museum and ticket office for the popular steamships, the restored Segwun and the newly built Winona, stands in its place.

Railway steamer stations also appeared at many Canadian ports. But they were not just for tourists; they were fundamental to Canada's transportation system. One of the first important Great Lakes steamer stations was that built at Collingwood on the Northern Railway in 1854, an attractive station with a tower, landscaped with gardens, and offering music from its bandshell. The Northern Railway provided steamer connections from its station at Bell Ewart to the Lake Simcoe ports of Barrie, Orillia, Beaverton, and Sutton and to the railway's popular Couchiching Hotel.

In 1874 the Whitby and Port Perry Extension Railway began to provide steamer service from its wharf station in Port Perry to Lindsay. Service ended just three years later when the railway line itself reached Lindsay. At Deseronto, Ontario, a combination freight warehouse and station linked the trains of the Napanee, Tamworth, and Quebec Railway (later the Bay of Quinte Railway) to the New York state ports of Oswego and Sodus Point.

One of Ontario's oldest stations was that built in 1856 by the Grand Trunk Railway at Kingston, Ontario. In 1860 it extended a branch from the main line "Outer Station" into downtown Kingston and built a brick mansard-roofed station to provide travellers with steamer connections to New York State. Although it is now surrounded by high-rise apartments, the downtown station still stands, its facade little altered in over 130 years.

At Owen Sound on Georgian Bay, a pair of steamer stations stared across the harbour at each other until 1912, when the CPR moved its steamer operation farther east to Port McNicoll. The new port quickly became the busiest on the lakes, transferring coach-loads of tourists as well as hopper-loads of grain to and from CPR's Great Lakes steamers.

Other Great Lakes wharf stations included those on the St. Lawrence River at Brockville and Prescott, that of the Thousand Islands Railway in Gananoque, the Michigan Central's Niagara-on-the-Lake station, and those on Lake Erie at Port Dover and Port Burwell. Toronto, however, despite its importance as both a railway centre and as port, never had a steamer station.

Following the Second World War, the increased use of trucks and larger trains eliminated many wharfside stations. The last of CPR's fleet of Great Lakes steamers puffed out of Port McNicoll in 1963. The era of the steamer station was over.

Although scant evidence remains that many were even there, a few have survived. The CPR summer station at French River near Sudbury was moved to a nearby lot. At Owen Sound two stations still stare across the harbour at each other. That of the CNR has become a marine museum, while that of the CPR, a "new era" style structure that never saw steamer service, is now trackless.

Canada's other major lake-studded playground was the Kootenay area of southern British Columbia. In the beginning, recreation travel was minimal. But the discovery of gold, silver, copper, and coal attracted a half-dozen railway lines, all requiring steamer stations.

Eventually the CPR and the Great Northern acquired the smaller lines and both maintained steamer fleets. The CPR continued passenger service on the lakes until 1957 and barge service for another two decades.

Most stations were built along standard plans. Survivors include the GNR's small station hotel at Kuskonook and the

CPR's station at Kaslo. Both lines, however, have been long abandoned. Fittingly, the former CPR steamer *Moyie* has also survived. It has been drawn onto the shore at Kaslo and converted into a museum.

Algonquin Park

While the CPR was touting the Rocky Mountains as Canada's great natural resource, the GTR had a natural treasure of its own, Ontario's Algonquin Park.

In 1893 the area became a provincial park. Although long promoted for its "wilderness," 75 percent was actually set aside for logging, a role that it retains to this day. Nevertheless, its tourist allure was strong and did not escape the owners of the railway.

In 1904 the GTR acquired the Canada Atlantic Railway from John Rudolphus Booth. It had in part served as Booth's logging railway between Ottawa and Parry Sound, built to not only haul lumber from Algonquin Park, but to ship grain from the West to the Atlantic.

The GTR wasted little time in going after the tourists. In 1908 they built the Highland Inn hotel in the middle of the park. Hugely popular, it was expanded to seventy-five guest rooms in

To counter the CPR's tourist promotion, the Grand Trunk heavily promoted its hotel properties in Algonquin Park. Photo courtesy of the Public Archives of Canada, A 84261.

1913. Just steps from its front door the GTR placed one of its own stations, a standard plan used commonly in southwestern Ontario. Tourists, apprehensive at staying in rooms that overlooked a noisy and smoky railway track, were assuaged by the rules at Algonquin Park station that prohibited switching at night, or blowing the whistle near the hotel, and that ordered engineers to shut off steam when passing.

West of the Highland Inn the line swung north to hug the shores of Joe Lake. Here, the railway built another hotel, the Hotel Algonquin. To complement a wilderness aura that the railway was trying to sell, the engineers built the station out of logs.

The GTR heavily promoted its recreational experience. It placed pictures of Algonquin Park on playing cards and offered packaged wilderness canoe excursions that originated at Canoe Lake station, included overnight stays at the Nominigan Lodge and ended at the Highland Inn itself.

Algonquin Park was not the only opportunity on this GTR line in which to enjoy nature. On the shore of Georgian Bay, west of Parry Sound, tourists disembarked at the twin-towered Rose Point station and crossed the small bay to the Rose Point Hotel. Farther inland, travellers from Buffalo rode the "Buffalo Flyer" to the Maple Lake Hotel located near Swords.

The 1930s marked the decline of the recreational stations in Algonquin Park. In that decade, the government of Canada responded to the crushing unemployment of the Depression by initiating a road-building program, one that included extending roads into Algonquin Park. Then, in 1933, a railway bridge east of the Highland Inn was damaged. Unable to obtain government funds to repair the bridge, the CNR, since 1923 the owner of the GTR, simply cut off through service.

Nevertheless, recreational trains continued rumbling as far as the Algonquin Park station from the west until 1959. But by then cottages had replaced hotels as the preferred summer recreational form, and the private auto had replaced the passenger train as the way to get there. There was, after all, no other way to travel to the private cottages. Unable to compete with the new road and the private cottage, CN simply demolished the Highland Inn (the Algonquin had burned some years earlier) and sold the Nominigan. Soon after, it ripped down

the stations and tore up the tracks.

The short-sighted love affair with the car is regretted to this day by harried wilderness seekers who must now endure mind-numbing traffic jams, and by families with young children who would prefer seeing Algonquin Park from the comfort of a lodge rather than from remote and rocky campsites.

The Campers' Specials

Although eastern Canada is perceived as the urban and agricultural heartland of Canada, much of it has remained undeveloped, primarily in the rocky lake-strewn reaches of

Remote fishing camps attracted many train travellers and, in remote regions of Ontario and Quebec served by VIA Rail, still do. Photo courtesy of CPR Archives, A 20674.

northern Ontario and Quebec. From the early days of railway travel these remote regions attracted fishermen, canoeists, and cottagers or "campers," as they are called in these areas.

"Cacoma is a quiet enough way station during the greater part of the year," noted one traveller in the 1920s, "but during July and August it is one of the busiest on the line. Big trunks line the platform and crowded omnibuses fly to and fro … boats dance upon the water while the gay and festive dance upon the land … in the winter it subsides into an ordinary village, empty houses abound, the great hotel is abandoned to darkness."

During the 1920s recreation began to play a greater role in the lives on Canadians. The two-week vacation, unheard of before the First World War, became a common part of the year's routine. Wherever railway lines twisted through the romantic wilds of northern Ontario and Quebec, tourists followed. Fishing and hunting camps began to appear along the routes of the former National Transcontinental west of Nakina, along the route of the CPR between Sudbury and While River, along the route of the Algoma Central Railway north of Sault Ste Marie, and along the CNR between Shawinigan and Jonquière in Quebec.

Special trains were put on just to transport the tourists. One of the more famous and enduring was the "Campers' Special." Departing Winnipeg each sultry summer Friday evening, it carried eager cottagers to shores of Malachi, Ottermere, and Farlane Lakes in northwestern Ontario. Many were employees of the CNR who had received their cottage lots directly from the railway. The cottages remain accessible only by train to this day. However, in 1990, the federal conservative government forced VIA Rail to reroute the *Canadian* from CPR to CN trackage, replacing the Campers' Special with a less convenient schedule that no longer permits the cottagers to take Friday–Sunday round trips.

The stations that serve the cottagers vary in style. In northwestern Ontario, those at Farlane and Malachi are former operator stations designed by the CNR in the 1920s largely for northwestern Ontario locations, while those at Ottermere and Wade, dating from the same period, are simpler flag stations with no accommodation for operators. Although no longer used by the railway, most are carefully maintained by the cottagers.

For the campers and natives along the ACR line north of Sault Ste Marie, Ontario, umbrella stations provide shelter, while elsewhere in northern Ontario along the CN and CPR lines, passengers are unloaded onto bare and grassy trackside meadows with only a signpost to mark the location.

Newfoundlanders were not even that lucky. On October 28, 1989, the last passenger train of the Newfoundland Railway (CN) departed Bishop's Falls for Corner Brook. Although townspeople along the way could resort, if unwillingly, to their cars as an alternative, the cottagers and campers of the Deer Lake area

LEFT: Happy hunters proudly show off their trophies of moose, deer, and even skunk, on the platform of Ontario's Haliburton station. Though much altered, the building still stands, and now displays art. Photo courtesy of Ontario Archives, Acc, 9912-1-2. RIGHT: Canoeists and other wilderness enthusiasts prepare to board the Algoma Central's local train at Hawk Junction. Its popular Agawa Canyon tours attract tourists from around the world. Photo by author.

One of Ontario's most popular rail adventures remains that of the Polar Bear Express, *here arriving at the refurbished Cochrane, Ontario, ONR station. Photo by author.*

could not. The train was their only access. These landowners, most of them elderly, were in effect forced to abandon their cabins, which had become inaccessible and nearly worthless.

Recreation stations are not yet a thing of the past. The popular Agawa Canyon tour train, often with as many as eighteen coaches, winds from the sleek modern station in Sault Ste Marie on a day-long train ride to the spectacular mountain passes and gorges of Algoma. Deep in the Agawa Canyon it deposits awestruck tourists onto the platform of the Canyon Station, a converted section house. From here they hike to waterfalls, picnic by the river, take pictures of the soaring canyon walls, or just inhale the clean air amid the silence of this remote region.

In Ontario, the Ontario Northland Railway also promotes its *Polar Bear Express* from Cochrane to Moosonee, as well the fall colour train, the *Dreamcatcher Express,* from North Bay to Temagami. The opportunity to visit the Cree communities of Moosonee and Moose Factory, Ontario's oldest European settlement, attracts more than forty thousand travellers each summer. In response to the growing demand, the town of Cochrane and the ONR have converted the upstairs of the CN/ONR station into a motel. Downstairs, the traditional station functions such as baggage check-in, ticketing, and even a new restaurant are part of one of a very few such traditional stations left in the country.

The spectacular scenery of the Forks of the Credit Canyon attracts tourists by the busload to the Credit Valley Explorer, *a single-day excursion from Orangeville, Ontario. Photo by author.*

Trains that specialize in the tourist trade have heralded a whole new era of recreational stations. The popular *Rocky Mountaineer* uses the former CPR station in Banff for its excursions, while the *Dreamcatcher Express* calls at the beautifully restored stone station at Temagami as its destination. The Orangeville and Brampton short-line railway has constructed a new station in a traditional style in Orangeville for its scenic *Credit Valley Explorer* tour train. And in Uxbridge, the historic "witch's hat" station is now a museum and the terminus for the York and Durham Heritage Railway.

Ski Trains

Not all Canadian recreation is summer sport. During the 1920s, in the steep, spectacular Laurentian Mountains north of Montreal, the sport of skiing suddenly surged to the fore.

It was through these same mountains that the Montreal Ottawa and Western Railway (renamed as the Montreal and Western) had in 1891 opened a colonization line as far as Ste-Adèle, and in 1909 to Mont-Laurier. The original purpose of the line was to help the government of Quebec and the Roman Catholic Church implement their joint policy of colonizing the relatively fertile mountain valleys with settlers from the overcrowded parishes of the St. Lawrence Valley.

A string of stations, many copying the earlier QM and O style, were constructed at villages like Shawbridge, Val-David, and St-Faustin. While the long and snowy winters made pioneering life difficult for the early settlers, they had considerable appeal to a ski enthusiast named Herman Johannsen. Born in Horten, Norway, in 1875, he migrated to Canada in 1919 and became a salesman of engineering equipment. In Norway, Johannsen was the best skier of his time and he soon devoted his efforts to the sport in his adopted country as well. In 1920, known better as "Jack Rabbit" Johannsen, he cut the Maple Leaf cross-country ski trail between Shawbridge and Mont Tremblant, a distance of ninety kilometres, and turned the Laurentians into a skiers' mecca.

During the 1930s, the trains to Mont-Laurier began to bulge with skiers, and for many years thereafter the "P'tit Train du Nord" was a popular Quebec institution. Although the train departed Montreal daily, the Friday ski train was what everyone waited for. Up to twelve coaches would leave Montreal's Park Avenue station, the puffing steam locomotives dropping skiers at stations such as Mont Tremblant and Ste-Agathe. By 1960, however, the province of Quebec had carried its highway construction programs deep into the Laurentians and train frequency dropped to three a week.

Ski trains were once popular throughout Ontario and Quebec, but none more so than the "P'tit Train du Nord," which led to ski slopes of the Laurentian Mountains such as those near Ste-Marguerite station shown here. Photo CP Archives, A 24196.

Then in 1975, a special "Jack Rabbit" ski train, laid on to celebrate Johannsen's one-hundredth birthday, carried more than one thousand skiers to Val-David. Sensing the resurgent popularity of the train as a way to avoid crowded and treacherous highways, the Laurentian Regional Development Council and the local tourist association restored the train service and once more skiers tumbled out at their favourite station. Then, on November 15, 1981, Canada's then transport minister, Jean-Luc Pepin, insensitive to the needs and wishes of Montreal skiers, eliminated the train.

Johannsen outlived the ski train and skied until he died at the age of 114 in 1989. Finally, in 1988, the CPR ended all train service into the area and abandoned the line.

Montreal was not the only city where skiers enjoyed the proximity to Quebec's mountains. Another pioneering railway, the Montreal and Western, snaked from Ottawa through the Gatineau Hills of Quebec to the lumber town of Maniwaki. In between lay a landscape of snow-covered mountains and hills. Here, too, skiers crowded onto trains that took them to such renowned ski resort towns as Wakefield. While regular passenger service had ended by the early 1960s, popular summer steam excursions operate from Hull to Wakefield, the line's sole surviving station.

Ontario's hills offered another skiers' paradise. Although the hills were neither as inviting nor as close to the large cities as were those of Quebec's Laurentians, Ontario nonetheless boasted its own ski trains. Overlooking the blue waters of Georgian Bay, ten kilometres west of Collingwood, are the Blue Mountains. By the 1930s ski trails had been carved into the forested faces of the slopes. On weekends, ski trains from Toronto would chug through Collingwood and puff to a halt in front of the tiny turreted Craigleith station where the skiers were whisked away by horse-drawn sleighs to the primitive ski lodges. The ski trains ended in 1966 and the tracks lifted shortly thereafter. The Craigleith station, however, survived for many years as a popular local restaurant, especially for skiers who now must travel by car and can only envy their predecessors who could travel relaxed in the ski trains.

During the late 1960s a commercial jingle floated from the radio urging skiers to take the "first train to Huntsville," another popular ski region. But this rephrasing of the hit song "Last Train to Clarksville" fell victim to the car craze and corporate hostility to passenger trains, and soon disappeared from the airwaves as surely as the ski trains disappeared from the rails.

The Huntsville station, now owned by the town, still welcomes visitors travelling on the fabled *Northlander*, a route popular during Ontario's spectacular fall colour season. In fact, many of the stations along the ONR between North Bay and Toronto have been revived as destinations for vacationers and tour groups. The town has cleaned up and partly restored the Huntsville station, while the attractive station in Gravenhurst has been renovated and now houses a bus and rail ticket office as well as a snack bar. In South River, the historic wooden station, an original on the line, has been acquired by the municipality and given a new coat of paint. Bracebridge, long deprived of a station stop, has reopened a small waiting room, once more restoring rail service to this scenic riverside community.

Red Lights

Although it seldom appears in local histories, the most popular form of recreation associated with Canada's stations was prostitution. While most eastern cities already had red-light districts before the arrival of the railways, the brothels of western Canada came with the railway and were located close to the station.

In most western railway towns, the main street ended at the back door of the station. The hookers, however, preferred to stay out of sight. They tended to locate on side streets that led off the main drag to avoid citizen protest and police scrutiny.

Few of the smaller towns were bothered by prostitution. As one prairie pioneer recalls, "Our town was pretty small; it only had one brothel." The occasional overnighting salesman or travelling preacher were seldom enough to warrant a full-blown red light district.

Instead, the hookers headed for the divisional towns. Here, they were sure to find restless train crews looking for ways to fill the hours until their return shift, passengers waiting for the train to be serviced, or travelling salesmen yearning for companionship while waiting to display their goods to the local merchants.

One of western Canada's most boisterous brothel towns was Saskatoon. When the Canadian Northern, the Canadian Pacific, and the Grand Trunk Pacific all laid rails into what had until then been a tiny prairie outpost, only a few years apart, the place became a boom town. Young single men flocked into the growing settlement, confident of finding work, and salesmen funnelled in and out on the many lines that radiated from the town. It was a hookers' haven. Twentieth and 21st Streets between the CNR station and the river became a twenty-four-hour parade of men padding from door to door, the "painted women" often hurling abuse behind them.

Moose Jaw was another hot spot. Although the CPR first built its maintenance shops in Regina, where a red-light district immediately popped up around the corner of 10th and Ottawa Streets, the railway relocated its divisional facilities to Moose Jaw and most of the hookers followed. The red-light district there was concentrated along River Street, west of the main street and just a block north of the busy station. Here in a string of hotels, bars, and restaurants, the flesh trade was plied. Moose Jaw became Regina's red-light district as well, and during American prohibition gained a reputation as a hideout for American rum-runners. (Tunnels discovered beneath the downtown streets are said to have been created by associates of the notorious Al Capone.)

Hotel strips such as this on Moose Jaw's River Street were once the hotbed of prairie prostitution. Times, however, have much changed. Photo by author.

Compared to this "Wild West," prostitution played a relatively minor role around eastern Canada's stations. Older and better established, they were family towns, lacking large populations of young and restless men. But the prostitutes were there. Although they rarely frequented the stations themselves, young men with oats to sow had only to ask a cab driver for directions to the nearest brothel.

Pimps, however, were a problem in the large urban stations. Here they would lurk in the concourses — Toronto's Union Station was a favourite — and carefully scan the arriving crowds for unaccompanied young girls, naive and vulnerable, many of whom were fleeing the crushing boredom and predictability of life in rural Canada to seek money and independence in the big cities. Once in the hands of the pimps, however, they became little more than slaves. The Travellers' Aid Society, working with railway security and plain-clothes police, were in the stations too, ready to pounce upon the pimps before they could claim their prey.

Far from the cities, in the remote railway towns and the mining camps of northern Ontario and Quebec, the proportionately high male population brought with it the expected gaggle of painted ladies.

Biscotasing, north of Sudbury, Ontario, during its early years was a divisional point and construction camp for the CPR. Here the hookers' two-room shacks, known as "cribs," crowded the dirt lanes close to the station. The pimping, the drinking, and the gambling turned the little shantytown into a wild and woolly frontier outpost. Within a few years, however, the construction crews had moved on, and the CPR moved its divisional point to Chapleau. Again, the red lights followed, and Biscotasing settled down to become a more sedate and sober mill town.

Sudbury, Ontario, was originally called Sudbury Junction, the point at which two branches of the CPR met the short-lived Algoma Eastern Railway. Here, the CPR built sorting yards, repair shops and a large divisional headquarters. Behind the CPR station on Elgin Street, a string of hotels appeared where train crews and travellers alike could find accommodating companionship.

Sudbury remains a busy divisional point. Although the prostitution trade has largely disappeared, many of the hotels still stand and suffer yet from a lingering reputation of having once been the less savoury part of town.

Railway towns from coast to coast were the same, although history seldom reflects this colourful era. Most are quiet now. As the towns grew, more women moved in. The young men married and settled down to raise families. The end of prohibition diverted the hookers from the brothels into the taverns. Then the Depression, with its lower salaries and hoards of unemployed, meant few had money to spare. By the start of the Second World War, the station red-light districts had nearly vanished from the landscape. Prostitution will continue to flourish, although in less obvious ways. However, its days when the hookers were just a few paces from the back doors of the stations have ended forever.

The Railway YMCAs

The inclination of the railway crews to tumble off the trains at the end of their run and toddle off to the taverns or the tarts was viewed with considerable concern by the railway companies. Not only was the practice giving the railways a poor reputation, but the crews were showing up for their return shifts in less than top shape. As a result, the railways, along with the Young Men's Christian Association, started a series of Railway YMCAs, located at divisional points, to give the crews a home away from home and keep them out of the bars and brothels.

In many of Canada's larger railway towns the railway YMCA became a sight and activity as much a part of the station as the garden, the waiting room, or the water tank.

Founded in London, England, in 1844 to provide youthful workers with an alternative to the depressing and dirty urban environment created by the Industrial Revolution, the YMCA first appeared in North America in Montreal in 1851. The first informal links to the railways began in 1866 at Pointe-Saint-Charles near Montreal, where the huge Grand Trunk yards employed twelve hundred men. The first formal association for railway workers was that formed at St. Thomas, Ontario, in 1881.

But it was out along the remote sections of the main line where the crews faced horrible conditions. Accommodation often consisted of cold and barren bunkhouses; some of them converted boxcars. In 1896 D.A. Budge, General Secretary of the Montreal YMCA, visited the Grand Trunk Railway's divisional points and, in 1906, those of CPR. The dreadful conditions that he witnessed on these tours so disturbed him that he resolved to provide workers with comfortable beds and a Christian environment, and to do this by establishing a string of hostels run by the YMCA.

Money was scarce and existing structures had to be converted for the first Ys. The first structure of any size to become a railway Y was the former Canadian Northern office at the foot of Toronto's Spadina Avenue. The Grand Trunk fitted the building with a dormitory, a small gym, a restaurant, baths, and an outside play area and turned it over to the Y.

The program soon became a nationwide success story. Within twenty years, twenty-eight Railway Ys were in place. Built and owned by the railways, they were staffed by the Y and offered theatre, cards, bowling, and Bible reading. They were comfortable and warm, and welcomed by the lonely crew members. All were located at larger railway yards such as Revelstoke, Cranbrook, and Field in British Columbia, Moose Jaw in Saskatchewan, and Moncton in New Brunswick. In Ontario, railway Ys were scattered through the north at Sioux Lookout, Capreol, Cartier, Chapleau, Hornepayne, Ignace, Kenora, Schreiber, and White River and in the south at Allandale (Barrie), Fort Erie, Niagara Falls, St. Thomas, Sarnia, and Stratford. Four were located in Toronto, and three in Montreal, the birthplace of the movement. There was even a Canadian Railway Y in the U.S., located at CPR's Brownville Junction in Maine.

Many of the buildings were large and architecturally attractive. That at Sioux Lookout was three storeys high, constructed of brick in the beaux-arts style and containing a two-lane bowling alley, a fireplace, lecture rooms, and a library. The stone Y at Ignace had tennis courts, a verandah, a reading room, and a horseshoe pitch. In Field, British Columbia, the Mount Stephen House hotel was converted into a Y and replaced in 1935 by a larger structure that contained the station as well.

Many of these railway communities were small and remote and enjoyed few social or recreational facilities. Here, the railway Ys quickly became the centre for dances, teas, bake sales, and movies.

As with many of Canada's railway traditions and scenes, the end of the railway Y era began in the 1960s with dieselisation.

The railway YMCAs often became the focus for community recreation. This former railway Y in Sioux Lookout was demolished by the CN in 1989. Photo by author.

Because the diesel engines no longer had to stop every 150 kilometres to change the water in the boilers as the steam engines were required to do, the crews bypassed many of the old divisional points. Where layovers did continue, the railways built their own bunkhouses with larger rooms and more modern facilities.

In larger towns the Ys were turned over to the community and became community Ys. In smaller places this was not feasible and the railways, still the owners of the buildings, demolished them. The Ignace Y was demolished in 1967. That in Sioux Lookout, one of the largest, became railway offices, with new bunkhouses added. Then, in 1989, the CN pulled most of its crew out of Sioux Lookout and demolished the building, one of the largest and most substantial in this northwestern Ontario outpost. A few former railway Ys still stand and enjoy other uses. That at Allandale, a fine nineteenth-century brick building, is now a hotel and popular lounge.

Crews still lay over, and they are still lonely, but today they relax in modern motel-like bunkhouses. Most have forgotten, perhaps many never even knew, of the days when the Railway Y stood just behind the station and was their home away from home.

And so, whether it was to enjoy a fine meal, unload a canoe or skis, sleep over, or pursue less savoury activities, Canada's stations were often a gateway to recreation; recreation that, for the most part, the railway companies promoted and capitalized on, even to the point of creating special station designs. But with only a few exceptions, it is just another of those many once-loved station functions that survives only in the memories of those who lived it.

Although posed for the camera, this Craigleith, Ontario, scene is typical of a family reunion at the station. Photo courtesy of CNR Archives, X 33845.

THE STATION WAS THEIR STAGE:
THE RAILWAY STATION IN SMALL-TOWN CANADA

To three generations of small-town Canadians, the station was the heart of their community. Here they met, worshipped, socialized, danced, and even married. They gathered to greet teary-eyed relatives or to bid fearful farewells to soldier sons. They cheered royalty and jeered at politicians. They congregated on the station platform to meet the mail, crowded into the waiting room to hear the news on the telegraph or strolled by just to see who was arriving. The station was their stage.

The Station Kids

Many of the station memories that Canadians cherish the most were those obtained as children. To a child the lure of the station was irresistible.

I grew up in North Toronto, an area with an urban population that preferred to move in cars or TTC buses. The closest station to us was the CPR station at Leaside. Although few passenger trains used it — and we never did — our most eagerly anticipated summer entertainment was to drive to that station and watch the shining black steam engines puff and hiss past dragging a load of creaking, lurching freight cars. Of course, this was before most of us had a television set. But there was just something about a station.

In an early version of today's "hanging out at the mall," youngsters in small-town Canada would buy their sweets at the local store then bicycle, skip, or run to the station to meet their friends. Then, when the daily train arrived, all attention was on the hissing engine and the coaches it pulled. Curious eyes would peer cautiously into the baggage car to see if any convicts lurked in its dark recesses, chained glumly to the wall. In late summer they would skulk around the station to catch their first glimpse of a newly arriving teacher.

Fans crowd the platform of the Grand Trunk's York station to attend a football match in 1906. Photo courtesy of Metro Toronto Reference Library, T-12196.

Young Jeri and Ria try their balancing act on the rails before the abandoned ACR station at Wawa, Ontario. Photo by author.

If a train from the United States were to pass, as often happened in southern Ontario and Quebec, an ambitious youth might persuade a vendor to part with a prized American newspaper. For those brief moments he was the centre of attention, for in his hands was the news of those faraway and forbidden cities south of the border. Others would push and shove towards the travelling salesmen, out-shouting each other with offers to carry his heavy satchel to the hotel, usually just across the dusty street, for a nickel or a dime.

In a Canada that knew nothing of TVs or public playgrounds, the station became the playground for town youngsters, usually to the annoyance of the agent. When games of chase around the platform wore out, or when the agent shooed them off, the gang might scramble to the water tank and climb to its lofty summit, or turn the hand-operated turntable into a slow motion and creaking merry-go-round. Many children would experience their first train ride by secretly boarding at the coal dock or water tower and riding the train to the station just a few yards away.

In quieter and more curious moods, they would simply watch the agent carry out his daily duties, peeking from beneath a desk to watch him clack out a message on his telegraph key, or peering around the corner of the station as he manipulated the baggage carts over the wooden platform.

Sometimes the station was their escape, their gateway to the world outside. Youngsters would hurry to the station, often hours early, coins clutched in their hands, and fidget impatiently until a distant whistle announced the train that would carry them to town to see the current movie, or to the crowds and commotion of the local fall fair.

When the sultry summer nights gave way to the cool winds of fall, the station lost much of its allure. For those of high-school age fall meant bundling up against the morning chill to trudge to the darkened depot and await the distant light of the train that would take them to school.

As youth bloomed into adulthood, courtship blossomed at many a country station. Young couples would walk, hand in hand if they dared, down the main street, past darkened shops, to the station where a setting sun would turn the rails into golden ribbons. And as the sun inched below the horizon they might walk along the rails balancing awkwardly until one would slip onto the cinders, and both would laugh.

Some evenings other couples would join them. If someone had brought a harmonica and if the agent had children of like age, then all might crowd into the waiting room. Simple tunes would fill the air and boots would clomp a two-step upon the shiny oiled floors. From such evenings love often bloomed and many a marriage took place within a railway station.

Just as today, some youths were more interested in rowdyism. This account has been left of youthful antics around the Central Ontario Railway station at Gilmour, Ontario: It was "as is no other place in the north … well stocked with uncontrolled drunkenness … a Saturday, even Sunday, drunks pitching quoits and shooting at a target … attempts at train-wrecking have been made several times at the station."

One of the most eagerly awaited arrivals was the mail. After the mail-car clerk handed the bags to the agent and the agent to the postmaster, a throng of people would follow him eagerly into the station, anxious to clutch the long-awaited, perhaps perfumed, love letter, the newspaper from the old country, or the latest Eaton's catalogue. At Christmas the carts bulged with parcels that contained gifts of fruits, cakes, and toys.

The All-Purpose Station

As the railways unrolled across unsettled regions of Canada, the station was often the town's first community structure, and as such might need to play unusual roles. While stores and hotels quickly followed the laying out of a town, churches took longer. A congregation had to organize, and let the church headquarters know of their existence, then somehow find the money to build their first church buildings. Until then many a railway station served as the community's first church. Reverend Silas Huntington, whose territory in the 1880s and 1890s included the CPR lands in northern Ontario, was frequently forced to preach in railway stations, lamenting that, "Such places are not suitable for our evangelistic work."

One of the northern Ontario stations used for church services was that at Franz, situated where the main line of the CPR crossed that of the Algoma Central Railway. Here, the lower half of the ticket agent's door served as an altar from which the travelling Anglican priest preached to ardent parishioners and hapless passengers alike.

On the Canadian Northern Railway in Peebles, Saskatchewan, worshippers at first found nowhere to worship and resorted to the station water tank. Sheltered from the elements by a wooden exterior wall, and heated by a stove that was intended to keep the water in the tank from freezing, they huddled against the curving wall to sing their praises to the Lord, and perhaps to offer a silent prayer that no hissing steam engine would rumble along side and lower the creaking and leaky spout to fill its boilers and douse the wary worshippers.

Meanwhile, in Quebec, where the railway had come long after the village cathedrals had pointed their silver steeples skyward, the village curé could be seen pacing the platform to greet arriving villagers and visitors alike.

Before the prairies filled with pioneers who shunted Canada's Indians onto reserves, the stations were a popular gathering spot for native people. At first simply curious at the puffing and belching steam engines, they quickly began to recognize the commercial potential of train time and of their own attraction to tourists. In his 1887 account of a cross-country train trip, W.H. Withrow recalled how "at many of the stations a few Indians or half breeds may be seen … They were selling buffalo horns from which the rough and outer surface had been chipped or filed off."

Gateways

For arriving immigrants, the station was a gateway to a whole new life. It was from those railway station platforms that 3 million Canadians first saw their new homelands. They came from America where their tumultuous frontiers had been closed, from England and Scotland where they were shut out the Industrial Revolution, and Clifford Sifton's "stalwart peasants in sheepskin coats" from eastern Europe.

For the CPR and the Canadian Northern Railway it was a windfall. These railway companies held more than 30 million acres of rich (and not-so-rich) farmlands and hundreds of townsites. However, a worldwide recession slowed sales, and the railways began to pursue foreign immigration more rigorously.

European farm families gather on the platform of Winnipeg's CPR station to await processing before heading off to their prairie farmsteads. Photo courtesy of Glenbow Archives, 2660-1.

Clifford Sifton, the federal minister responsible for immigration between 1896 and 1904, joined the CPR in touting the fertility of the West. By 1914 more than 3 million immigrants piled into the immigration sheds at Quebec City, Saint John, or Halifax, while others trekked north from the American plains states.

In April 1893, the *Quebec Chronicle* described four hundred immigrants disembarking from the SS *Lake Huron* and into the Levis station across the river from Quebec City. Their one thousand pieces of luggage were placed onto carts and wheeled into the disinfecting room. Here, the doors were sealed and boilers heated water to 230 degrees to steam the contents.

From the immigration stations, the newcomers crowded into the colonist cars for a tiring and bone-jarring journey west. At the Winnipeg station they huddled about their belongings, waiting for an immigration official who spoke their language. In the immigration hall they would find beds and enough food and tools to allow them to start up their homestead. But also stalking the station were unscrupulous boarding-house operators who whisked many away to overpriced boarding houses, never bothering to tell them that accommodation was available in the immigration halls themselves, and for free.

But it was when they eventually disembarked at their final station that they got a look at their new home. In established communities, a kindly agent might take them in and give them food and a bed until they could locate their homestead. In other cases, the station might be little more than a converted boxcar, sometimes with no other building in sight and here they would wonder where their path led, or even where it lay.

Prior to the radio and the telephone, the station telegraph brought the residents of many Canadian communities their daily news. When the telegraph was not clacking with train orders, it might be sending out the latest grain prices that were vital to the prairie communities. During elections, the men of the community crowded into the smoky waiting room to hear the latest victory or defeat of John A. Macdonald or Wilfred Laurier.

Sports events drew even larger crowds into the station such as the Stanley Cup playoffs or a heavyweight fight drew even larger crowds into the waiting room.

The war years brought news that many did not want to hear.

During the heavy fighting at Dieppe or Ypres in the First World War, the messages were those bearing the names of sons or husbands killed or maimed on the sodden battlefields of France and Belgium. One station, near the base in Borden, Ontario, was renamed Ypres following the horrific battle near that village in France.

First Trains

The first big community event for any station was the arrival of its first train. Bands, banners, and politicians were all on hand to herald a new era for their community.

The opening of the Great Western station in Hamilton, Ontario, in 1854 saw, according to the *Toronto Globe*, "Every stage, steamboat and railroad train … loaded with guests; the hotels were crowded to excess and the merry groups on the street showed that the entire population was in a high state of excitement."

Festivities marking the opening of the London and Port Stanley Railway in 1856 lasted four days. According to the *London Herald* of October 17, 1856, "In the morning [London] presented an animated appearance, flags flying and firemen in their various uniforms parading the streets. About 10 o'clock they formed into a procession and proceeded to the Port Stanley Railway Station on Bathurst Street where the station house and the cars were tastefully decorated with green arches."

A correspondent accompanying the first transcontinental train of the CPR in June of 1886 recalls that it was an occasion for the town's people to flock to the station. At Winnipeg the militia fired a salvo of artillery as the train rolled into the station. The mayor gave a welcoming speech and crowds piled through the coaches.

Further west at Swift Current, the correspondent noted the preponderance of Indians. "Mr Red Skin showed up in all his glory of blankets of various colours trappings and feathers … one Indian boy had his pony on the platform and rode it about for inspection."

At Crowfoot station a celebrity was waiting for the train. "The great chief of the Blackfeet, Crowfoot, came to meet us at the station named after himself. He is a good looking old Indian, sharp featured, black hair and bright eyes. We composed an address to him interpreted by a clergyman we found at the station … the old fellow expressed his 'ughs' of satisfaction."

Troop Trains

Even before the CPR had finished its continental link, one particular train drew a lot of attention. This was the train carrying troops sent to crush the second Riel Rebellion, which began in 1885. The horrendous problems in sending troops to counter Riel's first rebellion a decade earlier, when no railway existed, had awakened the government to the need for a quick completion of a transcontinental railway. A CPR artist who accompanied the

troops has left images of crowds lining the hillsides beside the original Dalhousie Square station in Montreal to bid the troops farewell. Another photograph shows the militia mustered on the platform of the Winnipeg station, while still another shows them at the Qu'Appelle station ready to march out after the rebels.

At the battle of Ridgeway during the 1870 Fenian raids, two stations played a military role. To counter the Americans who had landed at Fort Erie and were advancing westward, the Canadians massed eight hundred troops at the Port Colborne station and boarded flatcars to Ridgeway, where they engaged the Fenians. During the battle the Americans gained the upper hand and forced the Canadians back to the Ridgeway station, where they hurried back onto the train and retreated to Port Colborne.

Some of the most moving photographs of station activity were those depicting the tearful farewells to troops during the First

The CPR's first transcontinental train is greeted by troops at the Qu'Appelle station in Saskatchewan. Photo courtesy of Saskatchewan Archives, R-B 10183.

WRA-325

Canadian troops head off to the front in high spirits during the Second World War, a period when train travel reached historic highs in Canada. Photo courtesy of the Public Archives of Canada, PA 114800.

and Second World Wars. Troops massed at the stations closest to the military bases to board the trains that would eventually take them to the Atlantic ports and then perhaps onward to a muddy grave in the trenches of France or Belgium, or to die on a boulder-strewn beach at Normandy. Stations like Orillia and Whitby, Toronto's Exhibition station, or Camp Borden, which had two stations of its own, were the focus for troop farewells. They would change trains at Toronto and Montreal, where special rooms were set aside for them.

As the wars progressed, the stations hosted arrivals of a different kind. In Europe, as the German war machine began to crumble, prisoners were marched onto ships and back to

the POW camps in Canada. Many of them were processed at Quebec, where they were transferred onto trains that would take them to northern Ontario communities such as Kapuskasing, where a large POW camp was built.

Not all wartime prisoners were the enemy. Fostered by flimsy fears that were fanned by racism, the federal government on February 24, 1941, passed its infamous order-in-council, PC 1486, that ordered the RCMP to round up Canadians of Japanese origin, to confiscate their property and inter them. After first being processed at Hastings Park in Vancouver, they were herded onto eastbound trains. Many were hurried off the trains and onto the platform of the New Denver (British Columbia)

LEFT: Not all station gatherings were glad. Here, a train-load of Japanese-Canadians is being sent to internment camps at a B.C. ghost town during the infamous Second World War roundup. Photo courtesy of the Public Archives of Canada, C 46356. RIGHT: Although forgotten today, J.J. Maloney led the Canadian Ku Klux Klan during the 1930s and attracted curious onlookers until he ended up in jail. Photo courtesy of Glenbow Archives, ND 3-5991.

station, from where they were allocated to the ghost towns of Kaslo, Slocan, Greenwood, or Sandon. Others were kept on the train until it reached the Taber, Alberta, station where ruddy-faced sugar beet farmers met them and escorted them to the farms where they would toil long hours in the fields. Still others ended up in Tionaga, Ontario, a remote and stationless ghost town on the CNR.

Finally, the war over, the stations thronged with happier crowds, wives holding high their children for the first glimpse of the fathers they had never seen, and mothers who had sent a boy to war and welcomed home a hero.

The end of the Second World War also brought with it a new breed of immigrant — the war bride. Thousands of women married or became engaged to Canadian soldiers stationed in England or Europe. When the war ended they thronged into steamships bound for Canada. Here, they were taken by train to their respective destinations, escorted by army officials, and released only when their spouses signed their custodial papers. Station scenes were often chaotic — anxious brides disappearing into crowds before the papers were completed. On occasion they were tragic; the bride standing forlornly with no one there to meet her.

The Education Trains

Canadians looked to their stations not just for their entertainment, but for their education. Special trains were a particularly strong pull. In 1901 A.W. "Good Roads" Campbell coordinated a "Good Roads" train full of the latest road-making equipment, to tour southern Ontario towns and villages. His efforts to encourage better roads by using the train was an irony that no one would understand until decades later, when roads brought about the downfall of much rail service.

In 1913 a "Made in Canada" train toured the stations of the CPR. Canadians flocked to their stations to see the variety of products then made in Canada. Free trade deals might prohibit a repeat of such a train.

Every June and July between 1915 and 1918, the Saskatchewan College of Agriculture sent out the "Better Farming" train to the many stations throughout rural Saskatchewan, carrying exhibits of livestock, field crops, and farm machinery. Nicknamed the "Weed Train," this travelling classroom offered crop displays and farming seminars.

TOP: Edmontonians engulf the CPR station to welcome home First World War veterans of the 49th battalion. Photo courtesy of Glenbow Archives, NA 1337-10. BOTTOM: Veterans of the 1991 Gulf War form up in front of Toronto's Union Station for a triumphal march up Bay Street. Photo by author.

The Saskatchewan government's "weed train" was a travelling classroom offering crop displays and farming seminars. Photo courtesy of Saskatchewan Archives, R-B 3751-3.

Not all special trains were universally welcomed. Unknown today, J.J. Maloney, head of the Canadian Ku Klux Klan, drew the curious to Alberta's stations during the 1930s until he ended up in jail.

Schools on Wheels

Isolation drew people even closer to their station. In the pre-highway era, travel between communities was limited, and many communities in northern Ontario and Quebec were utterly isolated one from the other. Dense swamps, swirling rivers, and the world's hardest rock thoroughly discouraged any kind of settlement apart from the railway towns. Indeed, such settlement was impossible. Here, the station was literally the residents' lifeline, their only contact with the outside. So isolated and small were these tiny train towns that most lacked dentists, doctors, or schools, services taken for granted in the towns and villages of the south.

One man recognized the inequity and cared. In 1922, J.B. McDougall, a North Bay Ontario school inspector, convinced the Department of Education to experiment with a rolling schoolroom. Between 1926 and 1967, that branch of government along with the CNR, CPR, and the Temiskaming and Northern Ontario railways (later the Ontario Northland Railway),

converted seven passenger coaches into travelling classrooms.

These classrooms on wheels were equipped with desks, books, blackboards, and living quarters for the teacher and his family. They would travel back and forth along a predetermined stretch of railway line and spend a week on the sidings of the smallest communities. From the native communities, the trappers' shacks, and the railway workers' homes nearby, the children would emerge, books and homework in hand, ready for another week of lessons.

But the teachers' jobs did not end with the afternoon bell. Most evenings adults from the community would crowd the coach to learn arithmetic, English, or just to pick up the latest news of the outside world that they so seldom saw.

In a similar vein, the Ontario Department of Health created rolling dentists' offices. Although they spent less time in each community, the two dental cars were responsible for over two thousand kilometres of CNR trackage and eighteen hundred kilometres of CPR. One such car sits in the Smiths Falls Railway Museum in eastern Ontario.

By the late 1960s highways had reached Ontario's remotest railway villages and the school cars and the dental cars were backed onto sidings and forgotten. One school car has been preserved at the CRHA railway museum at Delson, Quebec, another has become a school-car museum in Clinton, Ontario, the home of Fred Sloman, Ontario's longest-serving school-car teacher. Sloman brought his school to hundreds of youngsters for more than forty years on the lines north of Capreol, raising a family of his own as well. His school car was spotted by chance, sitting derelict on a storage siding and rescued.

The Harvester Specials

During the 1920s both the CNR and the CPR advertised special harvester trains. For special fares ($12) the railways lured eastern Canadians to the West to help with labour intensive harvests. These special trains equipped with aging colonist coaches were among the busiest. The *Globe* of August 15, 1922, reported that, "all day yesterday every inch of space on the floors and platforms

TOP: For many years the trains brought travelling classrooms to remote settlements in northern Ontario. Photo by author.
BOTTOM: This former school on wheels was rescued from demolition and turned into a museum in Clinton, Ontario. Photo by author.

at Union Station was crowded with outgoing harvesters and their baggage.

Andrew Daniel Clement, a teacher bound for the Rainy River area of Ontario, lamented of boarding such a harvester special. "I was the lone figure on the platform waiting to board … I had two suitcases and this branded me as unwanted. As I walked along, the protruding heads took up a chant 'Pas place ici' [no space here]." The hungry harvesters turned each divisional restaurant into a madhouse. "When the train stopped there was a mad rush. The restaurants were swamped . The all-aboard signal by the conductor was delayed till long past leaving time and even then at two stops men were left behind."

By 1928 the railways were carrying nearly a half million harvesters. But, after 1929, drought and depression combined to end the harvester specials. Another similar institution continues to this day. Each May thousands of university and high school students, largely from Quebec, crowd onto VIA Rail's *Canadian* to travel to Manitoba to plant trees. This writer witnessed one such train with thirty-two coaches, a length one crew member claimed was VIA's longest-ever train.

Celebration Trains

In 1936 the CPR celebrated the fiftieth anniversary of the first transcontinental train by sending its special "jubilee train" out west. As it rolled into the Moose Jaw station, engines in the massive yard let out a cacophony of hoots and whistles, completely drowning out the efforts of the Canadian Legion band to entertain the travelling dignitaries. More than two thousand people turned up at Regina's imposing classical union station to greet the train. And among the thousands who lined the platform at Portage la Prairie stood one Fred Newman, who had been at Craigellachie for the driving of the last spike more than fifty years before.

In 1948 the Edmonton Chamber of Commerce sponsored a special friendship train to visit the remote communities of the Peace River country. With eighty Edmonton businessmen on board, the train passed through several little agricultural towns.

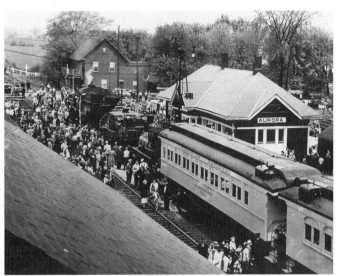

The CNR's historic Museum Train attracts a crowd to the Aurora station in 1953. Photo courtesy of York University Archives, 3216.

At Slave Lake the travellers were met by a huge throng who launched into a spontaneous singsong and dance on the station's rickety wooden platform.

In 1953 the CNR's special museum train drew thousands of Canadians to the stations to see vintage coaches and wood-burning locomotives. Fourteen years later the federal government's centennial Confederation Train crossed the country with its displays and decorations. Line-ups lasted hours as Canadians eagerly crowded their stations to celebrate their country's first hundred years.

While many crowds were on hand to see the first steam trains, even more turned out to see the last. On April 25, 1960, train 76 puffed and hissed to a halt at Winnipeg's CN station. A large crowd was on hand for the train was the CN's farewell to steam.

The Sports Trains

Some of the largest and most ecstatic crowds to besiege the stations were those who welcomed home their sports heros. Early in Canada's history, as towns battled each other for supremacy on the soccer field, the baseball diamond, or the hockey rink, it was the trains carrying the victorious teams home that drew the biggest crowds to the station. Screaming fans would choke Montreal's Windsor station or Toronto's Union station to roar their adulation as the Leafs or the Canadiens brought home the coveted Stanley Cup.

In 1948 fans of the Canadian Football League's Calgary Stampeders added a new dimension to the station celebrations. That year their beloved "Stamps" would battle the Ottawa Roughriders for the Grey Cup at Toronto's Varsity Stadium and, to urge them on, the fans brought a little bit of the West with them. Toronto residents gaped as the Calgarians unloaded their horses and chuckwagons, and turned Union Station into a scene of pancake breakfasts, square dancing, country singalongs, and good old-fashioned Grey Cup whoop-ups.

For many years, when the Grey Cup was fought between the best team from the West and the best from the East, Toronto remained the site of the Grey Cup. The "Stampeder Special" became an instant institution, carrying as many as fifteen coaches, with a special baggage car where fiddles and guitars filled the air with square-dance music. All along the route, wherever a long stop was scheduled, crowds gathered to cheer on the team and dance to the music of the revellers.

Trains from the West would disgorge a mass of cheering,

hollering, and occasionally staggering football fans into Union Station, a tradition that would continue until other cities built large stadiums and until airplanes took over from the trains.

A high point for the Grey Cup train was the 1955 Grey Cup "Goodwill" train. Led by Metropolitan Toronto's first Chairman, Fred Gardiner, two hundred Torontonians paraded down Yonge Street and onto the special train that would carry them across the country to the site of that year's Grey Cup game in Vancouver.

At the Winnipeg station the goodwill ambassadors were met by Mayor George Sharpe. There, they gathered in the waiting room to parade down Main Street, where they gamely battled a foot of fresh snow, bone-chilling temperatures of minus fifteen degrees Celsius and winds of fifty-five kilometres per hour. The parade met similar conditions three days later in Regina. Nevertheless, their spirits were so high that newspaper writer Val Sears enthused, "Not since World War Two has there been a train like this one. It may possibly make railway history."

The Royal Tours

One of Canada's longest-standing traditions and one of its biggest station attractions has been the Royal Tour. Ever since Albert

LEFT: A tradition is launched as Calgary fans cheer their Stampeders football team en route to the 1948 Grey Cup match in Toronto. Photo courtesy of Glenbow Archives, NA 3354-1. RIGHT: In 1955 Toronto follows Calgary's example and sends a "Goodwill" train off to the Grey Cup in Vancouver, pausing in Winnipeg on the way. Photo courtesy of York University Archives, 3020.

Edward, Prince of Wales, travelled past dozens of garlanded stations between Toronto and Collingwood in 1860, Canadians have jammed their stations to get a fleeting glimpse of royalty.

In 1901 the Duke and Duchess of Cornwall and York took the CPR to Vancouver. "It was a continual triumphant journey," gushed a CPR reporter, "the train dashing past gaily decorated stations. A brief stop was made at Three Rivers where an official welcome was extended the royal couple by the mayor. [In Montreal] a tremendous crowd of people occupied every available foot of space from which Place Viger Station could be seen."

A writer for the *Winnipeg Tribune* arrived early at that city's station. "Before the sun was up people began to assemble in the vicinity of the station … the 13th Field Battery thundered forth a royal salute." Thousands again jammed the station that evening when "rockets were sent high in the air as the train pulled out and the scene was one long to be remembered."

In 1919 W.D. Newton, a British journalist, accompanied the Prince of Wales on his memorable cross-country tour of Canada. In his book, *Westward with the Prince of Wales*, he left many descriptions of the scenes at the stations: "At every station people were gathered. They had come sometimes from heaven knows where for in the wide plain or the lonely valley there was no sign of habitation. They had come in by automobile or by rig or they had walked. They were content if all they could

accomplish was to send a hearty cheer after the train as it sped by at express speed."

But the grandest royal tour of all was more leisurely and lured to the stations more Canadians than had assembled there before or since for a single event. It was the royal tour of 1939.

Never before had a reigning monarch visited Canada. Beginning in late May of 1939, King George VI and Queen Elizabeth (the late Queen Mother Elizabeth) began their memorable cross-country train trip, a journey that would last more than three weeks. Special "Royal Hudson" engines were brought in and polished, and coaches were newly painted in royal blue and gold.

The tour began on May 17 in Quebec City and rolled westward along the CPR line. Fifty thousand cheering people crowding the Three Rivers Station sang "God Save the King" and cheered again when the Queen spoke to them in French. On May 22 the train made an unexpected stop at Brockville to greet the throng of twenty-five thousand strong that engulfed the station.

As the train rolled on, the crowds grew larger, undaunted by the time of night or the conditions of the weather. "Never before has such a crowd gathered at one place in Belleville," noted the

LEFT: Football fever flared in front of Toronto's Union Station following the Argos' Grey Cup victory in 1994. Photo by author. RIGHT: Nothing brought Canadians to their station like a Royal tour, the grandest of which was that of King George VI and Queen Elizabeth in 1939. Photo courtesy of the Public Archives of Canada, C 85095.

Toronto Telegram, "Early in the afternoon people started to take up positions along the barriers. By 6 o'clock 15,000 were at the station. Early in the evening rain started to fall but the crowd refused to leave."

Farther west stood Cobourg where the train was scheduled to overnight. Here, crowds began to gather at midnight, staying up all night, and were joined in the grey pre-dawn by the Cobourg Citizens band. At 8:30 the train appeared to a tumultuous roar, but rolled through without stopping, offering not even a glimpse of the royal couple.

In Toronto, the royal couple disembarked at the CPR's former North Toronto station to review a guard of honour. Officially closed a decade earlier, and converted to a liquor store, it was redesignated as a station for one day so that the train could legally stop and the royal couple could disembark.

When the King and Queen departed Toronto, thousands jammed the front of Union Station to send them off. But, as the train rumbled on northwest of Toronto, the station crowds were not so lucky. At stations like West Toronto, Weston, Woodbridge, Palgrave, Kleinburg, Bolton, and even the now vanished Blackhorse Crossing, crowds jammed the tiny platforms, peering impatiently for the train that was an hour late and then had to watch it roar through at one hundred kilometres an hour. The *Telegram* reported "At Kleinburg a group of 500 watched in vain for a sight of their majesties. The crowd included villagers, farmers, and cowboys in full western regalia from a nearby ranch. The only persons on the train who came into view were 2 coloured porters who waved towels at the crowd."

As darkness fell that day, the train rumbled into Carley, north of Barrie, for a watering stop. Here, a startling sight awaited the royal couple. Surrounding the station, and parked on the hillsides, were a thousand automobiles, while higher on the hills, five piles of pine stumps were stacked ten feet high. As the King and Queen watched, the headlights came on and the pine piles were set ablaze. The King glanced in amazement at the brilliant spectacle, and the Queen commented, "Aren't they beautiful? This is the prettiest sight of the trip."

Disappointment again greeted crowds across Ontario's northland. A reporter with the pilot train noted, "As the train passes, lonely figures show by the track silently waiting for a flash of the royal special. At Franz station a little crowd stood clustered, waiting. They may be lucky to glimpse their 2 majesties if they do not sleep late."

White River, Ontario, residents were treated to a longer stopover. Natives canoed for days from their wilderness settlements to see the royal couple. "Shivering squaws with papooses bundled in their arms stood in snow to greet the King and Queen here today (May 23)," wrote the on board reporter. "In Michipicoten near Puckasaw River a group of Indians 100 miles away heard that the King and Queen might be in White River. They took to their canoes immediately over treacherous waters all because the royal train is stopping here for 20 minutes." Trains from all around the northland, as there were no roads, brought in beds and people from outlying communities. It was the grandest twenty minutes White River would ever know.

The story was repeated all across the country, with thousands congregating at flag-bedecked stations in Regina, Calgary, and Vancouver. The train then made its way back east along the CNR line through Jasper, Edmonton, Winnipeg again, and then back into southern Ontario. Thousands converged upon the stations big and small. Many had came from faraway farms to spend an entire day in town, because for prairie kids, a rare visit to Moose Jaw or Melville was in itself almost as exhilarating as was the sight of royalty was to their parents.

Two more royal visits brought Canadians out to the stations. In 1951 Princess Elizabeth and the Duke of Edinburgh spent a portion of their tour on the train, although much of it was by air. The queen-to-be retraced some of the same ground covered by her parents twelve years earlier, pulling in crowds between Nova Scotia and Windsor, including thirty-five thousand at Cornwall and Brockville.

Then, in 1978, Canadians went to the station grounds (for by then many of the stations were gone) to witness royalty by rail for the last time. In token homage to the glorious 1939 tour by rail, Queen Elizabeth and Prince Philip boarded a train in Regina and journeyed to four communities northeast of Regina. At the Fort Qu'Appelle station the Gordon Indian Dancers entertained the royal party with a hoop dance and presented them with a ceramic plaque. In contrast to the tour of 1939, which lasted three weeks, the Saskatchewan trip — the last time Canadians would go to the station to see their Queen — was over in a scant sixty-two hours.

Whistle-stopping

If Canadians looked to their stations as the stage on which to cheer royalty, they saw it equally as an opportunity to jeer at their politicians.

In the days before radio and television, the only way a politician could really reach his constituents was from the vestibule of a rail car. With only a few minutes to spend in each station, the candidate's organizers would hustle a crowd together, usually supporters, and assemble them at the stations. A few moments were spent listing accomplishments achieved and promises that would be kept, and the train would give a whistle and grunt and chug its way to the next station.

Although it is likely someone started whistle-stopping before John A. Macdonald came along, he was Canada's first prime minister who is most closely identified with it. The CPR was, after all, his creation and he used it to maximum advantage. Laurier, Bennett, and King followed, all reaching out to voters from their vestibules.

Peter C. Newman, writing in the *Toronto Star*, suggests that John Diefenbaker was the last politician in history to campaign from the back of a train as the "Dief the Chief" made his way through the farming communities of southern Saskatchewan. As recounted by Newman, during the day the platform crowds varied from six to sixty. At one stop, Mortlach, only four turned up. "We had no idea the chief would be aboard," one said. A rousing welcome, however, awaited at the next stop, Morse. The local band waited with over two hundred cheering supporters, including high school students who had been bussed in. Diefenbaker stood before the band and "directed" it through a march.

Newman noted that, "For some reason station agents in those days were musical (or thought they were) and organized ragged marching bands to welcome the Tory leader. Those of us in the train's press corps were constantly trying to file stories but seldom could, because the station agents were usually on the platform serenading the chief."

Funeral trains also drew Canadians to the platforms. The most memorable was that of Sir John A. Macdonald, who died June 6, 1891. A reporter for the *Dominion Illustrated* magazine wrote: "As the train was leaving Ottawa an old man, standing bareheaded on the platform called out 'Goodbye, Sir John, goodbye' … Stops were made at Carleton Place and Smiths Falls where crowds of people pressed around the funeral car … at the latter town a floral offering was made by the Liberal-Conservative associations … The Kingston station … and the large square immediately opposite were densely crowded with citizens eager to see the last homecoming of their representative …" From that station, Macdonald's body was taken to Cataraqui for burial. That Kingston station stands today as a tourist information centre, beside it a decommissioned steam engine appropriately labelled "The Spirit of Sir John A."

The funeral train of John Diefenbaker was similar to that of Macdonald. In accordance with his wishes, Diefenbaker's remains were returned to Saskatchewan by train for burial. Like Macdonald's, the train drew huge crowds. Indeed, the crowd that mobbed the Kenora station was so huge that it forced the train to make an unscheduled stop.

Prime Minister Pierre Trudeau revives the whistle stop as he campaigns through the Maritimes during the 1974 election campaign. Photo courtesy of the Public Archives of Canada, PA 136972.

The election of Pierre Trudeau as prime minister ushered in the electronic age in politics. Although TV had greatly influenced the outcome of the 1960 U.S. election through its much watched "Kennedy–Nixon" debate, where Nixon's facial stubble overshadowed the issues, Canada had to wait another eight years before Trudeaumania cast its spell over the new 1960s generation of Canadians.

Jet airlines replaced the trains and the thirty-second "photo-op" replaced the five-minute whistle-stop. Nevertheless, Trudeau did engage in electioneering from the platform of a train. The 1974 election saw him make his way through a number of Maritime communities and dazzle the spectators from the platform of his coach.

But later crowds were not as friendly. In 1982, as Trudeau and his two sons made their way through western Canada on a vacation, an angry mob besieged the train at the platform in Salmon Arm, British Columbia. Trudeau responded by prominently giving the group "the finger" through the window of the train, an image captured by a newspaper photographer, and later dubbed the "Salmon Arm salute." But the unfortunate prime minister's trial by mob didn't end there. When the residents of Canmore heard of Trudeau's gesture, they mobbed the train, throwing eggs and tomatoes. When the train eased into Sudbury station, the crowd was so hostile that the scheduled forty-minute stop was reduced to just a few minutes.

Ironically, Trudeau's own funeral train on October 2, 2000, also attracted thousands to the stations, as well as special television coverage, even through his train, accompanied by his two sons, Justin and Sacha, travelled the relatively short distance between Ottawa and Montreal.

As with Trudeau's ill-fated western train trip, crowds often flocked to the station to vent their anger. One of the most memorable station demonstrations of all occurred on the platform of Ontario's Brockville station in 1989. September 6 was a hot and sticky day. Ontario Premier David Peterson was due in town by train for a rally. Waiting for him amidst the Grit supporters were a number of "English rights" groups there to oppose the premier's support for bilingualism in Ontario.

After most of the demonstrators had dispersed and as the TV cameramen were packing up their equipment, a few remaining

The decision by the federal government of Brian Mulroney to decimate Canada's rail passenger service in 1990 was met by angry demonstrations across the country as here in Medicine Hat. Photo by Chuck Nisbett, courtesy of the Medicine Hat News.

members of the groups laid the flag of Quebec on the platform and began to parade across it. As the cameras crews scrambled to unpack their cameras, one malcontent set the Quebec flag aflame. Images of the burning fleur-de-lis were played and replayed on the TV screens of Quebec, enraging the residents of that province as well as many in English Canada.

That station demonstration was by no means the last. On January 15, 1990, the Tory government of Brian Mulroney eliminated half of Canada's rail passenger services, contradicting a campaign promise to improve rail service. It also meant the end to Canada's longest-running transcontinental train service, that of the *Canadian* over the CPR's tracks. (It continues to operate on the tracks of CN.)

As the last train to follow that historic route edged its way out of Toronto's Union station on that frigid Sunday afternoon, demonstrators paraded with placards protesting the short-sightedness of their government. At stations all along the route, protestors showed up with placards, banners, and coffins. In Vancouver, even the VIA employees joined in a mock funeral march and laying of a wreath.

But rail passenger service has seen a resurgence in Canada. Thanks to far-sighted transport ministers like David Collenette, and clever marketing by VIA Rail, many train routes are frequently sold out. Urban gridlock and concerns over global warming have put the importance of rail travel higher on many political agendas, although passenger trains still must contend with freight service, which on many lines still receives priority from the CN and CPR dispatchers. Getting widgets to their destinations on time seems to be more important than the timely arrival of people. As passenger travel increases, remaining stations will remain a focus for many of Canada's communities, and in some ways will always be their heart and their stage.

The Stations and the Arts

From the beginning Canada's stations were a stage not just for ordinary Canadians living out their daily routines, but for writers, poets, artists, and photographers.

Poet Archibald Lampman, in his 1900 poem, "The Railway Station," vividly depicts the night-time arrival of a train at a small station, briefly filling the platform with the "hiss and the thunder … the faces that touch and the eyes that are dim with pain." Stephen Leacock contrasts the hustle of Union Station in Toronto with the tranquillity of his fictional "Mariposa" in his short story, "The Train to Mariposa." But perhaps Canada's most famous fictional station scene occurs on the platform of the "Bright River" station in Prince Edward Island. Matthew Cuthbert arrives to meet the "boy" that he and his wife were to adopt. Instead he finds a red-haired girl named Anne. So begins the much-loved and much-read *Anne of Green Gables*, written by Lucy Maud Montgomery and first published in 1908.

Dr. Harry Colebourn, a Canadian army veterinarian, while on his way to Valcartier, Quebec, in 1914, disembarked onto the platform of the station in White River, Ontario, and for $20 bought a bear cub. He named his pet "Winnipeg" after his adopted hometown. He could not have known then that he would be giving the world its best-loved children's book character, Winnie the Pooh. But when he was forced to leave "Winnie" with the London Zoo in order to join the front lines of the First

LEFT: Were it not for a Canadian army veterinarian named Harry Colebourn, the children of the world would never have come to know Winnie the Pooh. Photo courtesy of the Archives of Fred Colebourn and the town of White River. RIGHT: It was on the platform of this White River divisional station in Ontario that Colebourn purchased a bear cub from a hunter and named the little bear "Winnipeg." Photo courtesy of CPR Archives, A 4808.

World War, the bear became an instant favourite of the young Christopher Robin Milne. The boy's father, A.A. Milne, used his son's fascination with Winnie as the basis of his enduring series of children's books. A statue has been raised in White River to celebrate the link between Winnie and White River.

Stations have appeared in a number of early paintings, such as that of Toronto's first Union Station by artist William Armstrong, James Hamilton's portrayal of London's Great Western station, and W.T. Smedley's lively woodcut of Hamilton's station platform. The vanished era of steam locomotives has been captured by artist Wentworth Folkins in his series of paintings that depict steam train operations at various railway stations. Even artist David Milne depicted a distant silhouette of a prairie station in his 1929 painting *Railway Station*. Famed artist William Kurelek captured the fear of new arrivals to the Canadian west with his painting entitled *They Sought a New World* prepared for his book, *Jewish Life in Canada*. This work depicts immigrants huddled on the platform of a tiny and lonely prairie station, no other buildings in sight.

Some chance encounters on Canadian station platforms have had a significant effect on world literature. Had a young Englishman named Archie Belaney not impulsively hopped off the train at Temagami, Ontario, and happened to meet woodsman Bill Guppy, he might never have been introduced to the life of Canada's natives. And the world might never have come to know "Chief" Grey Owl who claimed to be part Sioux and who went on to become a leading writer and lecturer on animal conservation. Only after his death in 1938 did a shocked world discover that Grey Owl was no Indian at all, but Belaney.

Fresh from the success of the Woodstock Folk Festival in 1969, Janis Joplin, The Grateful Dead, The Band, and Buddy Guy chartered a CN Train the following year to cross the country, performing in Toronto, Calgary, and Winnipeg. They were not allowed into Montreal or Vancouver, however. In 2004, a movie about the excursion, *The Festival Express*, was produced by Gavin Pullman.

In June of 1990 the Pepsi soft drink company and Toronto's popular MuchMusic TV channel rented a VIA train that would bring Canadian youth rushing to their station, many for the first time. On June 7 the eight-car train, painted in the Pepsi colours of red, white, and blue, left Vancouver for stops at Jasper,

If an Englishman named Archie Belaney (right) had not met a trapper named Bill Guppy on the platform of the station in Temagami, Ontario, he would not likely have adopted the guise of an Indian, naming himself "Grey Owl" and going on to promote the preservation of the Canadian beaver. Photo courtesy of Ontario Archives, S 14531.

Edmonton, Saskatoon, Winnipeg, Toronto, Ottawa, Montreal, Quebec City, Moncton, and Halifax. Among those on board were noted Canadian artists Jeff Healey and his band, Blue Rodeo, Jane Siberry, Paul Lane, and National Velvet.

At many of the stops the bands would mount a makeshift platform and throb out the rock beats of the '90s for swaying and handclapping youngsters. But it was at one of Canada's smaller communities that the largest crowds turned out. Capreol, Ontario, lies about a half hour north of Sudbury. Although a stop had not been scheduled, the organizers acceded to a request from a local Pepsi bottler and added a stop at this historic railway centre. Long before the train appeared down the track more than one thousand people were milling around the station, most of them young and anxious to see their favourite Canadian music artists. An elderly

LEFT: MuchMusic's "Pepsi" train is met by an enthusiastic crowd at Jasper, Alberta. Photo by author. RIGHT: Sometimes small-town residents would simply pass time on the platform waiting for the evening train. Photo by author.

couple likened the gathering to the atmosphere they remember from old time small-town station gatherings. For indeed it was.

Every December, since the year 2000, the CPR has decorated a train with Christmas lights and rolled it across Canada, as well as the United States, drawing sightseers to their stations to enjoy such entertainers as Widemouth Mason and Melanie Doane, an effort that has raised millions of dollars for local food banks since its inception.

Many of Canada's surviving stations have attracted producers of movies, television shows, and commercials. Ontario's Gravenhurst station appears in *Boy in Blue*, the life of Ned Hanlon; the Avonlea station in Saskatchewan substitutes for the demolished Wilcox station in the *Hounds of Notre Dame*; while the Esquimalt and Nanaimo station at Parksville, British Columbia, became the turn-of-the-century Kamloops station for the climax of the movie version of the story of train robber, Bill Miner, *The Grey Fox*. Union Station in Toronto has substituted for a number of U.S. stations, including the Chicago station in the movie *The Silver Streak*, where it is the victim of a runaway train that crashes through the wall.

Union Station also portrayed itself in Murray Brattle's 1974 short film, *Union Station*, a tribute to the grandeur and moods of the building. It was a film that, along with the book *The Open Gate*, helped save the station from demolition.

A replica of the Grimsby, Ontario, station (the original was later destroyed by fire) built in 1978 by the Hamilton Region Conservation Authority has become a star station for commercials and such films as *Mark Twain and Me*, *Beautiful Dreamers*, and *Anne of Green Gables*. This is due to the faithful attention to detail and to the fact the station is not part of an operating railway.

The loss of Canadian stations has led to a sudden surge in Canadian station portraits. Stations now appear on calendars, collectors' plates, and even postage stamps and lapel pins. The renewed interest, however, is mainly a lament for the past, for many of the stations are gone forever. It is often only in our books, our films, and our art that they live on.

Sadly, the last crowds to come down to the station were those to watch it razed. While stations at West Toronto and Arnprior were demolished secretly in the middle of the night, most were routinely reduced to rubble during a few short working hours. Many spectators watched with tear-reddened eyes, some remembering the excitement of past crowds and the sights sounds and sentiments of the station's heyday that would never be repeated. Others fumed at the intransigence of the railway companies over preserving the structure. In any event, the station would have no like again. The heart of the community was gone; the stage was bare.

The station at Rogers Pass, shown here in its active days, is where the Trans-Canada Highway was formally opened in 1962. Photo courtesy of CPR Archives, A 11436.

"THE TRAIN DOESN'T STOP HERE ANYMORE": DECLINE OF THE RAILWAY STATIONS IN CANADA

Beginning of the End

On June 7, 1939, at St. Catharines, Ontario, Queen Elizabeth, queen consort of King George VI, stepped into the late spring sunshine and opened the Queen Elizabeth Way, a ceremony that symbolically commenced the demise of Canada's railway stations. The new four-lane road was the latest in superhighway design. With its controlled access and clover leaf intersections it was the first of its kind in North America (the Pennsylvania Turnpike would not even be started until the year after) and was a concept that would free the personal automobile from stop signs, congestion, and multiple accesses. It heralded a new era in transportation, the superhighway, and the decline of Canada's stations.

But some stations were in decline long before that. While Canada's rail era was still in its infancy, wood-burning steam engines were replaced by those that burned coal. These larger engines could pull longer trains and travel farther before refuelling. Suddenly, stations were no longer needed to provide wood at frequent intervals. And so, by 1880, before most of Canada's railway network was in place, some stations had lost one of their earliest functions.

At this time Canada's railway network was expanding rapidly, with nearly one hundred separately chartered railway lines. Then three giants slowly began to emerge. Between 1880 and 1900, the CPR, the Canadian Northern, and the Grand Trunk began to consume the many smaller lines through direct purchase or through 999-year leases.

Within that huge spider's web the three giant corporations discovered they possessed duplicate lines, lines that had once been fierce rivals. The CPR, for example, after it had taken over the Credit Valley and the Toronto Grey and Bruce railways, had two lines that ran nearly side by side from Toronto to Orangeville. As

While much of the Credit Valley line has long gone, its coaches await restoration in Tottenham, Ontario. They will then be hauled by the restored steam engines of the South Simcoe Railway Society. Photo by author.

a result, in 1932, the CPR abandoned the TG and B line south of Orangeville and removed the tracks and the stations.

By coordinating service and eliminating duplication, fewer trains puffed along the separate lines. The trains that appeared were longer and less frequent. Redundant lines were lifted, while on the lines that remained, stations were downgraded from operator to flag stations and agents were demoted to caretakers.

The 1920s and 1930s nevertheless remained the heyday of Canada's stations. More branch lines were built, and along them, new stations with new styles. In the late 1920s the CPR timetables listed nearly 2400 stations while the CNR network claimed nearly 4000.

The Second World War witnessed a tremendous upsurge in rail travel. Soldiers, sailors, and air force pilots crammed onto troop trains to and from the Atlantic ports where ships waited to carry them to the war. The CPR alone saw passenger travel jump from 7 million a year just before the war to 17 million in 1943.

Throughout the 1950s train travel remained highly popular. The CPR introduced its stainless steel passenger train, the *Canadian*, while the CNR countered with its *Supercontinental*. However, the clouds that would ultimately doom rail travel and eliminate nearly all of Canada's stations were forming. Dieselisation, the rush of passengers from the trains to their cars, automatic signalling, and the end of mail and local freight service combined to end Canada's station era.

For decades, the use of diesel to power locomotives had been regarded as superior to the use of coal. Diesel trains could travel half the continent before refuelling. The first diesel locomotive in Canada was built by the CNR in 1929. However, the major changeover from steam did not start until the late 1940s. By 1960 diesel and electric power had completely replaced steam power. Water tanks were dismantled and coal docks were sold for scrap. Many divisional stations became redundant and were downgraded or closed.

The CPR's much-publicized Canadian, *with its sleek chrome coaches, hadn't been on the rails long before the CPR began slashing its passenger service. Here it sits at the Golden, British Columbia, station in 1966. Photo by author.*

The years that followed the First World War also marked another rush of innovations that diminished the role of Canada's stations. Block signalling and centralized traffic control (CTC) had begun to replace the telegraph and the train order. Under block signalling the train itself tripped a switch that automatically changed the train signals and alerted the dispatcher as to its whereabouts. CTC eliminated a major role of the station operator altogether, for under this revolutionary new system, all train movement was coordinated from a central dispatcher. On his board at a large central location, he would watch the train movements and push a button to regulate train speeds and meets. But because of the enormous cost involved in changing the signals along thousands of kilometres of track, these new methods were implemented only slowly.

Following dieselisation CTC was eventually extended along most of Canada's main railway lines. Agents and operators were removed, and stations no longer needed for maintenance crews or as passenger shelters were demolished.

The New Rival

But it would be the spectacular popularity of the private car and the subsequent growth of highways like the Queen Elizabeth Way that would draw Canadians away from the trains and doom most surviving stations. In 1893 Canadians saw their first car. In 1908 Henry Ford opened his Model T assembly line and within ten years 200,000 cars were chugging and sputtering along Canada's muddy roads.

Most traffic, however, remained within urban areas. Interurban travel was still difficult. It took, for example, eleven hours to travel from Toronto to Walkerton along the narrow dirt roads, while a trip by train was less than four hours by train. Today the travel time is less than two by car while trains no longer run.

But Canada's new car owners were a determined lot. "Good Roads" associations began popping up even before the turn of the century, and in July of 1901, A.W. Campbell, an Ontario provincial instructor in road-making machinery, launched a "good roads" train. For fourteen weeks he drew crowds to their local station to see road-making machinery built by the Sawyer Massey Co. of Hamilton and cement from the Canada Portland Cement Co. in Deseronto, a relatively new product at that time.

After the First World War ended, work began on interurban roads. Ontario and Quebec both established government departments to build and maintain highways. Between 1920 and 1930 Canada added more than a million cars to its highways, and governments spent $93 million to build and improve even more roads. This prompted Dr. Robert James Manion, then minister of railways, to criticize the use of taxes paid by railways for the construction of highways that would give an advantage to its competitors such as trucks and buses.

During the 1930s the federal government, as a Depression-era make-work project, assisted the provinces to construct "trunk" roads and marked the beginning of the Trans-Canada Highway. Then in 1949, the federal government passed the Trans-Canada Highway Act, legislation under which the federal government subsidized 50 percent of construction costs for the provinces to build this new national link. In 1962 at Rogers Pass, the Trans-Canada Highway was formally opened.

In 1956 the new Highway 401 had been completed around Toronto (within three years it was carrying twice the volume of traffic for which it was designed) and by the 1960s Canadian governments were spending $1.25 billion on highways. Canadians had decided. They had chosen cars over trains. Born of the auto, suburbs sprawled across the farmlands and more and more Canadians began living farther and farther from the stations. Within a few short years, stations had gone from being the heart and focus of the community to another forgotten deteriorating building.

Express bus service began rolling along the new roads, competing with the railways for interurban service. The CPR actually had its own bus service south of Montreal.

In 1936 C.D. Howe created Trans-Canada Airlines and in 1942 the CPR established Canadian Pacific Airlines. New international airports were opened at Toronto and Montreal, and by the late 1960s jet aircraft carried contented passengers coast-to-coast from modern uncrowded terminals in four or five short hours, rather than the five days it took by rail.

Derailing Passenger Service

But to the railways the writing was clearly on the wall and they began to terminate, some say with undue haste, their passenger services. In arguing before the Board of Transport Commissioners in 1965 for the discontinuation of its transcontinental train, less than ten years after it had opened to great fanfare, the CPR stated that the "continuing demonstration by the public of a marked and increasing preference for the private automobile for shorter trips and jet aircraft for longer trips, there appears to be no foreseeable change in this trend. [We have] no choice but to consolidate, substitute, reduce and eliminate [rail passenger] services which have shown deterioration."

Ironically, at the same time as the CPR set out these arguments, the CN was advertising the inauguration of a "A Fast Railliner to Saskatoon and Prince Albert [from Regina]. Comfortable, fast CN Railliner service is the worry free way to travel."

More interested in freight profits than in unprofitable passenger lines, the CPR began to request permission to close passenger service and demolish stations on most of its branch lines, claiming they were unprofitable. There were accusations that decline in passenger travel was deliberately orchestrated by the CPR through inconvenient scheduling. At Transport Commission hearings into some of that company's shut-down requests, these accusations were upheld. But still the shut-downs continued.

Railways were also accused of making passenger lines look unprofitable by assigning shared passenger and freight costs completely against passenger revenues. With the advent of VIA Rail to assume operation of the so-called "unprofitable" passenger services, the CN and the CPR could charge costs against VIA for use of their lines, equipment, and personnel in a way that was often arbitrary and unaccountable. For example, according to the Task Force on VIA Rail, a fuse bought by the CN from Bombardier for $2.78 was later re-sold to VIA for $48.

The once busy terminus of Cape Tormentine, the link between New Brunswick and Prince Edward Island, lies silent and overgrown. Photo by author.

It has also been demonstrated that the CN charges Amtrak one-third less to use its tracks than it charges VIA.

It is little wonder that Canada's rail passenger service has always looked "unprofitable." Still, much of the shift away from rail travel was due to the growth of the car and the airplane. From an all-time high of 55.4 million passengers carried by trains in 1945, ridership had plummeted to 27.2 million by the mid-1950s and by 1970 most branch line passenger service had ended. The federal government cut more of VIA's services in 1982 and 1990 until barely 6 million Canadians could use the railway.

Along the popular commuter line between Toronto and Peterborough, for example, towards the end of the 1970s the CPR demolished every station, Canada's only surviving Van Horne styles, and replaced them with wooden "tool sheds." The CN opted for the aluminum steel and glass "bus shelters."

The 1960s, 1970s, and 1980s signalled the swift demise of the railway station in Canada, spurred on by the recommendations of the MacPherson Royal Commission, which recommended that passenger service end on all uneconomic passenger lines, and by the blinkered political philosophy of Transportation Minister Jack Pickersgill, who wanted to end railway passenger service entirely.

The 1960s did indeed witness the end of much of Canada's branch line passenger service. In Ontario, service along the Sault Ste Marie line, the Orangeville line, the Goderich line, and the Kingston and Pembroke line all ended. In the Maritimes, service along the CN Yarmouth line and the famous *Newfie Bullet* all stopped. In 1981 the Liberal government of Pierre Trudeau cut a further 20 percent of Canada's passenger service, some of which was briefly restored by a Conservative government in 1985. However, in 1990, that same government proceeded to eliminate a devastating 50 percent of Canada's passenger lines, outraging thousands of Canadians who had depended upon the trains. Service from Montreal to St-Hyacinthe ended when local municipalities refused to pay their share of the train's annual $1 million deficit, while in Ontario the popular commuter

Tracks being lifted from the CPR line in Harrowsmith, Ontario, as they have been from most of Canada's branch lines. Photo by author.

LEFT: The popular commuter train between Peterborough and Toronto became a victim of the Mulroney government's service cuts in 1990. Its restoration is still being discussed. Photo by author.
RIGHT: Symbolic of the Mulroney government's rail passenger cutbacks, these VIA coaches sit idly at the Ottawa station, awaiting shipment to Mexico. Photo by author.

service between Peterborough and Toronto also fell victim to the sweeping cuts.

Seen as a panacea during the Pickersgill days, the fumes spewed by cars, trucks, and jet aircraft have proven to be such environmental disasters that rail travel is once more being seen as a solution to gridlock and global warming. Despite the reluctance of governments to increase funding, ridership on such lines as VIA Rail and the Ontario's government's GO Transit and the ONR's *Northlander* are steadily increasing.

Trucks Take Over

But cuts to passenger service alone were not responsible for the decline in stations. The railways continued offering telegraph service as CN/CP telecommunications long after the telegraph ended any relevance it had to railway operation. Once telephones had become a feature in each home, the telegraph service was removed from the station and operated centrally. With the dramatic decline in passenger traffic after the Second World War, and the elimination of passenger service from many routes, station functions were reduced to that of handling freight. Cattle, crops, timber, and factory products had kept many stations open. But the competition from trucks loomed ominously on the

horizon. In 1948 the first freight truck rumbled along the Trans-Canada Highway between Fort William and Winnipeg, breaking the CPR's long-standing freight monopoly. In 1950 a nine-day railway strike drove shippers to willing truckers and many never returned to the railways.

By the year 2000 most new industries were locating on cheap suburban land and relying on "just-in-time" truck deliveries to re-main competitive. Except for large bulk-hauling industries located near rail lines, the link between trains and industries was gone.

By the mid 1970s one station in fifteen generated enough revenue to cover costs. Even though agents were paid for full eight-hour shifts, some stations were experiencing less than fifteen minutes worth of business per day. To halt this tremendous inefficiency, the railways ended one of Canada's longest railway traditions, local freight service, and replaced it with piggybacking and containerization. Instead of booking through a local station agent, shippers would deal by telephone through a central or regional carload centre.

Trucks sped off along multi-lane highways carrying products that had, until then, been shipped from the local way station, directly to massive railway yards. Here the trailer, or the container, was hoisted directly onto the railway car and shipped on unit trains to a similar central yard near the destination where trucks would again take over. (Piggybacking was nothing new to

Quebec and the Atlantic Provinces: A Portfolio

Ste-Agathe, Quebec

Prevost, Quebec

St-Marc-des-Carrières, Quebec

Port Daniel, Quebec

Venosta, Quebec

Pictou, Nova Scotia

Avondale, Newfoundland

Burtts Corner, New Brunswick

A blank chalk schedule board at St-Basile, Quebec, symbolizes the drastic decline in Canada's rail passenger service. Photo by author.

railways. In 1855 Joseph Howe instituted a form of piggybacking on Nova Scotia short-lines where he would hoist farmers' wagons onto flatcars for the trip to their destination.)

The End of an Era

With the advent of containerization and piggybacking, stations by the hundreds were deprived now of their last community function and closed their doors forever. By the 1970s most stations had lost their functions entirely; mail, signalling, and freight all disappeared. Only along those few lines that still offered passenger service were stations left up to provide shelter for waiting passengers, often with peeling paint and broken windows. Unattended, these rambling old buildings became expensive to maintain and sometimes impossible to insure. Often these were bulldozed into rubble and replaced with small shelters in which waiting passengers might huddle against the cold.

The death of Forward, Saskatchewan, is typical. Once a busy farm town with both CNR and CPR stations, by the 1930s the drought and depression had turned it into a near ghost town, and the CNR proposed closing its station. The local reaction was swift. "There will be no service between Radville and Forward," complained the local council. "It is the people of these districts

With the abandonment of many prairie branch lines, the little towns, like Ensign, Alberta, which depended upon them, became ghost towns. Photo by author.

whose wheat going from prairie farms to the Atlantic that contributes to keeping these stations open."

It was to little avail. The Board of Railway Commissioners noted that only twenty-seven tons worth $234 were shipped out of Forward and downgraded the agent to "caretaker" status. By 1962 both revenue and people were gone and the station was removed. Today, the site of this once bustling spot is an overgrown field with even the railway roadbed barely discernible.

The 1960s witnessed the first wave of wholesale station demolition. Of more than 270 stations that stood on the dense network of lines throughout Quebec's eastern townships, fewer than 25 survived the decade. Between April and July of 1975 the CN applied to the Transportation Commission for permission to demolish nearly 100 stations in Saskatchewan alone. From 1979–1980, that province lost another 100 stations. On August 9, 1974, the Commission agreed to allow the CN to demolish 50 stations in Manitoba. Between 1970 and 1980, railways in

Ontario were given permission to remove more than 140 stations. In 1979 the CN announced to Newfoundlanders that 29 of their stations were to be closed and 14 agents made redundant.

In a 1970 *Toronto Star* article, Tom Ford offered that, "Toronto is gobbling up industry at the expense of Ontario's small towns. As a result the CNR wants to close 350 country stations where it is losing business."

Towns that depended heavily or solely upon the station and the business that it generated were often reduced to ghost towns. The remote rock land of northern Ontario was particularly hard hit, for many of the towns there were built solely to support the railway. One-time divisional towns like Reddit, Foleyet, and Nakina, remote and surrounded by miles of silent bush land, were reduced only to their maintenance of way crews. The roundhouses have been demolished; the maintenance shops are mere foundations. The stores and hotels have closed and many residents have moved away. The massive station at Reddit was

The once bustling hotel at Melaval, Saskatchewan, fell silent after the trains stopped calling. Photo by author.

torn down in the 1970s, that at Foleyet in 1990, although the station at Nakina has been restored by the town and converted into a multi-modal facility.

Across the prairies, towns closed down by the hundreds and today Canadians can in places find ghost towns literally every twelve kilometres simply by following the abandoned branch lines.

In just two short decades the railway stations of Canada had gone from being the most important institution in town to usually a hole in the ground, its many vital functions distant memories to the millions for whom the station had been the heart of the community.

The clandestine demolition of the CPR's West Toronto station enraged citizens and helped launch a nationwide campaign to save endangered stations. Photo courtesy of Metro Toronto Reference Library, T 33895.

"BOARDED-UP SHACKS": THE FIGHT TO SAVE OUR STATIONS

West Toronto Comes Down

"Just a boarded-up shack," was how CPR lawyer Donald Maxwell dismissed the West Toronto Junction station before three Federal Court of Appeal judges as he tried to justify the CPR's pre-dawn demolition of the building.

In 1979 the CPR closed the station and told anyone who cared to listen that they wanted to tear it down. But the station, a large Tudor Revival building, had been a West Toronto Junction landmark since it was built in 1912 and residents and politicians alike were determined that it should stay.

Station closings had become rampant during the 1970s in both the U.S. and Canada and the buildings began to be put to a variety of alternate uses. Libraries, museums, seniors' drop-in centres, municipal offices, and private uses could all be found in redundant stations, usually without moving the building. Nevertheless, some railway companies, the CPR among them, insisted that the stations must be moved.

The preservationists, however, were hoping to change the CPR's mind. The City of Toronto, the West Toronto Junction Historical Society, and the CPR had been in the midst of conducting a feasibility study into turning the building into a farmers' market, but after four years of talking, the CPR had

had enough. During the pre-dawn hours of a November day in 1982, a CPR wrecking crew quietly fenced off the site and began to demolish. By the time the city awoke the station was rubble. A furious Toronto mayor, Arthur Eggleton, rushed to the scene and handed the crew orders to stop work. They refused. It was too late anyhow.

Denounced as "corporate vandalism" and likened to a "commando raid," the West Toronto demolition made headlines across the country. But it had also struck a responsive note. Too many Canadians had stood by teary-eyed and enraged as they watched their stations fall under the bulldozer's blade.

Among these were the residents of Renfrew, Pembroke, Almonte, and Arnprior. In 1982 these Ottawa Valley towns had pleaded with the CPR to save their magnificent stone stations. Built of local limestone to a special architectural plan, these stations were unlike any other in Canada. In all cases the CPR told the communities that the stations must be moved. But the costs of moving the large stone structures would have exceeded $150,000, more than the small communities could afford.

Nipigon was another victim. The frame CPR station in this northern Ontario railway town was a community landmark. Since 1928 it had stood grandly on the main street opposite the town's four blocks of stores. Carefully tended lawns and gardens stretched along each side.

The CPR station in Nipigon was ripped apart when the town could not raise the extra funds upon which the railway insisted in order to save the historic building. Photo by author.

When the CPR told the town of its intentions to demolish the station, the residents agreed to move it. Although the $20,000 price tag for the move was steep for a town of just two thousand, the determined residents raised the amount. Then, just two days before the move, the CPR advised them that they would need $8,000 more to remove the signal arm, and $30,000 more for re-wiring. The coffers were dry and the people of Nipigon could not come up with another cent. The CPR demolished the station.

In 1982 the CPR declared its intention to demolish its Streetsville, Ontario, station and replace it with an aluminum prefab. The citizens of Streetsville joined with the provincial government to try to prevent the removal of the 1914 brick station. Using economic arguments they pointed to a cost study showing that the CPR would save $60,000 if it upgraded the station instead of replacing it. John Cox, CPR's regional manager of public relations, announced that the CPR was not in the heritage business and the station came down.

During the dark period of station demolition the CPR removed every station that stood between Toronto and the Quebec border, with the exception of the divisional station at Smiths Falls (from which it derived rental revenue from VIA

Rail). Lost were the elegant former Canadian Northern station at Belleville (which the CPR had temporarily allowed to be used as a Moose Lodge and bus terminal); the Tudor Revival station at Trenton, a look-alike to the West Toronto station; a two-storey custom-built station at Chesterville; as well as a variety of standard plan stations constructed variously of brick or wood. The stone station at Perth, with its arched entrance, was dismantled and unceremoniously dumped into a landfill site.

Meanwhile, the CNR wrecking crews were busily knocking down the ancient stone stations between Toronto and Montreal, the original stations built by the Grand Trunk Railway, as well as the eclectic collection of stations built by the Intercolonial Railway in the maritime provinces. Many of these buildings were among the oldest stations in Canada.

In some cases municipalities themselves were to blame. When offered the opportunity to preserve its station, a rare example of an early Canadian National style, complete with its original wood shingle exterior and board platform, the town of Smooth Rock Falls, Ontario, declined. The station is now gone. By contrast, the town of Kapuskasing, on the same line, bought their station and today successfully operates out of it a travel agency and a bus

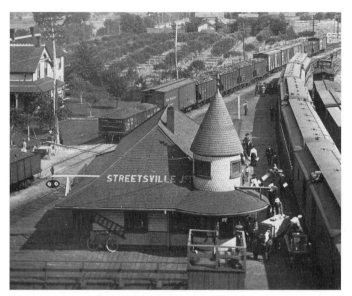

TOP LEFT: The Credit Valley Railway's Streetsville station was moved off to become a home when the CPR replaced it with a new structure in 1914. Photo courtesy of the Streetsville Historical Society collection, RPA 1990.075. TOP RIGHT: Down comes the handsome CPR station in the Port Arthur section of Thunder Bay. The adjacent road needed widening. Photo courtesy of the Thunder Bay Museum. BOTTOM LEFT: Local indifference sealed the fate of the little country station in Consecon, Ontario, near Picton. Photo by author. BOTTOM RIGHT: A concerted local drive helped to restore Port Hope's threatened Grand Trunk station. Still a VIA stop, it is now Canada's oldest continuously operating railway station. Photo by author.

depot. Train service to Kapuskasing was suspended only in 1990 with the Tory government's infamous rail passenger cuts.

In other cases the railway insisted upon conditions that were simply too unreasonable for the municipality to accept. When the CN offered the Glencoe station, a rare example of a turreted frame Grand Trunk station, to the town, council found the CN's conditions too onerous. These conditions included fencing, liability insurance

for the building and the grounds, and the questionable condition that if the railway eventually wanted to develop the land, the town would still be required to return the station to the railway for $1.

The town ultimately did buy the station and moved it a short distance back from the tracks.

Station demolition is nothing new in Canada. As communities grew, small stations were replaced with larger ones; older

Unlike its neighbour at Smooth Rock Falls, the town of Kapuskasing purchased the brick CN station and now operates it as a bus terminal and travel agency. Photo by the author.

buildings deteriorated and were replaced with buildings that were sounder and warmer. But stations were always there.

The Rescues Begin

Canada's early station recycling had little to do with heritage preservation. It was simply a practical way to acquire a cheap building. The first recorded station to be recycled was the Great Western station in Toronto. Built in 1856, it was abandoned in 1872 when the new Union Station was opened. It survived as a farmers' market until 1952 when it burned down.

In the early 1900s, when the CPR was replacing many of the old stations that it had inherited from the Credit Valley Railway, two of these intriguing turreted stations, those at Milton and at Streetsville, were moved away to become houses and yet survive.

One of the more impressive recycling examples occurred on the former Bay of Quinte Railway in central Ontario. When the line was abandoned in 1942, nearly every station between the villages of Queensville and Newburgh, six in all, was preserved. These solid two-storey stuccoed stations all survive on site, all but one are private homes, and all retain their original appearance, including freight sheds, trademark narrow cement platforms, and unusual two-storey bay windows.

One of the first stations to be preserved for its heritage value was that at Petrolia, Ontario. By the 1930s the oil boom, which had fuelled the town's prosperity and which had inspired the Grand Trunk to build a twin towered brick station on the main street, had gone sour and the station was closed. Recognizing the heritage value of the building, the town acquired the station, eventually converting it to a library. The former ticket office became the librarian's office, the baggage room the children's library, while the ladies' waiting room has become the library boardroom.

After the Second World War, and more particularly in the 1960s, Canadians began to realize that their stations were going for good. By then most functions had gone; passenger lines had been closed, computers had replaced the telegraph, local freight had been bumped by containerization, and the mail had been given over to the airlines.

Another postwar craze was urban renewal. During the 1960s planners and politicians felt that the solution to downtown deterioration was demolition. Low-cost houses were targeted as "slums" and bulldozed, while fine old commercial buildings were replaced with faceless blocks of glass and concrete. Then the urban renewalists turned to inner city railway tracks. Regarded as unsightly and a nuisance, many downtown tracks were removed. Newer stations, designed to look more like airport terminals, were relegated to the suburbs within easier reach of the car-driving public. In Saskatoon and Oshawa, when new CN stations opened in the suburbs during the 1960s, their historic downtown predecessors were demolished. In the 1960s, plans to beautify Ottawa called for the removal of all downtown railway tracks. A new station opened farther out, and the historic Union Station was threatened with removal. Ottawa, however, has long prided itself on its heritage and the station was preserved as a conference hall. Unfortunately, the public may see only the exterior. Uniformed security guards sternly prohibit unauthorized persons from viewing the former grand waiting hall and concourse.

Heritage also won the day in Quebec City. The preoccupation with suburbia and the nuisance of several level train crossings led to the removal of rail passenger service from the old Gare du Palais in 1976 to a newer suburban station in

Since becoming a conference centre, the high-ceilinged waiting room at Ottawa's former Union Station is now off limits to ordinary citizens. Photo by author.

Sainte-Foy. Then, with the subsequent removal of freight traffic in the core area, passenger train movement became perceived as less of a problem. In 1985 VIA Rail and the City of Quebec pumped $28 million into restoring the magnificent chateau-esque building and passenger trains rumbled in once more. It was a rare example of a train station being recycled as a train station, and is also the focus of community events such as those in conjunction with Quebec's four-hundredth anniversary celebrations in 2008.

After having for generations taken their stations for granted, Canadians began to value stations for their architectural merit, for the vital role they played in their community, and simply for nostalgia, and they became more active in saving them. Stations by the hundreds were being dragged off to become homes, cottages, and chicken coops. Others were being plunked down in museum grounds sandwiched inappropriately between pioneer log cabins and pioneer churches. Few were being saved as "stations," fewer still on their original site.

On the prairies, when branch line abandonment and station demolition became rampant during the mid 1970s, most communities were more concerned with the closure of grain elevators and factories and the loss of the jobs than they were over the loss of the station buildings. But the concern over stations was not far behind.

LEFT: VIA Rail helped fund the restoration of Quebec City's grand Gare du Palais while also restoring its role as the city's rail passenger terminal. Photo by author. RIGHT: Montreal's Parc Avenue CPR station has received new life as a liquor store. Photo by author.

Communities rallied to find ways of saving them. Many became museums such as those at High River, Alberta; Frenchman's Butte, Saskatchewan; and Avonlea, Saskatchewan. Manitoba's Miami station became a senior citizens' drop-in centre. These stations were all preserved on site. The St. Albert station was moved to a site north of Edmonton where the Alberta Railway Museum has added a wooden water tower as well as rolling stock, and runs a steam excursion along a mile of track.

The former CPR stations at Laggan (now Lake Louise) and

Shepard, Alberta, were moved to the Heritage Park in Calgary where they relive their traditional role as the focus of the rebuilt community and are the points of embarkation for a vintage steam train that puffs around the perimeter of the park.

History is even better served when the station remains beside the tracks and continues to play a "station" role. The former St. James station in Winnipeg was relocated to become Inkster Junction and is the point of departure for the popular Prairie Dog Special excursion steam and diesel excursion along CN trackage. In Alberta, the Alberta Prairie Railway operates a popular steam excursion from Stettler to the preserved Big Valley station, while the Canadian Northern Society has undertaken to preserve a string of ten stations in Alberta and Saskatchewan, along with a roundhouse and grain elevators. In Ontario, the Smiths Falls Railway Society has preserved the former Smiths Falls Canadian Northern station on its original site where, amid vintage rolling stock, including a dental car, it has established a museum.

When the CN abandoned rail operations on Prince Edward Island in the 1980s, many stations were still around. Some ended up simply as farm storage buildings; others became garages, stores, houses, or restaurants. Four of the architecturally more pleasing stations, those at Montague, Elmira, and the stone

LEFT: The CPR's prairie station at Miami, Manitoba, has become a senior citizens' centre. Photo by author. RIGHT: The Canadian Northern Association in Alberta has managed to preserve more than a half-dozen stations, as well as grain elevators and a roundhouse, including Big Valley's Canadian Northern station from which it runs steam excursions. Photo by author.

stations at Alberton and Kensington, have become either museums or tourist centres and remain on their original sites. Meanwhile, the large urban terminal at Charlottetown became a farmers' market. In Newfoundland, several stations have been converted to museums, including the attractive mansard-roofed Avondale station, and the St. John's terminus.

In Nova Scotia, nearly two dozen stations are being reused on site; the stations at Musquodoboit and Louisbourg are tourist centres, while the fascinating station at Pictou is a community centre. On Cape Breton Island, the ancient wooden Intercolonial station at Orangedale belongs now to the municipality and displays many of the station's original furnishings. The 1905 station in Liverpool is now the Hank Snow Music Centre. The Tatamagouche station has become an inn while its similar neighbour in Pugwash has become a library. One of Canada's oldest on-site stations, the Rothesay, New Brunswick, station of the former European and North American Railway (built in 1858) is an artist's studio.

In Ontario, the Ontario Northland Railway not only contributed its demolition costs towards the preservation of the Cobalt Ontario station, but has allowed its reuse on site. An ambitious building designed by John Lyle, its grandeur reflects the long-vanished days when Cobalt was the centre of a frenzied silver boom and one of the richest and most promising towns in Canada before becoming a near ghost town. One of the few relics of those glory days, the station houses a private collection of military memorabilia and offices.

Just down the track, an even more ambitious effort has not only saved the exotic stone station in Temagami, but has restored it to its former grandeur. Built in 1907, it was designed as a Tudoresque structure in order to appeal to tourists arriving at this wilderness area to embark on the Lake Temagami steamers. Following the demise of the steamer era, the station stood derelict for many years with only a small room serving as a shelter for passengers on the *Northlander* train. Then Claire and Richard Smerden rode into town. While first engaged in saving an endangered forestry tower, they then turned their attention to the deteriorating station. With the aid of a board of directors and considerable fundraising, the vaulted waiting room has now been restored and currently houses a gift shop. Structural repairs were completed and the building became a local attraction as well as a multi-functional venue. And the train still stops.

Similarly, the Port Stanley and Union stations in southern Ontario have been restored and are part of the London and Port Stanley Terminal Railway excursions. The historic witch's hat station in Uxbridge is now a museum and the terminus for the York and Durham Heritage Railway.

ABOVE: The attractive stone station at Kensington, Prince Edward Island, has kept some rail and a diesel locomotive as it serves as a tourist centre. Photo by author. RIGHT: Cooperation between the town of Temagami, the Ontario Northland Railway, and the determined drive of a pair of heritage-minded individuals has helped restore the magnificent Temagami station to its original glory, both outside and in. It remains a stop for the daily Northlander *passenger train. Photo by author.*

Preservation Problems

The CN and the CPR, however, continued to insist that most of their stations must be moved. While smaller way stations were relatively inexpensive to move, larger stations, especially urban stations, were prohibitively expensive to relocate and were often demolished. In a few instances, the CPR financially aided the relocation of a station, often contributing an amount equivalent to the cost of demolition.

Much, however, is lost when a station is removed from its site. For the historic role of the station was that of gateway between the community and the outside. Removed from that location, it can become just another building and is often altered beyond recognition. Even when they are preserved in pioneer villages or relocated to a vacant village lot on some back street they can look awkward and out of place.

Moving a station can be costly and difficult. When the Canadian Railway Museum purchased the Barrington station in Quebec, it paid the CN a token $1. Then the hard part began. The procession that hauled the station along Quebec's roads to the museum in Delson included the contractor's 3 trucks, 6 Bell

Telephone cars, 3 vehicles from Quebec Hydro, one truck each from the Shawinigan and Southern power companies, and 2 Quebec Provincial Police vehicles, a veritable parade that included 17 vehicles and 26 staff.

As with the Barrington station, relocation is more successful when it is incorporated into a railway theme. The Bellis, Alberta, station became the centrepiece of the Ukrainian heritage village east of Edmonton. Several relocated prairie buildings were placed along a typical prairie street. Dominating the street is the station, reflecting the role that stations played in the prairie communities. The interior of this former Canadian Northern station was accurately furnished as a turn-of-the-century station. Operator's paraphernalia clutters the office, period furniture fills the living quarters, while outside, the baggage carts, boxcars, and the distant grain elevators complete the authentic scene.

However, despite the best intentions of concerned citizens and preservationists, many obstacles remained in the way of

LEFT: The "last spike" is driven in front the historic station in Uxbridge, Ontario, in 1996, opening the line of the York and Durham Heritage Railway, a volunteer-run tourist train. Photo by author. RIGHT: The CPR's London, Ontario, station was saved on site, and is now a popular cocktail lounge. Photo by author.

preserving stations. First, there were the railways. The CPR's policy, and that of the CN in many instances, was that the station had to be moved for safety reasons. Non-railway uses, they argued, were incompatible adjacent to an operating railway and posed a threat to the public. It was a policy that was often applied even to lightly used branch lines and lines up for abandonment.

It is, however, a rationale that cannot be substantiated. Often, once the station has been moved, the railway sells or redevelops the property into a use that could just as easily have been incorporated into the station building itself. The retention of a station on site poses no greater threat to public safety than any other reuse of a vacant station site.

The policy also ignores local zoning. Once a railway sells the station to a non-railway purchaser, municipalities can, through their local zoning bylaws, control the reuse of the station and apply conditions that would set out fencing and parking requirements and even determine where the public can walk. In this way the preservation of a station by a new purchaser may be safer than if the station or the land were to remain in the railway's ownership and beyond the ability of the municipality to regulate.

It has, on occasion, been possible to sway the railway companies from this position. When the residents of Avonlea, Saskatchewan, first approached the CN to sell them the station for a museum, the CN ordered it moved. Persuasion from provincial

and federal politicians that the lightly used branch line posed no threat convinced the CN to allow the station to remain.

In the early 1980s the CPR had indicated that it no longer needed its unusual old station at Peterborough, Ontario. When the town first proposed buying the building, the CPR insisted upon its removal. However, the uproar over the West Toronto demolition, the debate that surrounded the new legislation, and a change in policy-makers at the CPR's head office all contributed to a softening of this attitude. In 1990, the Peterborough Chamber of Commerce, headed by general manager Don Frise, acquired the station and, using a $150,000 grant from the Ontario Heritage Foundation, and with $50,000 of its own funds, began to restore it. Now restored to its original yellow brick finish, the building remains where it has sat for more than 125 years and houses government offices.

One of the more interesting battles to save stations was that waged in the Laurentian Mountains north of Montreal. Passenger service along the Mont-Laurier line had survived into the 1980s thanks to the popularity of the winter ski trains. As a result, when Liberal minister of transport, Jean-Luc Pepin, closed passenger service in 1980, many of them original stations were still in place.

Shortly thereafter, the CPR began to remove them and, by 1985, nine of the stations had come down. That was when Adrien

Lobbying by the Peterborough Chamber of Commerce helped save and restore the CPR station in that town, although trains now pass it by. Photo by the author.

Gregoire, a municipal councillor and economic development officer in L'annonciation, went to work. Recognizing the historic and economic benefit of saving the old stations, he rallied other municipalities along the line to pressure the CPR to hold back the wrecking crews. In 1987 the CPR backed away from its standard position that the stations be removed and agreed to allow the municipalities to take over the stations. While the tracks have since been lifted, many of the historic stations survive and serve new uses.

It was not just small towns that faced the loss of their stations. In 1964 the president of the CN threatened to demolish what is considered to be one of the most magnificent stations in North America — Toronto's Union Station. The controversial "Metro Centre" plan proposed levelling the existing structure and replacing it with several office towers. Toronto rallied. A station committee was formed and authors Pierre Berton, Mike Filey, and several others pooled their considerable talents to produce *The Open Gate*, edited by Richard Bebout. It is a book that probes the social, architectural, and operational history of the station and is considered one of the best books on stations ever produced.

Its impact was stunning.

Rather than demolishing the station, CN, and later VIA Rail, and the federal government pumped $3 million into giving the station a facelift. The Great Hall, the largest room in Canada, was washed and the Indiana limestone that made up the exterior was scraped and scrubbed of its five decades of smoke, soot, and gypsum. The station was not just preserved; it was born again. Its burgeoning popularity, however, has rendered it once more obsolete and plans, much delayed, are under way to improve it once again.

In 1973 Canada's other grand old station, CPR's Windsor Station in Montreal, was likewise threatened with demolition. As in Toronto, Montrealers formed a committee to save the station and convinced the CPR to preserve the historic structure. Instead of tearing it down, the CPR poured $18 million into its restoration. And so the words that William Van Horne placed on a six-foot sign a century ago when he opened the station apply once again today: "Beats all creation, the new CPR station." Commuter trains today stop a short distance west of the station in a new facility built in conjunction with the new Molson Centre.

Many once redundant and tattered old stations have been revived as commuter stations. The Quebec Ministère des Transports has spent $2 million to alter former CPR stations at Beaconsfield, Vaudreuil, Montreal Ouest, and Valois for use by commuters on the SCTUM. Improvements have included new platforms, period lighting, pedestrian tunnels, and building

Considered one of North America's grandest stations, Toronto's Union Station was rescued from demolition by a determined community drive in the early 1970s. It is awaiting further restoration. Photo by author.

restoration. All stations were built in the early years of the twentieth century. Sadly, however, the original CPR station at Dorval, much loved by railway photographers from all across North America, was demolished just before it could celebrate its one-hundredth birthday.

Ontario's GO Transit has retained and renovated the historic former Grand Trunk stations at Maple and Aurora. The handsome former Grand Trunk stations in Brampton and Georgetown have been used by GO for several years, and remain stops for VIA Rail as well.

VIA Rail has also been active in preserving stations. It now owns or leases many former CN and CPR stations and wants to present the best possible face to attract travellers. In 1987 the company spent $11.5 million in restoration and renovations to stations, in 1988 a further $13.7 million. Among its achievements were the facelifting of Toronto's Union Station, and the restoration and reactivation of Quebec's Gare du Palais.

Such success was far from universal. Commuters along a popular CPR line between Toronto and Peterborough fixed up and repainted up the several old "Van Horne" stations that lined their route. The buildings, however, remained the property of the CPR and between 1978 and 1983 the railway, which no longer needed them, demolished all but two. Today, only that at Peterborough survives. A short distance east, the Havelock station, a 1930 replacement for the original "Van Horne," has become a restaurant.

Under the federal-provincial division of power, only the provinces were allowed to designate buildings for heritage protection. However, because railways are federally regulated, provincial heritage legislation can't touch them. Even though most provinces have legislation that permits the provincial minister to designate and preserve historical buildings, railway stations remained exempt.

In many ways, Ontario led the early fight to preserve stations. The Ministry of Culture and Communications published kits that advised municipalities what strategies and techniques they might use to save their stations. The kit contained historical and architectural information on Ontario's railway networks and its stations, and provided users with legal information and how SOS (Save Our Station) committees might be organized.

A program initiated by Ontario's Ministry of Transportation helped finance the preservation of a small number of railway stations as intermodal terminals. Stations at Gravenhurst, Orillia (although now trackless), St. Marys, and Nakina were preserved under this program.

Another Ontario agency involved in station preservation was the non-profit Ontario Heritage Foundation. One of its notable successes was the restoration of the 1856 Grand Trunk station in Port Hope, Ontario. That agency along with CN, VIA Rail, and the town, contributed $180,000 to fully restore the station. The work involved replacing the exterior limestone and restoring the interior for both the CN railway crew and VIA passengers. Built in the classical five-arch stone Grand Trunk style of the 1850s, it remains the oldest continuously functioning railway station in Canada.

A Bold New Law

But it was the West Toronto demolition that awoke Canadians to the realization that the whole country was rapidly losing a vital component of its heritage. No longer would stations remain a local issue. The problem lay not just with the railway companies that considered the stations to be "shacks," but with a loophole in federal-provincial heritage laws. Simply put, stations could not

legally be preserved. Railways had only to apply to the Canadian Transportation Committee for approval to demolish. It was a committee that had no mandate to consider heritage factors. In hearings to consider a CPR demolition application, five of thirteen witnesses presented heritage-related arguments. The CTC dismissed them all in a single sentence.

The greatest hurdle, however, has been the federal law. While exempting federally chartered railways from all provincial laws, federal legislation makes no provision for history. Even though the National Historic Sites and Monuments Act allows stations to be designated as national historic sites, that legislation makes no provision to preserve them. (In Ottawa, an historical convent was demolished the day after it had been designated a national historic site.)

Spurred on by the West Toronto demolition, the Heritage Canada Foundation, led by its Ottawa director, the late Jacques Dalibard, was determined to finally plug the loophole. In 1983 the Foundation enlisted Liberal MP Jesse Flis (in whose riding the West Toronto station was situated) to introduce Bill C-253, a private members' bill "to protect heritage railway stations." But the bill was plagued by delays. In 1984 an election left it on the order paper, and again, in 1986, parliament prorogued before the bill had been through committee.

Its prospects appeared more encouraging when it was introduced for the third time in 1986. Thanks largely to heavy lobbying by Heritage Canada, and to the angry mood of the nation following the CPR's conviction in 1987 (later overturned) of criminal charges over its West Toronto demolition, the bill drew overwhelming support from MPs of all parties and from Tom McMillan, minister of the environment. It passed in the Commons unanimously.

But it ran into more hurdles in the Senate. One of them was Liberal senator Ian Sinclair, who, six years earlier as head of CP Rail had, "for the good of the people," as he put it, ordered the demolition of the West Toronto station. Sinclair, along with his Liberal colleagues, began to place a variety of procedural obstacles in the way of the bill, including referrals to committees, and skirmishes over the wording of the French text. But the public reaction against their tactics was so overwhelming that one by

Although the massive St. Thomas station was one of the first stations in Canada to be designated under the Heritage Railway Stations Protection Act, much work needs to be done to save it. This room once housed sleeping quarters for train crews. Photo by author.

one the Liberal senators backed off. Finally, on September 21, when the vote was taken, the only senator to oppose the railway station preservation bill was the man who demolished West Toronto, Ian Sinclair.

The Heritage Railway Station Protection Act heralded a new dawn for station preservation, at least for those few that remained. Under the new law, once a station was given a heritage designation, the railway company could neither demolish it nor alter it. To place a station upon the protected list, any province, municipality, or individual may recommend to the Historical Sites and Monuments Board the station they want preserved. The Board then evaluates the historical, architectural, and environmental significance of the station and may then recommend it to the Minister of the Environment for protection.

When the legislation was proclaimed, twelve stations appeared on the list; today that number exceeds three hundred.

While this legislation places Canada in the forefront of station preservation, (in the U.S. even being placed on the National Historic Register does not guarantee preservation) problems remain. Most of the stations on the initial list were in no immediate danger of demolition. Other stations, in more immediate danger, were omitted. For example, none of the stations designated as "national historic sites" were there, especially when the latter designation does not guarantee preservation.

The second problem is the length of time needed for a station to be chosen. Only a limited number can be reviewed at one time, and even then it takes at least another year to make the

Sadly, even a federal heritage designation can't always save the day. Although designated, the St. Clair West station in Toronto was first vandalized and then torched. Photo by author.

protected list. The railway demolition crews do not take that long to demolish a station.

The third problem is the question of what to do with a redundant station once it is on the list. Designation still does not guarantee that a new use will be found for it. Many designated stations have been destroyed by vandals while awaiting a new owner. The classical Grand Trunk station in Kingston was gutted by fire and, although designated, at this writing sits crumbling under a tarpaulin. The designated St. Clair West station in Toronto sat vandalized until an arsonist put it out of its misery.

Following the passing of the legislation, station fever gripped the country and many success stories can now be counted. In London, Ontario, the CPR has allowed its turn-of-the-century station to be incorporated into a redevelopment proposal as a restaurant. The 1916 North Toronto or Summerhill station has become the centrepiece for Marathon Realty's redevelopment of its lands around the building, and has been restored both outside and in. Montreal's Parc Avenue station, similar in style to that at North Toronto, has, like the latter, been restored and it too houses a liquor store. Vancouver's CPR station now contains retail space and is a terminus for commuter trains and ferries. The elegant station at Fernie is now a municipal building while the CPR's Chinese pagoda-style station in Virden is a museum. In fact, since the legislation passed, more than 160 stations have

The former K and P station in Kingston, Ontario, now serves as a tourist information centre. The steam engine in front hauled Sir John A. Macdonald's funeral train. Photo by author.

been designated, and Canada can count more than 200 railway station museums.

Requiem

The fight to save Canada's stations is far from over. There have been victories and far too many losses, but at least there is the awareness that stations are part of a heritage that goes far beyond the style of the building or its size, or even beyond the specific role it played in a particular community. The station was much more. It was the gateway for many newly arriving Canadians, it was the social heart of small-town Canada, it was the gateway through which immigrants entered to seek new life in a new land, and it was the door through which many Canadians left their homes, some never to return. It was part and parcel of the creation of this land, a symbol of a nation. The station may be a thing of the past, for the most part, but it is a past that should never be forgotten, even though the train doesn't stop there anymore.

In 2001 then federal transport minister David Collenette uses the Grand Hall at Toronto's Union Station to announce a rail passenger "renaissance" in Canada. Photo by author.

BIBLIOGRAPHY

Adair, Daryl T. *Canadian Rail Travel Guide*. Markham, Ont.: Fitzhenry and Whiteside, 2004.

———. *The Guide to Canada's Railway Heritage*. Winnipeg: North Kildonan Publishers, 2007.

Alexander, Edwin P. *Down at the Depot, American Railroad Stations From 1831 to 1920*. New York: Clarkson N. Potter, 1970.

Andreae, Christopher, Geoff Matthews, and Mark Fram. *Lines of Country: An Atlas of Railway and Waterway History in Canada*. Erin, Ont.: Boston Mills Press, 1997.

Andreae, Christopher. *The Story of the London Port Stanley Railway*. Toronto: Gage Publishing, 1986.

Archibald, William. "All Aboard the Y Train." *Canadian National Magazine* (October 1956).

Artibise, F.J. *Prairie Urban Development*, Booklet #34. Ottawa: Canadian Historical Association, 1981.

Ashdown, Dana, *Railway Steamships of Ontario*. Erin, Ont.: Boston Mills Press, 1988.

Backhouse, Frances. "Glacier House; A Loving Look at a Lost Lifestyle." *Canadian Geographic* (Aug/Sept 1987): 34–41.

"Bag and Baggages." *Canadian Rail* (Jan/Feb 1988): 202–204. First published in CP Staff Bulletin (January 1944).

Baird, Ian. *Canadian Pacific Stations in British Columbia*. Victoria: Orca Book Publishers, 1990.

Baird, Ian. *A Historical Guide to the E and N Railway*. Victoria: Heritage Architectural Guide, 1985.

Ballentyne, Bruce. *A Guide to Canadian Railway Stations*. Ottawa: Bytown Railway Society, 1998.

Barnes, Michael. *Link with a Lonely Land: The Temiskaming and Northern Ontario Railway*. Erin, Ont.: Boston Mills Press, 1985.

Barr, Elinor, and Betty Dyck. *Ignace: A Saga of the Shield*. Winnipeg: Prairie Publishing Co., 1979.

Bedbrook, W.J. "The New Look in Railway Stations." *Canadian Rail* (1956).

Bébout, R., ed., with John Taylor and Mike Filey. *The Open Gate: Toronto Union Station*. Toronto: Peter Martin Associates, 1972.

Bell, Alan. *A Way to the West: A Canadian Railway Legend*. Barrie, Ont.: self published, 1991.

Bean, Audrey, and others. *La Gare Windsor*. Montreal: Les Amis de la Gare Windsor, 1973.

Bennet, Carol, and D.W. McQuaig. *In Search of the K and P*. Renfrew, Ont.: Renfrew Advance, 1981.

Berton, Pierre. *The Great Railway*. Toronto: McClelland and Stewart, 1972.

Bohi, Charles. *Canadian National's Western Depots*. Toronto: Railfare Enterprises, 1972.

Bohi, C.W., and L.S. Kozma. *Canadian Pacific's Western Depots*. David City, Ne: South Platte Press, 1993.

Booth, J. Derek. *Railways of Southern Quebec*. Vols. 1–2. Toronto: Railfare Enterprises, 1982.

———. "Railway Stations in Southern Quebec." *Canadian Rail* 256 (April 1973): 105–118.

Bouchier, M.F. "The Impact of the Northern Railway on the Sense of Place in Canada West, 1850–65." Master's thesis, York University, 1979.

Bousfield, A., and G. Teffoli. *Royal Spring*. Toronto: Dundurn Press, 1989.

Bowers, Peter. *Two Divisions to Bluewater*. Erin, Ont.: Boston Mills Press, 1983.

Boyer, B.A. *Muskoka's Grand Hotels*. Erin, Ont.: Boston Mills Press, 1987.

Broseau, M., J. Knight and John Witham. *Inventory of Railway Station Buildings in Canada*. Ottawa: Environment Canada, Parks Service, 1974.

Brown, Ron. *The Last Stop: A Guide to Heritage Railway Stations in Ontario*. Toronto: Polar Bear Press, 2004.

———. "It's Fun to Stay in the (Railway) YMCAs." *Beaver Magazine* (Feb/March 1999): 34–38.

Burnet, Robert G. "Darlington and Port Union Stations." *Canadian Rail* 412 (Sep/Oct 1989): 148–150.

Canada. Board of Railway Commissioners. *Annual Reports*. Various years.

Canada. Manitoba Ministry of Culture, Historic Resources Branch. *Railway Stations of Manitoba*, 1986.

Canada. National Liberal Caucus. *Report of the Federal Liberal Task Force on VIA Rail*. November 1989.

Canadian Pacific Railway. Chief Engineer's Office, *Standard Plans*, 1921.

Canadian Pacific Railway. *Get Your Farm Home From the CPR*. Calgary: Department of Natural Resources, 1915.

Cavalier, Julien. *North American Railway Stations*. Cranbury, Nj: A.S. Barnes and Co., 1979.

Chandler, Graham. "Canada's Silk Road." *The Beaver* (December 2005): 16–21.

Chartrand, Guy. "Les 100 Ans de la Gare Windsor." *Canadian Rail* 408 (Jan/Feb 1989): 12–13.

Chevrier, Giles. "Le Chef de la gare St-Lazare." *Canadian Rail* 236 (Sep/Oct 1970).

Collins, Robert. "The Day the King Came to Moose Jaw." *Reader's Digest* (March 1973).

Conlin Engineering. *CN Railway Station Feasibility Study*. Town of Rainy River, 1988.

Cook, Clayton D. *End of the Line: The Pictorial History of the Newfoundland Railway*. St. John's: Harry Cuff Publications, 1989.

Cooper, Charles. *Hamilton's Other Railway, 1853–2000: The Hamilton and Northwestern Railway in Retrospective*. Ottawa: Bytown Railway Society, 2001.

———. *Narrow Gage For Us*. Erin, Ont.: Boston Mills Press, 1982.

Cooper, Juanita. "Original Depot Hub of Hustle and Bustle." *Gravenhurst News*, 1 October 1986.

Cote, Jean-Guy. "Steam Hauled Silk Trains." *Canadian Rail* 293 (Nov/Dec 1974): 210–216.

"CPR's Royal Train." *Railway and Shipping World* (October 1901).

Crichton, V. *Pioneering in Northern Ontario*. Belleville, Ont.: Mika Publishing, 1975.

Cruise, David, and Alison Griffiths. *Lords of the Line* Markham, Ont.: Viking Penguin, 1989.

Curie, A.W. *The Grand Trunk Railway of Canada*. Toronto: University of Toronto Press, 1957.

Dalibard, Jacques. "Getting on the Right Track." *Canadian Heritage* 10 (1984): 2–3.

Davis, Jo. *Not A Sentimental Journey: What's Behind the VIA Rail Cuts*. Waterloo, Ont.: Gunbyfield Publishing, 1990.

Dempsey, Hugh A., ed. *The CPR West*. Vancouver: Douglas and McIntyre, 1985.

Denhez, Marc. "Railway Blues: Stations are Coming Down in a Legal Vacuum." *Canadian Heritage* 41 (1983): 12–14.

Droege, John. *Passengers, Terminals and Trains*. New York: McGraw-Hill, 1916.

Eagle, John A. *The Canadian Pacific and the Development of Western*

Canada, 1896–1914. Montreal: McGill-Queen's Press, 1989.

Easton, Mel. *Mel Easton's History of the K and P.* Perth, Ont.: The Perth Courier Publishing Company, 1978.

Edmonson, H. A., and R. V. Francavigulia. *Railroad Station Planbook*. Milwaukee: Kalmbach Books, 1977.

Facts and Figures, Canadian Pacific Railway, occasional report, 1937.

Ferguson, Ted. *Sentimental Journey: An Oral History of Train Travel*. Toronto: Doubleday, 1958.

Folkins, Wentworth, and Michael Bradley. *The Great Days of Canadian Steam: A Wentworth Folkins Portfolio*. Willowdale, Ont.: Hounslow Press, 1988.

Folster, David. "Why McAdam NB Has Such a Big Railway Station." *Canadian Geographic* (April/May 1982): 34–36.

Foran, Max. "The CPR and the Urban West, 1881–1930." In *The CPR West*, edited by Hugh Dempsey. Vancouver: Douglas and McIntyre, 1985.

Garland, Aileen. "Gardens Along the Right of Way." *Manitoba Pageant* (Winter 1977).

Geddes, Hilda. *The Canadian Mississippi River*. Snow Road, Ont.: self-published, 1988.

Golay, Michael. *The Old Railway Station Book*. Rowayton, Conn.: Prospero Books, 2000.

Graham, Allan. "One Every Two and a Half Miles: A Brief Look at the Railway Stations on the Prince Edward Island Railway." *Canadian Rail* 382 (Sept/ Oct 1984): 148–173.

Grant, H.R., and Charles Bohi. *The Country Railroad Station in America*. Sioux Falls, Nd: Centre for Western Studies, 1988.

Gray, James H. *Red Lights on the Prairies*. Toronto: Macmillan, 1971.

Greenlaw, C.N. *VIA Rail*. Osceola, Wi.: Voyageur Press, 2007.

Groupe, Harcart. *Inventaire des gares du Canadien Pacifique de la Région des Laurentides*. Ministère des Affaires Culturelles du Quebec (MAC), Direction du patrimoine, Montreal, n.d.

Hanna, D.B. *Train of Recollection* Toronto: Macmillan, 1924.

Hart, D.J. *The Selling of Canada*. Banff: Altitude Publishing, 1983.

Hedges, James B. *Building the Canadian West: Land Colonization Policies of the CPR*. Toronto: Macmillan, 1939.

Heels, Charles. *Railroad Recollections*. Edited by Alan R. Capon. Bloomfield, Ont.: Museum Restoration Service, 1980.

"Historic Station May be Saved." *Oshawa-Whitby This Week*, 16 March 1988.

Holmes, Ed. *Life at the Keewatin Station*. Manuscript.

Humphrey, Edythe. "Station Agents Job Hectic in Nokomis of 1907." *Regina Leader Post*, 31 December 1955.

Hungry Wolf, Adolf, and Okan. *Canadian Railway Stories*. Skookumchuck, B.C.: Good Medicine Books, 1985.

Jackson, John, and John Burtniak. *Railways in the Niagara Peninsula*. Belleville, Ont.: Mika Publishing, 1978.

Jones, David C. *Empire of Dust*. Edmonton: University of Alberta Press, 1987.

Kalman, Harold. "What to do with all those Redundant Stations." *Canadian Heritage* (December 1980): 4.

Kitigawa, M. *This is My Own: Letters to Wes and Other Writings on Japanese Canadians*. Vancouver: Talon Press, 1985.

Kozma, Leslie Steve. *A Building Survey and Brief Architectural and Graphic Examination of Railway Stations in Alberta*. Edmonton: Alberta Culture, 1976.

Kurelek, William, and I. Abraham. *Jewish Life in Canada*. Vancouver: Hurtig, 1985.

Lamb, W. Kaye. *History of the Canadian Pacific Railway*. Toronto: Macmillan, 1977.

Lampman, Archibald. "The Railway Station." In *The Poems of Archibald Lampman*, edited by D.C. Scott, 1900.

Lavallee, Omer. "The Saga of Barrington Station." *Canadian Rail* (December 1965).

———. "Windsor Station 1889–1964." *Canadian Rail* (1965).

———. *Van Horne's Road*. Toronto: Railfare Enterprises, 1974.

Laver, Ross. "Board Orders Public Inquiry into CP Station Demolition." *Globe and Mail*, 27 November 1982.

Leggett, Robert F. *Railways of Canada*. Vancouver: Douglas and McIntyre, 1973.

Leslie, Donald. *Donald Leslie Memoirs*. Calgary: Glenbow Institute Archives, n.d.

Liddell, Ken. *I'll Take the Train*. Saskatoon: Western Producer Prairie Books, 1977.

MacKay, Niall. *Over the Hills to Georgian Bay: A Picture History of the Ottawa, Arnprior and Parry Sound Railway*. Erin, Ont.: Boston Mills Press, 1981.

Marron, Kevin. "Preservation Attempt Destroys Rail Station." *Globe and Mail*, 1 January 1988.

Marsh, Lon. "The Edmonton Chamber of Commerce Friendship Train." *Canadian Rail* 402 (Jan/Feb 1988): 4–6.

Martin, J. Edward. *Railway Stations of Western Canada*. White Rock, B.C.: Studio E, 1980.

McCombs, Arnold. "The Agassiz Station." *Canadian Rail* 421 (Mar/Apr 1991): 39–41.

McDougall, Terry. "How We Won the Battle of the Railway Stations." *Canadian Heritage Magazine* (Winter 1988): 36–41.

———. "Making Tracks: Thanks to Adrien Gregoire Nine Country Stations Get a New Lease on Life." *Canadian Heritage Magazine* (Summer 1989): 35–36.

McIntyre, Katherine. "The Old North Toronto Station: A Landmark Revived." *Heritage Magazine* (Winter 2005): 4–9.

Meeks, Carol. *The Railroad Station*. New Haven, Conn.: Yale University Press, 1964.

McGregor, Don. *105th Anniversary of the Railway YMCAs*. Orillia, Ont.: YMCA Archives, 1985.

Mika, Nick and Helma, with Donald M. Wilson. *Illustrated History of Canadian Railways*. Belleville, Ont.: Mika Publishing, 1986.

Murphy, Gavin. "Canada's Train Stations: Destruction, Oblivion, or Protection." *Canadian Heritage* (August/September 1985): 28–33.

Neilson, Hugh. *The Diaries of Hugh Neilson: St Catharine's Station, 1861*. Manuscript. Toronto: Ontario Public Archives, n.d.

"New CPR Depot to be Opened This Month." *Edmonton Daily Bulletin*, 2 August 1913.

Newell, Dianne, and Ralph Greenhill. *Survivals: Aspects of Industrial Archaeology in Ontario*. Erin, Ont.: Boston Mills Press, 1989.

"North Toronto Station, Canadian Pacific Railway." *Canadian Railway and Marine World*. (August 1915).

"Old Station Being Razed on 49th Anniversary of First Trains." *Edmonton Journal*, 20 October 1951.

"Opening of New Canadian National Depot." *Edmonton Bulletin*, 16 March 1928.

O'Reilly, D. "Historic Orangeville Station Threatened." *Real Estate News*, 9 March 1984.

Patrick, Calvin M. "Early Railway Shipments of Canadian Livestock." *Canadian Rail* 407 (Nov/Dec 1988): 191–192.

Pennington, Myles. *Railways and Other Ways*. Toronto: Williamson and Company, 1894.

Planning for Heritage Railway Stations. 2 vols. Toronto: Ontario Heritage Foundation, Ministry of Citizenship and Culture in cooperation with Canadian National Railways and VIA Rail, 1987.

Poirier, Daniel. "Le P'tit Train du Nord." *Canadian Rail* 397 (March/April 1987) : 45–50.

Pope, Joseph. *The Tour of Their Royal Highnesses: The Duke and Duchess of Cornwall and York Through the Dominion of Canada in the Year 1901*. Ottawa: S.E. Dawson, 1903.

Public Archives of Canada. RG 46, Series C-11-1, volume 1415, File 11389.1. *Station Plans, 1945*.

Public Archives of Canada. RG 46, Series C-11-1, vol 1415, File 8883.4. *Telephones in Stations, 1909–1935*.

Public Archives of Canada. RG 46, Series C-11-1, vol 1448, File 17061. *Closings of Stations on Weekends and Holidays, 1911–1961*.

Public Archives of Canada. RG 46, Series C-11-1, vol 1538, File 18540.25. *Naming Railway Stations, Part 1, 1916–1929, Part 2, 1931–1952*.

Public Archives of Canada. RG 46, Series C-11-1, vol 1526, File 10729. *CP Standard Plans for Western Lines, 1929*.

Public Archives of Canada. RG 12, vol 1345, File 3350-3. *History of Government Control and Regulation of Railways in Canada, 1891–1953*.

Public Archives of Canada. RG 30, M ACC 78930/42. *Grand Trunk Railway Station Plans*, n.d.

Queen's University Archives. *1939 Royal Tour Scrapbook*, 2 volumes.

"Rail Demolition May Spark Man vs. Bulldozer Battle." *Edmonton Journal*, 28 March 1978.

A Railway Station Information Kit; An Aid for the Conservation of Heritage Railway Stations. Toronto: Ontario Heritage Foundation, 1988.

"Remembering: It Was an Event When the Train Came to Town." Special edition of *The Coupler*, BC Rail Employee magazine, BC Rail, 1987.

R.J. Long Consultants, Ltd. *CPR Station Redevelopment*. Orangeville, Ont.: Town of Orangeville BIA, 1984.

Richards, J., and John Mackenzie. *The Railway Station, A Social History*. Oxford and New York: Oxford University Press, 1986.

Ross, Murray G. *The YMCA in Canada*. Toronto: Ryerson Press, 1951.

Ruel, A., and B. Salomon de Friedberg. *Les Gares de Chemins de Fer au Québec, Analyse Typologique et Sélection*. Ministère des Affaires Culturelles du Québec (MAC), 1982.

"Saskatchewan Towns Finding Use for Empty Railway Stations." *Regina Leader Post*, 8 February 1978.

Sawchuk Peach Associates. *Cobalt Railway Station Feasibility Study*. Town of Cobalt, Sudbury, 1985.

Schuessler, Karl. *Schools on Wheels*. Erin, Ont: Boston Mills Press, 1986.

Scrivener, Leslie, and Jim Wilkes. "Art's Too Late to Save Historic Station." *Toronto Star*, 25 November 1982.

Smith, Doug. "A Tale of Two Stations: Quebec's Palais Station." *Canadian Rail* 394 (Sep/Oct 1986): 170–172.

"Society Wants CP Rail Buildings Saved." *North Bay Nugget*, 10 November 1987.

Spears, Tom. "CP Denies Demolished Building was a Station." *Toronto Star*, 6 December 1984.

Stamp, Robert M. *Riding the Radials*. Erin, Ont.: Boston Mills Press, 1989.

Standing Committee on Transport. *The Renaissance of Passenger Rail in Canada*. Ottawa: Transport Canada, 1998.

———. "Steel of Empire: Royal Tours and the CPR." In *The CPR West*, edited by Hugh Dempsey. Vancouver: Douglas and McIntyre, 1985.

Stevens, G.R. *Canadian National Railways*. 2 vols. Toronto: Clarke Irwin and Co., 1962.

"Storming the Station." *Hamilton Spectator*, 28 December 1895.

A Study of Canadian Pacific's Heritage Railway Properties. Toronto: Ontario Heritage Foundation in cooperation with CP Rail and VIA Rail, 1989.

Talman, J.J. *Impact of the Railway on a Pioneer Community*. Ottawa: Canadian Historical Association, 1955.

Tatley, Richard. *Steamboat Era in the Muskokas*. 2 vols. Erin, Ont.: Boston Mills, 1983.

Taylor, Sterling. "Vintage Rail Station Back in King after 22 Years Away From Home." *Toronto Star*, 15 December 1989.

Thompson, Allan. "Summerhill Station Slated for Yet Another Lease on Life." *Toronto Star*, 29 May 1990.

Thompson, John. "Does the Original Champlain and St. Lawrence Station Exist?" *Canadian Rail* 395 (Nov/Dec 1986): 199–201.

"Toronto Union Station, History and Description." *Canadian Railway and Marine World* (1927).

Town of White River. *The Birthplace of Winnie The Pooh, Our Discovery*. Information Kit, 1990.

Tozer, Ron, and Dan Strickland. *A Pictorial History of Algonquin Park*. Toronto: The Friends of Algonquin Park and the Ontario Ministry of Natural Resources, 1986.

Walker, Frank. *Four Whistles to Wood Up*. Toronto: Upper Canada Railway Society, 1953.

Von Baeyer, E. *Rhetoric and Roses: A History of Canadian Gardening*. Markham, Ont.: Fitzhenry and Whiteside, 1984.

Weaver, Martin E. "Union Station Gets the Cinderella Treatment." *Canadian Heritage* (Aug/Sep 1985): 36–38.

Welcome to Station Park. Promotional brochure. London, Ont., 1990.

Wilmot, Elizabeth. *Meet Me at the Station*. Toronto: Gage Publishing, 1976.

————. *Faces and Places Along the Railway*. Toronto: Gage Publishing, 1979.

Wilson, Dale. *Tracks of the Black Bear: The Story of the Algoma Central Railway*. Schomberg, Ont: Green Tree Publishing, 1974.

Wilson, Donald M. *Lost Horizons*. Belleville, Ont.: Mika Publishing, 1983.

————. *Ontario and Quebec Railway*. Belleville, Ont.: Mika Publishing, 1984.

Withrow, W.H. *Our Own Country*. Toronto, 1887.

Worthen, S.S. "Bonaventure Station, Montréal." *Canadian Rail* 293 (Nov/Dec, 1974): 204–207.

Selected Online Resources

Railway-related museums and excursions
www.canadabyrail.ca

CPR Archives
www.cprheritage.com

Nova Scotia's preserved stations plus several links
www.novascotiarailwayheritage.com

Heritage Railway Station Preservation Act
www.pc.gc.ca/clmhc-hsmbc

A list of all extant stations in North America along with many other railway related sites
www.rrshs.org

New website for Union Station restoration plans
www.toronto.ca/union_station

INDEX

Page numbers in bold refer to photgraphs and illustrations